THE ASTRONOMER'S SOURCEBOOK

The Complete Guide to Astronomical Equipment, Publications, Planetariums, Organizations, Events, and More

Bob Gibson

WOODBINE HOUSE ★ 1992

For information regarding bulk sales of this book, please contact:
Woodbine House, 5615 Fishers Lane, Rockville, MD 20852, 800/843–7323

Copyright © 1992 Woodbine House, Inc.

All rights reserved under International and Pan-American Copyright Conventions. Published in the United States of America by Woodbine House, Inc.

Cover photo: Eagle Nebula (M16); courtesy of National Optical Astronomy Observatories

Library of Congress Cataloging-in-Publication Data

Gibson, Bob.
    The astronomer's sourcebook : the complete guide to astronomical equipment, publications, planetariums, organizations, events, and more / Bob Gibson.
       p. cm.
    Includes bibliographical references and indexes.
    ISBN 0–933149–43–3 (pbk.) : $19.95
    1. Astronomy—Handbooks, manuals, etc. I. Title.
QB64.G43   1992   91–45817
520—dc20   CIP

Manufactured in the United States of America

1 2 3 4 5 6 7 8 9 10

TABLE
OF CONTENTS

CHAPTER 3: TELESCOPES AND ACCESSORIES

CHAPTER 4: FINDING YOUR WAY IN THE SKY

CHAPTER 5: ASTROPHOTOGRAPHY

CHAPTER 6: OBSERVATORIES

CHAPTER 7: PLANETARIUMS AND MUSEUMS

CHAPTER 8: U.S. SPACE-BASED ASTRONOMY PROJECTS

CHAPTER 9: THE HISTORY OF ASTRONOMY

CHAPTER 10: ASTRONOMY EDUCATION

APPENDIXES

GLOSSARY

CORPORATE INDEX

PUBLICATIONS INDEX

SUBJECT INDEX

INTRODUCTION

Not too many years ago, amateur astronomers had few choices when buying telescopes and other instruments for their hobby. A few companies sold small refractors; a company or two offered small reflectors through advertisements in the astronomy publications. Much of the equipment used by professionals was custom-made for the research organizations that employed them, and completely out of the reach of amateurs.

Amateurs, by and large, built their own equipment; a six-inch reflector was the norm and the components were military-surplus parts. Today, amateurs can buy "off the shelf" instruments that rival the equipment only professionals used a few decades ago. Telescopes with apertures of twenty inches or more are available without having to place a special order. And portable catadioptrics have opened new vistas for amateurs in terms of technology and ease of use; they have also proved to be excellent for astrophotography.

Concurrently, a flood of accessories, maps, atlases, videos, computer software, and books have hit the market. No longer are your choices limited to a few observing guides, two or three models of telescopes, and surplus military parts for filters and mirrors. In fact, the choices open to you today can be bewildering, the terms daunting, and the advertising claims overpowering. There are dozens of companies hawking seemingly identical goods.

Just where can you buy what you need to enjoy the night sky, and how can you find out what the costs are? Those are a few of the questions answered in the **Astronomer's Sourcebook.**

The **Astronomer's Sourcebook** lists sources for almost any product that beginning and serious amateurs could want. Listings include manufacturers and dealers of refractors, reflectors, and catadioptic telescopes; mounts, drives, filters, eyepieces, lenses, mirrors, and other accessories; reference guides, how-to books, maps, atlases, and catalogues; magazines, journals, and computer software; posters, slides, prints, and videos; space art,

T-shirts, and other gifts and novelties. For the most part, suppliers of these products are grouped together according to the types of products they sell. For example, all manufacturers of telescopes and accessories are gathered together in the Telescopes and Accessories chapter and most magazines and journals can be found in the **Periodicals** section in Chapter 1. Remember as you use these lists, however, that many categories overlap; a telescope dealer also may sell telescope-making supplies; some manufacturers also sell accessories; book publishers sometimes offer gifts or posters, etc. In many cases, when a firm offers products that fall into several categories, a cross listing refers you to the main section for that entry. Be sure, also, to check the Subject and Corporate Indexes if there is a particular type or brand of equipment that you can't find simply by scanning the Table of Contents.

The addresses and telephone numbers of manufacturers and dealers are as up-to-date as possible, as are the prices and model descriptions. The information has been culled from company brochures, advertisements, personal inspection where possible, and conversations with others. Bear in mind, however, that companies move, go out of business, and change their prices (usually, unfortunately, in an upward direction). In other words, call or write to check for current information before making a major purchase.

One positive note among all the advertising hoopla is that most firms want to supply you with high quality equipment. It's their reputation on the line, after all, and they know that the astronomy magazines report negative findings on equipment they review. Furthermore, even though most astronomy equipment purchases are mail-order out of necessity, there have been few reports of abuses.

The joy of astronomy, of course, need not be limited to accumulating tons of equipment and books. For most amateurs, a far bigger lure is learning more about the mysteries of the Universe. For that reason, the **Astronomer's Sourcebook** not only lists sources of equipment needed to make discoveries on your own, but also covers opportunities for learning from others. Because observatories and planetariums are a prime source of astronomical information (as well as entertainment), separate chapter are devoted to listing these facilities. Many of the observatories and planetariums in North America want and encourage public participation. They often work closely with local astronomers, professional and amateur, and respond to legitimate requests for information. For those anticipating a trip, the telephone numbers, addresses, admission prices, and visitor rules are provided, and are up-to-date at press time. A word of caution, however: check ahead before you travel to a location. Situations change, and sometimes an observatory may drop public tours because of money or staffing problems. Prices at a planetarium may be increased, or the hours reduced.

Amateur astronomers—and by some estimates there are between 200,000 and 300,000 in this country—make up another valuable resource for knowledge seekers. Clubs offer the beginner a place to learn about equipment and materials and enable the advanced amateur to test new ideas and equipment. They can also be a valuable resource for professional astronomers who need observations from an area of the country that is in the path of an eclipse, occultation, or other special event. The section on the ever-changing astronomy club scene is not intended as a final listing of every club in the country. Club presidents change, sometimes yearly, but the addresses listed will at least get you in touch with a member of the club who can tell you where to get further information.

For those interested in more formal types of learning, there is a chapter on Astronomy Education. Included are lists of summer camps and clinics; scholarships, grants, and internship opportunities; and universities across the U.S. and Canada which offer degrees in astronomy. A special subsection deals with sources of materials for teachers who need to locate written, audiovisual, or other teaching aids for class. It also contains the address and number of the NASA teacher resource centers throughout the country. Teachers might also want to check the **Photos, Slides, and Videos** section in Chapter 1 for sources of educational videos.

Information included in the **Astronomer's Sourcebook** is primarily intended to meet the needs of beginning, intermediate, and advanced amateurs. Maps only accessible to professional astronomers, for example, are not listed. Nor is there an attempt to include listings of books that would only appeal to a narrow branch of astronomers. The book does, however, contain several features that can help you make sense of more technically oriented publications. In the back of the book you will find a glossary of astronomical terms, as well as appendices with useful formulas and tables of astronomical constants and the like.

In parting, may the **Astronomer's Sourcebook** help you find whatever you are looking for—whether it be a better telescope, an affordable charge-coupled device, or a steady mount, or simply a congenial group of astronomy buffs to share your observing pleasure. May you always have dark skies and good seeing.

1

ARMCHAIR ASTRONOMY

BOOKS

Buying astronomy books that reflect your growing needs as an amateur or as a professional isn't as simple as running down to your local bookstore. Often, the big book chains carry only a few titles, usually geared to casual readers. There are, however, several sources that offer "bookstore services" by mail. You can also contact most publishers of astronomy books directly, or, if you're lucky enough to live near a university, you can stop by the bookstore for textbooks or observing guides.

Astronomy and **Sky & Telescope** each provide handy reference guides along with their book listings to let you know if a book is targeted for beginning, intermediate, or advanced readers. For reviews of new publications, see those magazines; the Astronomical League of the Pacific's **Mercury**; the National Space Society's **Ad Astra**; The Planetary Society's **The Planetary Report;** or the Astronomical League's newsletters.

Listed below are mail-order sources of astronomy books, plus a selection of suggested reading materials dealing with historical, theoretical, and descriptive aspects of astronomy. If you are looking for astronomy books of a hands-on nature, see Chapter 3 for "how-to" books about building telescopes; Chapter 4 for listings of observing guides, maps, and atlases; and Chapter 5 for recommended publications on photographing celestial objects.

Mail-Order Sources

★ **The Astronomical League,** 6235 Omie Circle, Pensacola, FL 32504–7625. Tel. (904) 477–8859. Members of the League receive discounts on astronomy publications. Write for list.

★ **The Astronomical Society of the Pacific,** 390 Ashton Ave., San Francisco, CA 94112. Tel. (415) 337–1100. The Society offers a wide variety of publications and astronomy-related items.

★ **The Astronomy Book Club,** 3000 Cindel Drive, Delran, NJ 08075–9889. Members can buy books from a variety of publishers. Selections are featured in the **Astronomy Book Club News,** which is sent to members 15 times per year.

★ **Black Forest Observatory,** 12815 Porcupine Lane, Colorado Springs, CO 80908. Tel. (719) 495–3828. Astronomy books and various astronomy-related items.

★ **Kalmbach Publishing Co.,** 21207 Crossroads Circle, P.O. Box 1612, Waukesha, WI 53187–1612. Tel. 1–800–446–5489. Books, atlases, and numerous other astronomy-related items. Also publishes **Astronomy** and other astronomy publications.

★ **Northern Sky Telescopes,** 5667 Duluth St., Golden Valley, MN 55422. Tel. 1–800–345–4202 or (612) 545–6786.

Fax (612) 545–9297. Astronomy supplies, including books, atlases, and self-help guides.

★ **Optica b/c,** 4100 MacArthur Blvd., Oakland, CA 94619. Tel. (415) 530–1234. General astronomy products, including books, maps, and atlases. Catalog, $1.00.

★ **The Planetary Society,** 65 N. Catalina Ave., Pasadena, CA 01106. Tel (818) 793–5100. Sells books and other astronomy-related items.

★ **Sky Publishing Corporation,** P.O. Box 9111, Belmont, MA 02178–9111. Tel. (617) 864–7360. Fax (617) 864–6117. Sells books, atlases, and numerous other astronomy-related items. Write for catalog. Also publishes **Sky & Telescope** magazine.

★ **U.S. Government Printing Office,** Superintendent of Documents, Washington, DC 20402. Tel. (202) 783–3238. This important source provides material on a vast variety of subjects. The GPO sells posters, books, and pamphlets. Because publications often are printed in limited quantities or go out of print quickly, it's wise to contact the GPO for a subject list of available publications. Write for a free Subject Bibliography Index. Astronomy and Astrophysics are listed under Subject Number 115; Space, Rockets & Satellites (mostly material from the National Aeronautics and Space Administration) is listed under Subject Number 297. Check your local library to see if it carries the subject bibliographies. You can copy the order form if you find a publication you want to order. If you know the publication number, you can also call to order at the number above.

★ **Willmann-Bell, Inc.,** P.O. Box 35025, Richmond, VA 23235. For orders, call 1–800–825–STAR. For information, or if you live in Virginia, call (804) 320–7016. Fax (804) 272–5920. Has more than 1,000 different astronomy book titles in stock. Catalog for $1.00.

Specialists in Old Books

★ **Warren Blake, Old Science Books,** 308 Hadley Drive, Trumbull, CT 06611. Tel. (203) 459–0820. Blake collects and sells old, used astronomy books and prints from the early 20th century and before. The books are available on a one-of-a-kind basis, and the list changes constantly. Write for a listing.

★ **The Gemmary Inc.,** P.O. Box 816, Redondo Beach, CA 90277. Tel. (213) 372–5969. Buys and sells old science and mineralogy books. Also sells 18th- and 19th-century mathematical and optical instruments, including telescopes, globes, orreries, and navigation instruments. Science books catalogs are updated twice a year and cost $2; scientific instruments catalogs are published once a year and cost $5.

Recommended Titles

General Interest

★ **The Amateur Astronomer's Handbook,** by James Muirden. Thomas Y. Crowell, HarperCollins Publishers, 10 E. 53rd St., New York, NY 10022. $10.95. A good introduction to observing the heavens. Another publication by Muirden, **How to Use an Astronomical Telescope,** also is a good choice for the beginner.

★ **The Astronomer's Universe,** by Herbert Friedman. W.W. Norton & Co., 500 Fifth Ave., New York, NY 10110. Tel. 1–800–233–4830. A popular introduction to astronomy designed for intelligent readers.

★ **Astronomy: From the Earth to the Universe,** fourth edition, by Jay M. Pasachoff. Saunders College Publishing Division, Holt, Rinehart and Winston, Independence Square West, Philadelphia, PA 19106. $24.95. A beginning astronomy textbook designed primarily for non-science majors. An easy-to-read, informative text that introduces students to the Earth, Solar System, stars, and the galaxies.

★ **The Decade of Discovery in Astronomy and Astrophysics,** by John N. Bahcall, et al. Available from Sky Publishing Corporation. $24.95. This volume surveys where astronomy is heading. The volume contains details of the 10–year plan for the future of American astronomy by the National Research Council, and presents data on the costs of specific projects and the technological needs of astronomy.

★ **Exploration of the Universe,** by George C. Abell, David Morrison, and Sidney C. Wolff. $50. Saunders College Publishing Division, Holt, Rinehart and Winston, Independence Square West, Philadelphia, PA 19106. A classic text, now in its sixth edition, which is an excellent introduction to astronomy for college students or the amateur ready to study independently. The latest edition includes information from space probes through 1990.

★ **Frontiers of Astronomy,** by David Morrison and Sidney Wolff. Saunders College Publishing Division, Holt, Rinehart and Winston, Independence Square West, Philadelphia, PA 19106. Includes information on current research, supernova explosions, and dark matter, plus discussions of the history of astronomy.

★ **A History of Astronomy,** by Antonie Pannekoek. Published by Dover Publications and available from Sky Publishing Corporation. $11.95. This text covers the history of astronomy from ancient times to the middle of this century.

★ **In the Stream of Stars,** edited by William K. Hartmann, Andrei Sokolov, Ron Miller, and Vitaly Myagkov. Workman Publishing Co., 708 Broadway, New York, NY 10003. $29.93. A Soviet-American space art book that includes images from the space programs of the U.S. and Soviet Union, plus representations of alien worlds.

★ **Men, Monsters and the Modern Universe,** by George Lovi and Wil Tirion. Willmann-Bell, Inc. $24.95. A look at the figures that make up the constellations of the night sky, along with a look at some observing targets for the amateur.

★ **Observational Astronomy for Amateurs,** by J.B. Sidgwick. Available from Sky Publishing Corporation. $5.95. An advanced handbook for amateurs covering observing techniques.

★ **The Sky: A User's Guide,** by David H. Levy. Available from Cambridge University Press, 40 W. 20th St., New York, NY 10011. $24.95. This self-described "owner's manual for the sky" provides a lively introduction to observational astronomy. Chapters cover naked-eye astronomy and choosing a telescope, plus tips on observing objects inside and outside of the Solar System.

★ **Starlight Nights,** by Leslie Peltier. Available from Sky Publishing Corporation. $12.95. A classic book about the pleasures of star gazing written by the late, well-known amateur.

★ **The Universe from Your Backyard,** by David Eicher. Cambridge University Press, 40 W. 20th St., New York, NY 10011. $24.95. Details objects you can view, along with tips on finding the best deep-sky objects. The articles are taken from the **Backyard Astronomer** column in **Astronomy Magazine.**

Astronomers

★ **The Astronomers,** by Donald Goldsmith. St. Martin's Press, 175 5th Ave., New York, NY 10010. $24.95. The book is a companion to the PBS television series **The Astronomers.** The television series is available as a video set. An excellent look into the way astronomers work and the way they approach their research projects.

★ **Clyde Tombaugh: Discoverer of Planet Pluto,** by David H. Levy. Available from University of Arizona Press, 1230 N. Park Ave., Suite 102, Tucson, AZ 85719. $35.00. An entertaining and inspiring story detailing Tombaugh's painstaking search for the ninth planet, as well as his discovery of clusters of galaxies.

★ **Lonely Hearts of the Cosmos,** by Dennis Overbye. HarperCollins Publishers, 10 E. 53rd St., New York, NY 10022. $25.00. A look at the people who observe the Universe, and those who develop theories of cosmology. Although about science and scientists, the book often takes a personal look at the people behind the theories, mathematics, and instruments.

The Solar System

★ **Astronomical Tables of the Sun, Moon, and Planets,** by Jean Meeus. Available

from Willmann-Bell, Inc. $19.95. A reference book that includes past and future predictable astronomical events. The tables cover planetary oppositions and conjunctions and solar and lunar eclipses from 1950 to 2050.

★ **Earthlike Planets,** by Murray, Malin, Greeley, et al. Available from Sky Publishing Corporation. $24.95. Covers Mercury, Venus, Earth, and Mars, with theories on how they formed and their characteristics today.

★ **Introduction to Asteroids,** by Clifford Cunningham. Available from Sky Publishing Corporation. $19.95. An amateur observer's book on the minor planets visible through a small telescope.

★ **Introduction to Comets,** by C. Chapman. Available from Sky Publishing Corporation. $13.95. A more advanced survey of cometary science.

★ **The Moon Observer's Handbook,** by Fred Price. Cambridge University Press, 40 W. 20th St., New York, NY 10011. $34.50. A guide to observing the Moon.

★ **The Mystery of Comets,** by Fred Whipple. Available from Sky Publishing Corporation. $12.50. Whipple, who first described comets as "dirty snowballs," tells the story of his half century of work in cometary science.

★ **The New Solar System,** edited by J. Kelly Beatty and Andrew Chaikin. Available from Cambridge University Press and Sky Publishing Corporation. $19.95 in paperback. Includes chapters by specialists in areas such as the Moon, Mars, Outer Planets, Comets, Asteroids, Meteorites, and more.

★ **Origin and Evolution of Planetary and Satellite Atmospheres,** by S.K. Atreya. Available from Sky Publishing Corporation. The papers are part of the University of Arizona's Space Science Series. $45 per set. Provides data from spacecraft missions to planets and satellites. The papers discuss the similarities and differences between the atmospheres of the planets and satellites of the Solar System.

★ **Planets Beyond: Discovering the Outer Solar System,** by Mark Littman. Available from Sky Publishing Corporation. $22.95. Covers Uranus, Neptune, and Pluto, the only major planets to have been discovered in recorded history. The book discusses how the planets were discovered and includes recent information from the Voyager spacecraft.

★ **The Restless Sun,** by Donat Wentzel. Available from Sky Publishing Corporation. $27.95. Includes the latest data on the Sun, with a perspective on solar science.

Beyond the Solar System

★ **Colliding Galaxies: The Universe in Turmoil,** by Barry Parker. Available from Plenum Publishing, 233 Spring St., New York, NY 10013. $23.95. Tells the story of the growing field of study of colliding galaxies. It is aimed at a popular audience, and includes stories of astronomers at work.

★ **Cycles of Fire,** by William Hartmann & Ron Miller. Available from Sky Publishing Corporation. $27.50. A coffee-table book that includes the work of space artists portraying scenes of other planets and stars.

★ **Handbook of Space Astronomy and Astrophysics,** by Martin V. Zombeck. Available from Cambridge University Press, 40 W. 20th St., New York, NY 10011. $75. Reference material about space-age astronomy and astrophysics. Includes tables, graphs, and diagrams.

★ **The Invisible Universe Revealed,** by Gerrit Verschuur. Available from Sky Publishing Corporation. $19.95. Presents the story of radio astronomy.

★ **Voyage through the Universe,** by the editors of Time-Life Books. Time-Life Books, 777 Duke St., Alexandria, VA 22314. A series of 20 titles, each costing $14.99, that cover topics such as The Sun, The Stars, Galaxies, The Far Planets, Life Search, The New Astronomy and The Visible Universe, among others. Designed for a popular audience.

Cosmology

★ **Bubbles, Voids and Bumps in Time: The New Cosmology,** edited by James Cornell.

Available from Cambridge University Press, 40 W. 20th St., New York, NY 10011. $22.95. Six cosmologists discuss their views on the "state of the Universe."

★ **Cosmology,** by Edward Harrison. Available from Sky Publishing Corporation. $37.50. An introductory textbook that covers how the Universe formed, how it is expanding and changing, and where it is going.

★ **Evolutionary Phenomena in Galaxies,** edited by J.E. Beckman and B.E.J. Pagel. Available from Cambridge University Press, 40 W. 20th St., New York, NY 10011. $69.50. The book is based on the proceedings of a conference held in July 1988. Topics covered include the formation of galaxies and their ages, stellar dynamics, galactic scale gas and its role in star formation, and the formation, production, and distribution of the chemical elements within galaxies.

★ **The Formation and Evolution of Cosmic Strings**, edited by G.W. Biggons, S.W. Hawing, and T. Vachaspati. Available from Cambridge University Press, 40 W. 20th St., New York, NY 10011. $59.50. The proceedings of a symposium held in Cambridge in 1989, in which 30 top scientists reviewed progress in understanding the physical structure of cosmic strings.

★ **Quasar Astronomy,** by Daniel W. Weedman. Available from Cambridge University Press, 40 W. 20th St., New York, NY 10011. $22.95. The text discusses aspects of quasar spectroscopy, with sections covering techniques for analyzing quasar data and statistics and the distribution of quasars in space time.

Search for Extraterrestrials

For at least thirty years now scientists have been listening for evidence of civilizations on other worlds. As yet, Earth remains the only place where life in any form has been detected. However, scientists continue the search for extraterrestrial intelligence (SETI) by scanning the radio waves for indications of some signal. The following books detail some of the searches and introduce some of the searchers.

★ **Extraterrestrials: Science and Alien Intelligence,** edited by Edward Regis. Available from Cambridge University Press, 40 W. 20th St., New York, NY 10011. $42.00 hardback; $12.00 paper. A collection of fourteen essays on the search for extraterrestrials.

★ **The Search for Extraterrestrial Intelligence,** by Thomas R. McDonough. Available from John Wiley & Sons, 605 Third Ave., New York, NY 10158. $19.95. An entertaining look at the search by a knowledgeable scientist.

★ **Search for Extraterrestrial Intelligence,** edited by Philip Morrison, John Billingham, and Jon Wolfe. A 1979 NASA publication which includes sections by several SETI researchers.

★ **SETI Pioneers,** by David W. Swift. Available from the University of Arizona Press, 1230 N. Park Ave., Suite 102, Tucson, AZ 85719. Tel. 1–800–426–3797. $35.00. The book includes interviews with seventeen people who pioneered SETI work, including Frank Drake, who mounted the first full-scale search using the large radio telescopes at Green Banks, West Virginia.

Technical

★ **Formulae for Calculators,** by Jean Meeus. Available from Willmann-Bell, Inc. $14.95. Written for users of programmable calculators. Includes step-by-step instructions to get a program to run such calculations as orbit computations of asteroids or comets, and other astronomical problems.

★ **Fundamentals of Celestial Mechanics,** by J.M.A. Danby. Available from Willmann-Bell, Inc. $19.95. The text places an emphasis on computations and includes sample programs. The book is written for those with an understanding of calculus and elementary differential equations.

★ **Stars and Their Spectra,** by James B. Kaler. Available from Cambridge University Press, 40 W. 20th St., New York, NY 10011. $29.95. This book provides details on stellar spectroscopy, and al-

though designed for astronomy students, is suitable for serious amateurs.

Directories and Reference Books

★ **Annual Review of Astronomy & Astrophysics,** 4139 El Camino Way, Palo Alto, CA 94306. Tel. (415) 493–4400. A review of findings each year in the field of astronomy and astrophysics.

★ **The Cambridge Atlas of Astronomy,** edited by Jean Audouze. Available from Cambridge University Press, 40 W. 20th St., New York, NY 10011. $90. A complete atlas that offers data on planetary science, astrophysics, cosmology, and space missions.

★ **Directory of Physics and Astronomy.** American Institute of Physics, 335 E. 45th St., New York, NY 10017. An annual listing of members of the American Institute of Physics.

★ **General Science Index.** H.W. Wilson Co., 950 University Avenue, Bronx, NY 10452. Tel. 800–367–6770 or (212) 588–8400. An annual index to scientific articles published in periodicals.

★ **Science Citation Index.** The Institute for Scientific Information, 3501 Market St., Philadelphia, PA. Tel. 1–800–523–1850 or (215) 386–0100. A source for articles of scientific interest, including astronomy.

★ **STAR (Scientific & Technical Aerospace Report).** Published by NASA and available from U.S. Government Printing Office at address given under Mail-Order Sources. A yearly review of space, aerospace, and astronomy papers from the previous year.

PERIODICALS

Letters and journals have been a major factor in the spread of knowledge about astronomy since the invention of the printing press. Even with the rise of telecommunications, computers, and videos, astronomers continue to air their views through magazines, journals, and professional publications. For amateurs, magazines and journals represent a way of peeking into the vast storehouse of knowledge that grows daily. They are also a means of sharing opposing viewpoints for people separated by oceans and continents.

Some publications, primarily for professionals, deal with technical subjects, and require expertise in mathematics, physics, and astronomy to follow. Other, more "popular" publications present information in varying degrees of complexity, running the gamut from articles that require little scientific knowledge to understand to those that assume a degree of scientific sophistication on the part of the reader. A representative sample of periodicals targeted at both laymen and professionals are listed below. Many of the special organizations and clubs listed elsewhere in this book also publish newsletters and other periodicals.

Magazines

★ **Ad Astra,** 922 Pennsylvania Ave. SE, Washington, DC 20003. Tel. (202) 543–1900. A publication of the National Space Society which focuses on explaining, in non-technical terms, the space program and related efforts. Subscription is included with membership in the National Space Society. See **National and Special Interest Groups** in Chapter 2.

★ **Almanac for Computers,** published by the U.S. Naval Observatory, Washington, DC 20392. Send orders to: Superintendent of Documents, U.S. Government Printing Office, Washington, DC 20402.

★ **American Association of Variable Star Observers Bulletin,** 25 Birch St., Cambridge, MA 02138. Predicted dates for maxima and minima of long period variable stars. Subscription, $25. Also publishes **AAVSO Journal,** $25 per year, which includes scientific papers on variable star research; the **AAVSO Circular,** $15 per year, which covers monthly preliminary observations; and the **AAVSO Reports,** $30.

★ **Association of Lunar and Planetary Observers Journal (Strolling Astronomer),** Box 16131, San Francisco, CA 94116. Quarterly publication targeted at astronomers interested in objects within the Solar System. Subscription, $14 per year.

★ **Astrograph,** Box 2283, Arlington, VA 22202. Tel. (703) 830–2229. A magazine devoted to astrophotography. Subscription, $10 per year.

★ **Astronomy,** Kalmbach Publishing Co., 21027 Crossroads Circle, P.O. Box 1612, Waukesha, WI 53187. Tel. (414) 796–8776. Subscription inquiries, call (800) 446–5489. A mostly non-technical monthly publication aimed at amateurs and serious observers. Features a monthly sky map, plus scientific articles, observing tips, and book reviews. Also publishes equipment reviews and telescope-building suggestions. Accepts advertisements. Has the largest circulation of the strictly astronomy magazines. Subscription price, $24 per year.

★ **Astronomy Now,** 193 Uxbridge Road, London, W12 9RA, England. Features articles for newcomers to astronomy, as well as professionals. Subscription: $35 surface, $55 air mail.

★ **CCD News,** 31651 Avon Rd., Avon, OH 44011. Provides in-depth technical tips on using charge-coupled devices, with articles from experts at the amateur and

professional level. One-year subscription (four issues) costs $5.

★ **Discover,** 114 Fifth Ave., New York, NY 10011. A popular science magazine, recently bought by Walt Disney Corporation, that frequently carries articles about astronomy. Seldom covers observational techniques or equipment. Subscription: $27 annually.

★ **Final Frontier,** P.O. Box 11519, Washington, D.C., 20008. A bi-monthly magazine covering the space program for a general newsstand readership.

★ **Griffith Observer,** Griffith Observatory, 2800 E. Observatory Road, Los Angeles, CA 90027. Tel. (213) 664–1181. Monthly publication; subscriptions cost $12 per year.

★ **Mercury,** Astronomical Society of the Pacific, 390 Ashton Ave., San Francisco, CA 94112. Tel. (415) 337–1100. Bimonthly, non-technical journal intended for the general reader, amateur astronomer, and science educator. Features articles on current research, innovations in astronomy, education, and issues in other fields that touch astronomy. Subscription comes with the Astronomical Society of the Pacific membership fee: $29.50 in the U.S.; $37.50 for foreign members.

★ **Nature,** P.O. Box 1733, Riverton, NJ 08077–7333. **Nature** covers a wide range of topics, and frequently includes astronomical subjects such as new findings by astronomers worldwide.

★ **The Observer's Guide,** Astro Cards, Box 35, Natrona Heights, PA 15065. Observing is the focus of this bimonthly publication, which publishes astrophotos, plus "Eyepiece" impressions of objects. Observing tips discuss the appearance of objects in different-sized telescopes, such as 16–inch to 8–inch. Runs some articles on general topics, but overall emphasis is, as the name suggests, observational. Subscription rates: $15 per year; $21 in Canada; $24 per year by surface mail for all other countries; $33 by airmail. Astronomy Clubs with five or more subscriptions can deduct $3 per subscription.

★ **Odyssey,** Cobblestone, 30 Grove St., Peterborough, NH 03458. Designed for children and teenagers, this monthly magazine features easy-to-understand articles about astronomy and projects for children. Subscription, $19.95.

★ **The Planetary Report,** The Planetary Society, 65 North Catalina Ave., Pasadena, CA 91106. Tel. (818) 793–5100. Bimonthly publication written mostly in non-technical terms. Covers space projects as well as observational astronomy. Subscription covered through $25 membership fee.

★ **Publications,** Astronomical Society of the Pacific, 390 Ashton Ave., San Francisco, CA 94112. Tel. (415) 337–1100. Aimed at a more technical audience than the Society's **Mercury** publication. It serves as an outlet for publication of astronomy observations of a scientific nature, and keeps members of the Society in touch with current astronomical research. Subscription is $65 annually, which includes membership dues and subscription to **Mercury.** Submit manuscripts for publication to: Dr. Howard E. Bond, Editor, Space Telescope Science Institute, 3700 San Martin Drive, Baltimore, MD 21218.

★ **Sky & Telescope,** Sky Publishing Corporation, 49 Bay State Rd., Cambridge, MA 02138. Tel. (617) 864–7360. Subscription requests and editorial material should be sent to **Sky & Telescope,** P.O. Box 9111, Belmont, MA 02178–9111. Monthly magazine which includes monthly sky map, columns on objects to observe and telescope building, and book reviews. Accepts articles from professionals and amateurs. Regularly covers topics such as determining distances to galaxies, gravitational lenses, pulsars, the life of stars, and cosmological theories. Columns are aimed at the beginner through serious amateur or professional. Subscription is $24 per year; $45 for two years; and $60 for three years.

★ **The Starry Messenger,** P.O. Box 6552, Ithaca, NY, 14851. (201) 992–6865. For $20 per year, the magazine offers an advertising outlet for anyone wanting to buy or sell used astronomy equipment, books, magazines, and just about anything else related to the field.

★ **Webb Society Quarterly Journal,** Wild Rose, Church Road, Winkfield, Windsor, Berks, SL4 4SF, England. Observing tips, technical data on findings, science articles.

Professional Publications

★ **AAS Newsletter,** American Astronomical Society, 2000 Florida Ave., NW, Suite 300, Washington, DC 20009. Tel. (202) 328–2010. Published five times annually. Reports on Society actions, information about federal agencies, and news items of interest to astronomers. Subscription comes with membership in the Society.

★ **Annual Review of Astronomy & Astrophysics,** 4139 El Camino Way, Box 10139, Palo Alto, CA 94306–0897. Tel. (415) 493–4400. Fax (415) 855–9815. Telex (910) 290–0275. A review of current developments in astronomy and astrophysics. Subscription, $51 in U.S. and Canada, $55 elsewhere.

★ **The Astronomical Journal,** a publication of the American Astronomers Society, published by The University of Chicago Press, 5801 S. Ellis Ave., Chicago, IL 60637. Editorial offices at Kitt Peak National Observatory, Box 26732, Tucson, AZ 85726–6732, Dr. Helmut A. Abt, Managing Editor. Tel. (602) 325–9214. The

Journal is among the leading professional publications and features research in all aspects of astronomy, from theory to observational findings. U.S. subscriptions cost $75 per year for members and $280 for nonmembers, and are available in paper, microfiche, or paper/microfiche editions. Foreign subscriptions are $105 for members, surface rate, ($135 air freight).

★ **Astronomy & Astrophysics,** order from Springer-Verlag New York Inc., Service Center Secaucus, 44 Hartz Way, Secaucus, NJ 07094. Tel. (201) 348–4033. Fax (201) 348–4505. Telex 0–23–125994. A European journal. Cost is $1804 per year, or $73 per issue.

★ **Astronomy Quarterly,** 1130 San Lucas Circle, Tucson, AZ 85704. Tel. (602) 297–4797. Examines the role of astronomy and cosmology in natural philosophy.

★ **The Astrophysical Journal,** a publication of the American Astronomers Society, published by The University of Chicago Press, 5801 S. Ellis Ave., Chicago, IL 60637. Provides in-depth articles on research from observatories around the world, plus new theories about astrophysics. Subscriptions cost $135 for members in the U.S., $261 for surface and $435 for airfreight for foreign members, $600 for non-members.

★ **Astrophysical Letters & Communications,** Gordon and Breach, Science Publishers

Inc., 50 West 23rd St., New York, NY 10010. Subscriptions sold on a volume basis, with varying rates for corporate and academic subscribers.

★ **Astrophysics,** a translation of **Astrofizika,** a publication of the Academy of Sciences of Armenia. A technical publication for professionals or "serious" amateurs. Subscription, for two volumes per year, is $695, available from Plenum Publishing, 233 Spring St., New York, NY, 10013.

★ **Astrophysics & Space Science, An International Journal of Cosmic Physics,** available from Kluwer Academic Publishing Group, P.O. Box 358, Accord Station, Hingham, MA 02018–0358 in the U.S., or from Kluwer Academic Publishing Group, P.O. Box 322, 3300 AH Dordrecht, The Netherlands. The journal features original contributions from "the entire domain of astrophysics and allied fields of cosmochemistry, dynamics of stellar, galactic & extra-galactic topics, excluding the sun." The emphasis is on topics opened up through space research, with observational and theoretical papers accepted, plus articles on techniques of instrumentation. Subscription is $183.50 per volume.

★ **The Bulletin of the American Astronomical Society,** a publication of the American Astronomers Society, published by The University of Chicago Press, 5801 S. Ellis Ave., Chicago, IL 60637. A quarterly publication of abstracts of papers presented at meetings of the American Astronomical Society and its divisions and reports of observatories. Send manuscripts to **Bulletin of American Astronomical Society,** American Institute of Physics, 335 E. 45th St., New York, NY 10017. The cost for members of the AAS is $20 in the U.S., $30 for foreign surface delivery, $35 for foreign airfreight, $50 for nonmembers.

★ **Cosmic Research,** a translation of **Kosmicheskie Issledovaniya,** a publication of the Academy of Science, U.S.S.R. Available from Plenum Publications, 233 Spring St., New York, NY 10013. Features work by Soviet researchers. Subscription, for six issues, is $855.

★ **Experimental Astronomy,** available from Kluwer Academic Publishing Group, P.O. Box 358, Accord Station, Hingham, MA 02018–0358 in the U.S., or from Kluwer Academic Publishing Group, P.O. Box 322, 3300 AH Dordrecht, The Netherlands. Subscriptions are $156.50 for 16 issues; individuals can receive a reduced rate of $74 per volume. Subscribers to **Astrophysics and Space Science** also receive **Experimental Astronomy.** The periodical bills itself as a "medium of exchange for people developing and using new instruments to observe astronomical objects in several wavelengths," and includes new techniques to analyze data.

★ **Fundamentals of Cosmic Physics,** Gordon and Breach, Science Publishers Inc., 50 West 23rd St., New York, NY 10010.

★ **General Relativity and Gravitation,** Plenum Publishing, 233 Spring St., New York, NY 10013. Available at a cost of $495, this journal features articles on general relativity and related topics.

★ **Icarus, the International Journal of Solar System Studies,** Academic Press Inc., 1 East First St, Duluth, MN 55802. Edited by Joseph A. Bun, Space Science Bldg., Cornell University, Ithaca, NY, 14853–6801. Tel. (607) 255–4875. Annual subscription is $792.

★ **International Amateur-Professional Photoelectric Photometry Communications,** Dyer Observatory, Vanderbilt University, Nashville, TN, 37235. Published six times a year for members of International Amateur-Professional Photoelectric Photometry. Subscription cost covered in $15 membership fee. Works with amateurs and professionals with articles about automatic telescopes and photoelectric photometry. Editorial submissions to Dr. Terry D. Oswalt, Dept. of Physics & Space Sciences, Florida Institute of Technology, Melbourne, FL 32901. Tel. (404) 768–8000, ext. 8098.

★ **International Comet Quarterly,** Mail Stop 18, Smithsonian Astrophysical Observatory, 60 Garden St., Cambridge, MA 02138. Established in 1978, the quarterly contains information on comets, including observations from amateurs.

★ **Journal of College Science Teaching,** National Science Teachers Association, 1742 Connecticut Ave. NW, Washington, DC 20009. Cost is $40; published six times per year, September through May.

★ **Meteor News,** American Meteor Society, Route 3, Box 1062, Callahan, FL 32011 (editorial offices). Quarterly which provides information about meteors and the Society.

★ **The Observatory,** published by the Rutherford Appleton Laboratory, Chilton, Didcot, OX11 0QX, Great Britain.

★ **Physics Today,** American Institute of Physics, 500 Sunnyside Blvd., Woodbury, NY 11797. Members of the society receive the monthly magazine for $15; nonmembers, $95 per year. Regularly carries articles related to astronomy.

★ **Science,** P.O. Box 1723, Riverton, NJ 08077. Published weekly by the American Association for the Advancement of Science. Subscriptions are $82 per year, with different rates for students.

★ **Science News,** Science Services Inc., 1719 N. Street NW, Washington, DC 20036. Tel. (202) 785–2255. Regularly carries news about astronomy research as well as other science topics. Published weekly. Subscription $34.50 per year.

★ **Scientific American,** Scientific American Inc., 415 Madison Ave., New York, NY 10017. Tel. 1–800–333–1199. Although not devoted strictly to astronomy, this monthly magazine regularly carries articles and papers about the subject.

★ **Solar Physics,** available from Kluwer Academic Publishing Group, P.O. Box 358, Accord Station, Hingham, MA 02018–0358 in the U.S., or from Kluwer Academic Publishing Group, P.O. Box 322, 3300 AH Dordrecht, The Netherlands, at a cost of $184 per year. Editorial offices at National Solar Observatory, P.O. Box 26732, 950 N. Cherry Ave., Tucson, AZ 85726–6732. Tel. (602) 325–9269.

★ **Soviet Astronomy Letters,** translation published by the American Institute of Physics, 335 E. 45th St., New York, NY 10017.

★ **Space Science Review,** available from Kluwer Academic Publishing Group, P.O. Box 358, Accord Station, Hingham, MA 02018–0358 in the U.S., or from Kluwer Academic Publishing Group, P.O. Box 322, 3300 AH Dordrecht, The Netherlands, at a cost of $202.50. Published eight times per year. Invites "review papers on scientific research carried by means of rockets, rocket-propelled vehicles" and by balloons.

★ **21st Century Science & Technology,** 21st Century Science Association, 60 Sycolin Rd., Suite 203, Leesburg, VA, 22075. Tel. (703) 777–4743. Bimonthly dealing with educational topics and science teaching tips. Subscription $20 per year.

★ **Vistas in Astronomy,** Pergamon Press Inc., Maxwell House, Fairview Park, Elmsford, NY 10523. An international review journal published four times per year. Covers new findings in astronomy.

COMPUTER-BASED ASTRONOMY

Software

In today's world of astronomy, it often seems remarkable that anything was accomplished before the age of the computer. Computers simulate colliding galaxies, plot orbits for space probes, permit "enhancements" of bits of information that grow into breath-taking photos of distant planets and their moons, and allow professional astronomers to test theories in ways never before possible. Computations that once took weeks can be completed in a fraction of the time with the most basic home computer. Even amateurs, using fairly simple programs, can look at the night sky 2,000 years ago, or 2,000 years in the future.

Types of software available range from public domain programs to advanced simulators that run only on large mainframe units. With a computer, you can control your telescope, enhance images, and flash a map of the night sky on your screen. Software versions exist for the book form of many atlases. Some programs are visually exciting, allowing you to zoom in on Saturn or Jupiter, or to view the planets from Earth or from an imaginary point far out in space. Other programs are utilitarian, calculating an ephemeris, or predicting an orbit of a manmade satellite.

The number of firms offering such software for sale continues to grow, almost by the month. If you have a computer and modem, you can also tap into many fine public domain programs through computer bulletin boards. (See the section on Bulletin Boards below.) Astronomy clubs often have programs available, some written by members, and someone is usually offering a program for minimal cost at almost any gathering of astronomy buffs.

Here are some commercial sources for computer software.

★ **Andromeda Software Inc.,** P.O. Box 605, Amherst, NY 14226–0605. Offers a number of science programs, either shareware at a modest charge, or public domain programs for minimal costs. Programs include beginner disks that depict the sky and constellations,

programs to calculate the position of comets, and programs that take you on a tour of the Solar System. Free catalog.

★ **Applied Research Inc.,** 6700 Odyssey Dr., P.O. Box 11220, Huntsville, AL, 35814–1220. Tel. (205) 837–8600. Fax (205) 721–1180. Markets a program that allows you to calculate the orbits of objects around the Earth, including manmade satellites. Also gives views of the Earth from a satellite, and shows ground traces of a satellite.

★ **A.R.C., Science Simulation Software,** P.O. Box 1974, Loveland, CO 80539–1974. Tel. (303) 667–1168 or 1–800–759–1642. Fax (303) 667–1105. A.R.C. features the "Dance of the Planets," a vivid representation of a journey through the Solar System. Excellent color and lots of extras so you can spend hours traveling to the planets from all angles. Cost is $195 plus shipping and handling. Write for more information.

★ **Arizona Database Project Inc.,** 3135 South 48th St., Suite 3, Tempe, AZ 85282. A database for IBM compatibles which lists more than 23,000 deep-sky objects.

★ **Astro-Computer Control,** RD 1, Alexandria, PA 16611. Tel. (814) 669–4483. Computer control software for telescopes.

★ **Astronomical Research Network,** 206 Bellwood Ave., Maplewood, MN 55117.

Tel. (612) 488–5178. A program, designed for CD-ROM users, which features Jupiter, Saturn, Uranus and Moons, in one volume, and the Moons, Neptune, and other images in volume two.

★ **Astronomical Society of the Pacific,** 390 Ashton Ave., San Francisco, CA 94112. Tel. (415) 337–1100. This world-wide astronomical society offers a variety of computer software from various authors. Write for a catalog.

★ **Black Forest Observatory,** 12815 Porcupine Lane, Colorado Springs, CO 80908–3503. Tel. (719) 495–3828. Sells computer software written by other companies. Write for catalog.

★ **Carina Software,** 830 Williams St., San Leandro, CA 94577. Tel. (415) 352–7328. Sells the Voyager program, which allows you to explore the past, present, and future of the sky from anywhere on Earth.

★ **Comsoft,** P.O. Box 44265, Tucson, AZ 85733–4265. Tel. (602) 797–1420. An earth satellite orbit propagation program. Write for more information.

★ **Future Trends Software,** P.O. Box 3927, Austin, TX 78764. Tel. (512) 443–6564. Call 1–800–869–3279 for more information. The EZCosmoso program features plots for more than 10,000 celestial objects, including the Sun, Moon, planets, stars, constellations, and NGC items.

★ **GAO Associates,** P.O. Box 60333, Florence, MA 01060. Tel. (413) 586–3999. Orbital simulation and display programs.

★ **Kalmbach Publishing Co.,** P.O. Box 1612, Waukesha, WI 53108–1612. The publisher of **Astronomy** offers a variety of software products from various sources. Write for details, or see current copy of the magazine.

★ **MMI Corporation,** Dept. ST–89, 2950 Wyman Parkway, P.O. Box 19907, Baltimore, MD 21211. Tel. (301) 366–1222. Fax (301) 366–6311. Sells computer software and much more. Catalog free to educators; $2 to others.

★ **Parsec Software,** 1949 Blair Loop Rd., Danville, VA 24541. Tel. (804) 822–1179. Software simulations of the sky at various dates, plus views of the Solar System from any object. Eclipses and occultations. Prices start at $95.

★ **PicoSCIENCE,** 41512 Chadbourne Dr., Fremont, CA 94539. Tel. (415) 498–1095. Software that plots stars down to 16th magnitude.

★ **SkyBase Software and Computers,** 450 Spring Hill Dr., Morgan Hill, CA 95037. Software that allows you to make your own finder charts for comets, deep sky objects, or astrophotography.

★ **Sky Publishing Corporation,** 49 Bay State Rd., Cambridge, MA 02138. The publishing company of **Sky & Telescope** also offers a variety of computer software, including data bases and catalogs.

★ **Softouch Applications,** 646 N. Bend Rd., Baltimore, MD 21229. Sells programs for Macintosh computers, including one that plots star maps, displays planets, shows eclipses, computes comet paths, etc. Write for more information.

★ **Softshoppe Inc.,** P.O. Box 3678, Ann Arbor, MI 48106. Tel. (313) 761–7638. To order, call toll-free at 1–800–829–BEST. Fax (313) 761–7639. Accepts major credit cards. Offers public domain software and shareware (for IBM and Macintosh) on a variety of subjects, including astronomy.

★ **Software Bisque,** 912 12th St., Suite A, Golden, CO 80401. Tel. (303) 278–4478. Features astronomy programs, including some that show the constellations, bright stars, and NGC objects. Software designed to guide telescopes, with a few hardware additions. Screen can display line drawings of the constellations, etc. Also permits calculations of the coordinates of Solar System objects and of periodic comets.

★ **StarByte,** P.O. Box 42324, Cincinnati, OH 45242. To order, 1–800–835–2246. For free color brochure, call (513) 244–1212. Creates science programs, including Solar System tours and lists of what's visible in the sky.

★ **Stellar Software,** P.O. Box 10183, Berkeley, CA 94709. Tel. (415) 845–8405. Fax (415) 845–2139. TLX (910) 250–9172. Software creates optical ray tracers on three levels, from basics for students working with lenses, mirrors, and irises, to Beam Four applications for professionals. Write or call for further information.

★ **Western Research Co.,** 2127 E. Speedway, Suite 209, Tucson, AZ 85719. Markets LunarCal, a program that allows you to estimate when the lunar crescent will be visible. Cost is $48 plus postage, for Apple Macintosh computers.

★ **Zephyr Services,** 1900 Murray Avenue, Pittsburgh, PA 15217. Tel. 1–800–533–6666; (412) 422–6600, in Pennsylvania. Fax orders to (412) 422–9930. Write for brochure.

Bulletin Boards

With a computer and a modem, you can tap into bulletin boards that pass on information, allow you to "talk" with other astronomers, or just let you "listen" to others. Some may transfer programs to your computer, or allow you to pass on bits of information or significant findings. It's a way of circulating data in ways and speeds never before possible. In a sense, the computer and telephone open up new worlds.

Some of the bulletin boards below have a hook-up fee or a per-minute charge, but most may be dialed into free of charge. Remember, however, that long-distance phone rates apply if you are outside the local calling area.

★ **Acom II,** Houston, Texas. Houston Space Society and astronomy- related data. Tel. (713) 879–1448.

★ **Aerospace Technology BBS,** Fairfield, California. Tel. (797) 437–5389.

★ **Albuquerque Astronomical Society Computer Bulletin Board** is available for Albuquerque Astronomical Society members for discussions, announcements, and transfer of files and newsletter articles in the software library. Tel. (505) 255–3623. Set your modem to 8 N 1.

★ **America Online,** a national network for Apple II and Macintosh computers. Features weekly conferences, message boards, sky information, and celestial events, as well as a library with programs. Call 800–227–6364 for subscription information.

★ **The Andromeda Galaxy,** Troy, New York. Board carries astronomy files and other data. Tel. (518) 273–8313.

★ **Arkansas Astronomy BBS,** Little Rock, Arkansas. Operated by University of Arkansas and the Mid-South Astronomical Research Society. Includes a list of planetarium shows, observatory hours, and celestial events. Tel. (501) 569–3001.

★ **Astro,** Washington, D.C. Messages, files, and software on astronomy. Tel. (703) 524–1837.

★ **Astro-Info,** Montreal, Quebec. Carries NASA and ESA news and observing tips. Tel. (514) 471–1222.

★ **Astronomical Society of the Atlantic,** Atlanta, Georgia. The Society operates a computer bulletin board accessible at 300/1200/2400 baud at (404) 985–0408. Features national access to FIDONET, USENET, and other communications resources. This bulletin board also serves as the regional BBS for the Southeast Regional division of the Astronomical League.

★ **The Comm-post,** Denver, Colorado. Contains sections for astronomy and message board and forum discussion. International Astronomical Union circulars are on-line. Tel. (303) 534–4646.

★ **CompuServe,** Columbus, Ohio. CompuServe is an international computer network with more than 500,000 subscribers. **Sky & Telescope** has an on-line service through CompuServe. To subscribe, call 1–800–848–8199.

★ **Datalink RBB,** Dallas, Texas. The Dallas Remote Imaging Group sponsors this service, which specializes in amateur radio, satellite tracking, and ham radio information. Tel. (214) 394–7438.

★ **Event Horizons,** 141 N. State St., Suite 350, Lake Oswego, OR 97034. Tel. (503) 697–5100. A commercial system with a section devoted to astronomical images. You may access the system for free to download sample images and a catalog of available files, but to download other images, you must become a subscriber. The cost is $10 an hour for transmission speeds up to 2400 baud and $40 per hour for 9600 baud. Subscribers must pay in advance. To download, set your parameters to 8 data bits, 1 stop bit, no parity, and dial the number.

★ **NASA Aerospace Information Reprography,** Orlando, Florida. Articles about NASA and space topics. Tel. (407) 774–7371.

★ **NASA JSC,** gives shuttle schedules from the Johnson Space Center, Houston, Texas. Tel. (713) 483–5817.

★ **NASA-Lewis Computer BBS,** Cleveland, Ohio. Has an astronomy section and programs produced by NASA Lewis Center. Tel. (216) 433–8035.

★ **NASA Spacelink,** Huntsville, Alabama. A service that gives NASA news and information. Tel. (205) 895–0028.

★ **National Space Society Computer Bulletin Board Service,** Pittsburgh, Pennsylvania. Available via computer modem at (412) 366–5208, (1200/2400/9600 baud N–

8–1). The NSS BBS contains information on space topics, particularly current events and public policy. NSS also contributes to commercial boards such as CompuServe, America Online, PC-Link, and Q-Link. The NSS has other links available through the Pittsburgh number.

★ **Naval Observatory BB,** Washington, D.C. Sponsored by the U.S. Naval Observatory. Tel. (202) 653–1079.

★ **NSS Mid-Cities Chapter BBS,** Arlington, Texas. Sponsored by the National Space Society, this board discusses space, space science, and related technology. Tel. (817) 261–6641.

★ **Orange County Astronomers,** California. Tel. (714) 738–4331.

★ **Science Resources,** a service of the National Science Foundation in Washington, D.C. Tel. (202) 634–1764.

★ **SCI-FIND,** a service of the University of Missouri's Science Journalism Center. Tel. (314) 882–3874.

★ **SpaceMet Physics Forum,** Amherst, Massachusetts. Sponsored by the University of Massachusetts, Five Colleges, Inc., and the National Science Foundation. A board primarily for teachers; has many space, physics, and astronomy program files. Tel. (413) 545–1959.

★ **SPACE NETWORK,** Boulder, Colorado. Gives space news and research. Tel. (303) 494–8446.

★ **StarBase III,** Fresno, California. Specializes in astronomy, space, and science. Tel. (209) 432–2487.

★ **Stargate BBS,** sponsored by The Astronomical League, Pensacola Florida. Programs and the text of the **Reflector.** The **Reflector** also is available on CompuServe. 300, 1200, 2400 Baud. 24 hours. Tel. (214) 578–7618.

★ **Stargazer's BBS,** Virginia Beach, Virginia. Serves amateur astronomers in the Tidewater area. Has astronomy and telescope-making information. Tel. (804) 424–9295.

★ **Starlight,** Marshall, Michigan. Covers astronomy and astrophysics. Tel. (616) 781–6639.

★ **Star Net,** Minneapolis, Minnesota. A not-for-profit scientific exchange. Includes data on astronomy. Tel. (612) 681–9520.

★ **Starnet,** offered by the Walker County Science Center, Georgia. Includes information on computer software and the latest space science and astronomical information. Call (404) 764–1629, 24 hours a day.

★ **Starry Night,** Blue Springs, Missouri. Sponsored by the Astronomical Society of Kansas City. Has local astronomy information, observing information, astrophotography tips, radio astronomy data. Tel. (913) 631–0761.

★ **Technical and Scientific Bulletin Board,** Anaheim, California. Provides photometry and astronomy software. Tel. (714) 883–7343, using 300, 1200, or 2400 baud modems with standard 8–N–1 protocol.

★ **Zephyr BBS,** Maumee, Ohio. Space-related files. Tel. (419) 893– 0121.

HOTLINES

When you want to know what's going on in the sky, you can often get information by simply calling one of the many "hotlines" around the country. Many hotlines give observing data for planets, comets, eclipses, and other astronomical events. Some, sponsored by clubs or planetariums, offer observing tips mixed in with club or planetarium news. Others provide up-to-the-minute coverage of space shuttle missions. Whatever your choice, however, it's easy to learn "what's up there."

★ **Abrams Planetarium Sky Information,** sponsored by the Abrams Planetarium, Michigan State University. Gives current sky information, 24 hours per day. Tel. (517) 332–STAR.

★ **The Astronomical Society of Kansas City,** Starwatch Hotline. Provides information on astronomical events for the month. Tel. (913) 432–9077.

★ **Astronomical Society of the Atlantic,** Atlanta, Georgia. Information on astronomical activities and astronomical lectures in Georgia. Tel. (404) 264–0451.

★ **Astronomical Society of the Pacific,** San Francisco, California. Carries current research news. Updated weekly. Tel. (415) 337–1244.

★ **Brooks Observatory,** Mount Pleasant, Michigan. The "Astronomy Hotline" from Central Michigan University. Observing data on the Moon, planets, and other sky objects. Tel. (517) 774–3759.

★ **Buehler Planetarium,** Fort Lauderdale, Florida. Sponsors a night sky information line, open 24 hours a day. Tel. (305) 475–6734.

★ **Davis Planetarium Starline,** sponsored by the Maryland Science Center. Night sky information. Tel. (301) 539–STAR.

★ **DePauw University, McKim Observatory,** Greencastle, Indiana. Sponsors an Astronomy Hotline, a 24–hour information line that provides updates about objects to look for in the sky, and the next public open house date for the observatory. Tel. (317) 658–4661.

★ **Detroit Astronomical Society,** Detroit, Michigan. Hotline has information about general observing objects, such as planets, comets, and meteor showers. Tel. (313) 837–0130.

★ **Dudley Observatory,** Schenectady, New York. General astronomy information, after 5 p.m. weekdays and anytime on weekends. Tel. (518) 382–7584.

★ **The El Paso Independent School District,** El Paso, Texas. Operates a "Star Line" after 5 p.m. Central Daylight Time. The recording discusses "what's in the sky each month." Tel. (915) 779–4317.

★ **Fernbank Astronomy Hotline,** Fernbank Science Center, Atlanta, Georgia. Provides up-to-date sky information. Tel. (404) 329–4500, then press 2027.

★ **Fleischmann Planetarium,** Reno, Nevada. Current sky information. Offers tips on sky events; sponsored by the University of Nevada-Reno and the Fleischmann Planetarium. Tel. (702) 784–1–SKY.

★ **Gates Planetarium,** Denver, Colorado. Astronomy hotline for current astronomical events. Pre-recorded information updated monthly. Tel. (303) 370–6316. For specific information, call (303) 370–6426 to talk with staff astronomer.

★ **Griffith Observatory,** Los Angeles, California. Has general observing information about the Moon, planets, and other objects. Tel. (213) 663–8171.

★ **Hawaiian Skies,** Honolulu, Hawaii. This sky guide carries information about the night sky over the islands. Refers to stars and constellations by both standard and Hawaiian names. Tel. (808) 948–0759.

★ **NASA Kennedy Space Center Spaceport.** Provides current launch information. Open 9 a.m. to dusk every day except Christmas. In the continental U.S., call 1–900–321–LIFT OFF (75 cents per call).

★ **NASA-Johnson Space Center,** Houston, Texas. News relating to U.S. civilian space program. Tel. (713) 483–8600.

★ **National Air and Space Museum,** Washington, D.C. This report from the Albert Einstein Planetarium provides observing information. Tel. (202) 357–2000.

★ **The National Space Society** offers the following telephone hotlines:

  ■ **Dial-A-Shuttle,** at 1–900–909–NASA, is a 24–hour toll telephone service NSS produces during civilian space shuttle missions. Callers hear live astronaut communications when available, as well as interviews, features, and frequent updates on the mission.

■ **Space Hotline,** at (202) 543–1995, gives general news about space exploration.

★ **Pacific Science Center Astronomy Hotline,** Seattle, Washington. Observing information. Tel. (206) 443–2920.

★ **Sky & Telescope,** Cambridge, Massachusetts. This Skyline from the magazine has observing information, reports of newly discovered comets, astronomical research news, and space program developments. Updated Friday afternoons or as needed. Tel. (617) 497–4168. **Sky & Telescope** also offers an expanded version of "Skyline," at 1–900–226–4477. Callers with touch tone telephones can choose from segments on buying a telescope, astrophotography, objects in the sky, and other topics.

★ **The Skyline,** Phoenix, Arizona. Gives general astronomy and skywatching information. Callers can leave messages. Tel. (602) 955–7597.

★ **Smithsonian Astrophysical Observatory,** Cambridge, Massachusetts. Has general observing tips on the Moon, planets, and other objects. Tel. (617) 491–1497.

★ **Southworth Planetarium Sky Watch Hot Line,** sponsored by the Southworth Planetarium, Portland, Maine. A weekly update of sky events—Moon and planet positions, eclipses, and other events. Tel. (207) 780–4719.

★ **Sperry Observatory,** Cranford, New Jersey. Sponsored by the Amateur Astronomers, Inc., and includes information on the Moon and planetary data, plus times the observatory is open to the public. Tel. (908) 276–7827.

★ **StarLine,** sponsored by the Houston (Texas) Astronomical Society. Features a recorded message about astronomical happenings and Society events. Tel. (713) 639–3452.

★ **United States Naval Observatory,** Washington, D.C. Current official time.

Call costs 50 cents for one minute. Tel. 1–900–410–8463.

★ **University of Illinois,** Urbana, Illinois. General observing information. Tel. (217) 333–8789.

★ **Ventura County Astronomical Society,** Moorpark, California. Information on the positions and magnitudes of the planets and comets currently in the sky. Also has club news. Tel. (805) 529–7813.

★ **WWV,** Boulder, Colorado. Time signals for precision observing work. Also available as shortwave broadcast at 2.5, 5, 10, and 15 megahertz. Tel. (303) 499–7111.

PHOTOS, SLIDES, AND VIDEOS

Transparencies, posters, and videos add a new dimension to your enjoyment of the Universe, whether your interests tend toward space mission videos, educational photos and transparencies, or posters just to hang on your observatory wall. Many observatories, as well as the National Aeronautics and Space Administration, sell copies of transparencies of celestial objects. In addition, some astronomy groups, such as the Astronomical League and Astronomical Society of the Pacific, regularly send catalogs to members. You need not be a member to buy their wares.

Two excellent video series are **The Astronomers,** a six-part series that was first aired on public television, and **Cosmos,** narrated by Carl Sagan. **The Astronomers** offers a look at astronomers and explores questions astronomers are seeking to answer, such as where is the "dark matter" that many believe makes up the largest portion of the universe. **Cosmos** takes viewers on a journey through the Universe, and, although several years old, still has much of value to offer armchair astronomers. Both series are available from a number of sources, including Sky Publishing Corporation, the Black Forest Observatory, and many public libraries.

For a taste of what's available, you can write to the following organizations for a catalog. Be sure also to scan astronomy magazines such as **Sky & Telescope** and **Astronomy** for photos taken by amateurs. Each magazine regularly devotes a couple of pages to amateur work, and many of these amateurs would jump at the chance to peddle their photos. The magazines are also a good source of slides.

★ **Aerospace Resources International,** 1514 Vivian Court, Silver Spring, MD 20902. Tel. (301) 649–3796. Videos, slides, and other audio-visual materials related to NASA and astronomy.

★ **The Astronomical League,** 6235 Omie Circle, Pensacola, FL 32504– 7625. Tel. (904) 477–8859. The League has 10,800 members and serves as an umbrella group for many of the amateur societies in the country. It offers a variety of benefits, including book services, free pamphlets, tips on organizing amateur societies, observing guidelines and manuals, slides, videos, audio tapes, and films that local member societies can borrow. See listing in Chapter 2.

★ **The Astronomical Society of the Pacific,** 390 Ashton Ave., San Francisco, CA 94112. Tel. (415) 337–1100. Sells slides, posters, video tapes, computer software, gift items, and calendars though its catalog. See listing in Chapter 2.

★ **Astroscience Video Club,** 1220 E. Greg St., #14, Sparks, NV 89431. Tel. (702) 331–1531. Offers space materials,

NASA video tapes, and a quarterly space report video.

★ **Black Forest Observatory,** Department AS1190, 12815 Porcupine Lane, Colorado Springs, CO 80908. Free catalog. Astronomy and science videos, slides, globes, etc. See listing in Chapter 6.

★ **Centrepoint,** P.O. Box 542063A, Dallas, TX 75354. Tel. (214) 750–8089 (evenings). Videos of the Moon walks of the American astronauts.

★ **Eyes on the Universe,** 472 Country Club, Tooele, UT 84074–9665. Tel. (801) 882–1209. Astrophotographer Patrick Wiggins specializes in custom-photography of the night skies.

★ **Kai-Dib Films,** P.O. Box 261, Glendale, CA 91209. Tel. (818) 248–7130. Offers a set of 200 slides designed primarily for educators who need visual aids for their astronomy classes. The set can be used with Jay M. Pasachoff's **Astronomy: From the Earth to the Universe**. Call or write for more information.

★ **Kalmbach Publishing Co.,** 21027 Crossroads Circle, P.O. Box 1612, Waukesha, WI 53187. Tel (414) 796–8776. The publishers of **Astronomy** magazine also offer for sale posters, videos, books, and other items related to the space program and astronomy. NASA mission patches, and educational materials also available. See listing in **Periodicals** section above.

★ **Lunar Science Institute,** Data Center, Code L, 3303 NASA Road #1, Houston, TX 77058. Tel. (713) 488–5200. Lunar photos, maps, etc.

★ **MMI Corporation,** 2950 Wyman Parkway, P.O. Box 19907, Baltimore, MD 21211. Tel. (301) 366–1222. Fax (301) 366–6311. Slides of celestial objects and videos on astronomy subjects. See listing in Chapter 10. Free catalog for educators; $2 for others.

★ **Movie Newsreels,** P.O. Box 2589–E, Hollywood, CA 90078. Tel. (213) 467–2488. Offers color slides and videos of NASA missions.

★ **NASA.** Various organizational offices produce slides and prints for educators, scientists, and others. See Chapter 8 and the **Teaching Resources** section in Chapter 10.

★ **NASA CORE (Central Operation of Resources for Education),** 15181 Route 58 S., Oberlin, OH 44074. Tel. (216) 774–1051, ext. 293. Serves as the national distribution center for NASA-produced educational materials, including slides, videos, audio/visuals, transparencies, NASA memorabilia, etc., to teachers and groups sponsoring educational programs. See **Teaching Resources** section in Chapter 10.

★ **National Geographic Society,** 17th & M Streets NW, Washington, DC 20036. Tel. (301) 921–1330 in Maryland. 1–800–638–4077. Filmstrips and videos for educators.

★ **National Optical Astronomy Observatories,** P.O. Box 26732, Tucson, AZ 85726–6732. Tel. 602–325–9204. Offers a wide variety of black-and-white and color photographs, slides, and transparencies taken at Kitt Peak National Observatory, Cerro Tololo Inter-American Observatory, and the National Solar Observatory. Images include galaxies, quasars, nebulae, stars, comets, and planets, as well as observatory scenes and instrumentation. Some images are over 20 years old, but are still "considered among the best available." Request the "Catalog of Images."

★ **Nolly Productions,** 5145 S. Lewiston Way, Aurora, CO 80016. Tel. 1–800–437–0800. Videos of the U.S. space missions, including the Apollo, Gemini, and Space Shuttle missions.

★ **Optica b/c,** 4100 MacArthur Blvd., Oakland, CA 94619–1990. Supplies all sorts of posters, slides, videos, etc., about space and astronomy. Write for catalog. See listing in Chapter 3.

★ **The Planetary Society,** 65 N. Catalina Ave., Pasadena, CA 91106. Tel. (818) 793–5100. The Society offers a variety of videos, slides, posters, and other items related to astronomy and the space program. See listing in **National and Special Interest Groups** section in Chapter 2.

★ **Pleiades Group,** Suite 148, Dept. A3, 189 Berdan Ave., Wayne, NJ 07470. Photo stickers with peel-and-stick backs.

★ **Science & Art Products,** P.O. Box 1166, Dept. A, Malibu, CA 90265. Tel. (213) 456–2496. Offers a full-color astronomy poster with 35 astrophotos. Descriptions of each object are beneath each photo.

★ **Sky Publishing Corporation,** 49 Bay State Rd., Cambridge, MA 02138. Tel. (617) 864–7360. The corporation offers a variety of videos, many from the National Aeronautics and Space Administration, and slides from NASA and major observatories. Also posters and other items depicting space scenes. See listing in **Periodicals** section above.

★ **SkyWatcher Video,** 619 Hanover Dr., P.O. Box 456, Allen, TX 75002. Toll-free, 1–800–423–6837 (U.S.), or 1–800–526–9269 in Texas. Offers a number of videos, on such topics as the Solar Sys-

tem, the Outer Planets, Apollo to the Moon, Life in the Universe, etc.

★ **Spaceweek National Headquarters,** 1110 NASA Road One, #100, Houston, TX 77058. Contact Regina Kakadelis. Helps plan events related to space and astronomy. For an $8.50 registration fee, event planners receive materials and merchandise discounts, discounts on annual posters and promotional materials. See listing in **National and Special Interest Groups** section in Chapter 2.

★ **Tersch Enterprises,** P.O. Box 1059, Colorado Springs, CO 80901. Tel. (719) 597–3603. The company uses the Tiara Observatory at Colorado Springs to produce astronomical slides, including color slides of solar eclipses, for schools, universities, colleges, and others. Write for free catalog. See Tiara Observatory in Chapter 6.

★ **United States Space Foundation,** P.O. Box 1838, Colorado Springs, CO 80901. Tel. (719) 550–1000. A good source for slides of space missions, astronomical objects, spacecraft, etc. See listing in **National and Special Interest Groups** section of Chapter 2.

★ **Willmann-Bell Inc.,** P.O. Box 35025, Richmond, VA 23235. Tel. (804) 320–7016. Fax (804) 272–5920. Sells items related to astronomy. See listing in Chapter 3.

GIFTS AND NOVELTIES

Just like any other group of hobbyists or professionals, astronomers often want to show off their interests. You may want to show the world your favorite galaxy on the front of your T-shirt, or maybe collect that little knick-knack or tie tack that lets others know that you enjoy "looking up" at the Universe. A number of companies cater to these kinds of desires with items that are sometimes scientific, but just as often designed just for fun. Your shopping choices include planetarium, museum, and observatory gift shops, plus several mail-order firms. The companies listed below can meet your needs for novelty gifts, NASA mission patches, posters, space art, bumper stickers, T-shirts, globes, meteorites, and the like.

★ **American's Historic Collectibles Firm,** 6886 N. 9th Ave., Pensacola, FL 32504. Tel. 1–800–235–7273; (904) 444–2908. Offers magazine covers depicting the space events of the 1960s and 1970s.

★ **Artistic Promotions Unlimited,** 8261 Golf Road, Suite 105E, Niles, IL 60648. Tel. 1–800–835–2246. Artistic posters and paintings.

★ **The Astronomical Society of the Pacific,** 390 Ashton Ave., San Francisco, CA 94112. Tel. (415) 337–1100. The Society offers a variety of specialty items, including books, slides, posters, novelty gifts, and more.

★ **Astronomy To Go,** 6233 Castor Ave., Philadelphia, PA 19149. Tel. (215) 831–0485. NASA patches, novelties, charts, etc.

★ **Bethany Sciences,** P.O. Box 3726–S, New Haven, CT 06525. Tel. (203) 393–3395. Meteorites, space collectibles, space jewelry, books, slides, collecting kits, metal detectors. Color catalog, $2.

★ **Black Forest Observatory,** 12815 Porcupine Lane, Colorado Springs, CO 80908. Tel. (719) 495–3828. The observatory bills itself as a non-profit independent educational corporation. Offers books, specialty items, novelty gifts, and knickknacks. Write for a catalog.

★ **Caledonian Graphics,** Dept. A., P.O. Box 875, Zephyrhills, FL 34283. Tel. 1–800–223–4607. Offers astronomy designs on T-Shirts and sweats. Call or write for a free catalog.

★ **Celestial Innovations,** H.C.R. Box 3228, 67 Beverly Circle, Oracle, AZ 85623. Tel. (602) 896–9109.

★ **Cygnus Graphic,** 1637 E. Roma Ave., P.O. Box 32461–K, Phoenix, AZ 85064–2461. Supplies three-dimensional prints with astronomical themes. Write for ordering information.

★ **Eclipse Productions,** 31–43 33rd St., Astoria, NY 11106. T-shirts, novelty sunglasses.

★ **Edmund Scientific Co.,** Dept. 11B1, N964 Edscorp Bldg., Barrington, NJ 08007. Tel. (609) 547–8880. Sells posters, astronomical gifts, celestial globes, etc.

★ **Geochron Enterprises Inc.,** 899 Arguello St., Redwood City, CA 94063. Tel. 1–800–342–1661; (415) 361–1771 (in CA). Sells a clock that shows global time in color. The illuminated clock map depicts sunrise and sunset, the Sun's declination and meridian passage, and the time, day, and date anywhere on the planet. Write or call for brochures or ordering information.

★ **Robert A. Haag Meteorites,** 2990 East Michigan St., P.O. Box 27527, Tucson, AZ 85726. Buys, sells, and trades meteorites. Write for a brochure.

★ **Hansen Planetarium Publishing Division,** 1098 South, 200 West, Salt Lake City, UT 84101. Tel. 1–800–321–2369. Sells posters, calendars, star charts, books, etc. Also offers free catalog of gifts, including T-shirts, toys, sweats, models, etc.

★ **Hubbard Scientific,** P.O. Box 104, Northbrook, IL 60065. Tel. (312) 272–7810. 1–800–323–8368. Sells several educational scientific items, including a planetarium; a celestial star globe; astronomy study aids; star charts. Free catalog.

★ **Kalmbach Publishing Co.,** 21027 Crossroads Circle, P.O. Box 1612, Waukesha, WI 53187. Tel (414) 796–8776. The publishers of **Astronomy** magazine offer posters, videos, books, and other items related to the space program and astronomy. NASA mission patches and educational materials also available. See listing in **Periodicals** section above.

★ **F.C. Meichsner Co.,** 182 Lincoln St., Boston, MA 02111. Tel. 1–800–3–2–1–View. A variety of astronomical gifts, such as watches, accessories, etc.

★ **Meteor Crater Enterprises, Inc.,** 603 N. Beaver, Suite C., Flagstaff, AZ 87001. Tel. (602) 774–8350. Meteorites, space art, gifts, etc.

★ **MMI Corporation,** 2950 Wyman Parkway, P.O. Box 19907, Baltimore, MD 21211. Tel. (301) 366–1222. Fax (301) 366–6311. Slides, videos, and teaching manuals available. Also specialty gifts and novelties. Free catalog for educators, $2 for others.

★ **National Space Society,** 922 Pennsylvania Ave. SE, Washington, DC 20003–2140. Tel. (202) 543–1900. A non-profit, educational organization dedicated to the creation of a spacefaring civilization. Offers novelty items, books, etc.

★ **The Nature Company,** P.O. Box 2310, Berkeley, CA 94702. Tel. 1–800–227–1114. A national chain of science stores. Astronomy-related items include a Moon-phase calendar that glows in the dark; asteroid T-shirt in adult and child sizes; adhesive, glow-in-the-dark stars; blown-glass sculpture of Saturn; Meade telescopes; binoculars; books; and videos. Catalog $1.

★ **David New,** P.O. Box 278–A, Anacortes, WA 98221. Tel. (206) 293–2255. Meteorites, tektites, etc. Free catalog.

★ **Novagraphics,** P.O. Box 37197, Tucson, AZ 85740. Tel. 1–800–821–1989, ext. 1014; (602) 743–0500. Features space art by various artists. Subjects include the planets, moons, stars.

★ **Optica b/c,** 4100 MacArthur Blvd., Oakland, CA 94619–1990. Supplies all sorts of posters, slides, videos, etc., about space and astronomy. Write for catalog. See listing in Chapter 3.

★ **PD Unique Products,** 484 Lighthouse Ave., No. 104, Monterey, CA 93940. Tel. 1–800–877–4738. Sells a clock that

reproduces the visible face of the Moon in each cycle.

★ **The Planetary Society,** 65 N. Catalina Ave., Pasadena, CA 91106. Tel. (818) 793–5100. Offers a number of slides, specialty items, and novelty gifts. See listing in **National and Special Interest Groups** section of Chapter 2.

★ **Pleiades Group,** Suite 148, Dept. A3, 189 Berdan Ave., Wayne, NJ 07470. Photo stickers with peel-and-stick backs.

★ **SCI/Space Craft International,** 953 East Colorado Blvd., No. 201, Pasadena, CA 91106. Models of space missions, such as the Galileo mission to Jupiter.

★ **Science & Art Products,** P.O. Box 1166, Dept. A, Malibu, CA 90265. Tel. (213) 456–2496. Offers a full-color astronomy poster with 35 astrophotos. Descriptions of each object are beneath each photo.

★ **Sky Publishing Corporation,** 49 Bay State Rd., Cambridge, MA 02138. Tel. (617) 864–7360. The publishers of **Sky & Telescope** magazine offer a variety of videos, many from the National Aeronautics and Space Administration; slides from NASA and major observatories; posters; NASA patches; watches; and numerous other items. See listing in **Periodicals** section above.

★ **United States Space Foundation,** P.O. Box 1838, Colorado Springs, CO 80901. Tel. (719) 550–1000. Offers books, educational packages, etc. Write for more information.

★ **Yerkes Observatory,** 373 W. Geneva St., P.O. Box 258, Williams Bay, WI 53191. Tel. (414) 245–5555. In addition to conducting first-rate research, the Observatory also has a gift shop that includes meteorite sales.

2 ORGANIZATIONS

NATIONAL AND SPECIAL INTEREST ORGANIZATIONS

Special organizations devoted to astronomy abound. Some are like tiny asteroids, circling about core groups—a part of them, yet following their own orbits. Others attract members worldwide, including some who are well-known enough to be mentioned on television sitcoms. Whatever their size, however, they link together people with a common interest, whether it be astronomy in general, asteroid searching, variable star observing, or keeping the skies free of light pollution.

As a member, you may belong to a group of twenty or thirty people who rush to the telephone at the hint of an aurora borealis, or with the click of a keyboard talk via computer links to transfer information about asteroids.

Newsletters form a common bond, although not all groups have regular publications, or, for that matter, regular anything expect a love for their particular field. Whatever your interest, however, there's likely to be a place for you in one of the following groups.

★ **Amateur Satellite Observers,** 5105 Crestway Dr., Austin, TX 78731, Tel. (512) 452–6081. Contact Mike Mc-Cants. Members receive a newsletter, **ASO Bulletin,** for a $12 membership. The

ASO Bulletin contains orbital elements for a number of satellites. Members supply observations detailing visual characteristics, positional measurements, and tumble period observations. That information is given to the Working Group for Artificial Satellites of the Belgium Astronomical Society. With a $24 membership, members also receive a computer data disk, which contains more detailed orbital information. There are approximately 50 members.

★ **American Association of Variable Star Observers,** 25 Birch St., Cambridge, MA 02138. Tel. (617) 354–0484. Contact Janet A. Mattei. Members are professional and amateur astronomers who observe variable stars. Members process, analyze, and publish descriptions of their observations. The AAVSO also publishes finder charts of variable star fields and light curves of important variables.

Maintains a library of more than 2,000 books and periodicals. Publishes monthly **AAVSO Circular,** the semiannual **Journal of the AAVSO,** and the monthly **Solar Bulletin.** Holds a semiannual conference.

★ **American Lunar Society,** P.O. Box 209, East Pittsburgh, PA 15112. Tel. (412) 829–2627. Contact Francis G. Graham. The Society is open to anyone age 15 or older interested in the Earth's moon. Dues are $10 per year, and members receive an annual subscription to the quarterly **Selenology.** Has 77 members, and holds a biannual general meeting, usually in conjunction with another astronomical society's meeting. Active in observing Transient Lunar Phenomena. Also involved in a project to map lunar

domes, and does lunar occultation timings.

★ **The American Meteor Society,** Dept. of Physics and Astronomy, SUNY, Geneseo, NY 14454. Collects and analyzes meteor observations made from diverse geographic locations. Fireball observations submitted to the Society are forwarded to the Smithsonian Museum of Natural History, department of meteorites. The Society is loosely organized, and does not hold annual meetings. Membership categories include active, $5 per year; associate, $6; and probational, for those 14 to 18, $5 per year. Full membership is open to all over age 18, with the stipulation that prospective members show a willingness to observe and record their observations. The Society distributes material primarily to active observers, and does not offer free materials to the general public. A staff of volunteers helps with the various research programs. The Society concentrates on meteor sporadic rates, meteor shower rates, and meteor magnitude distributions. Members submit their work for analysis. Members receive **Meteor News,** and occasionally circulars about research reports.

★ **Association of Binary Star Observers,** 306 Reynolds Drive, Saugus, MA 01906. Annual dues $15. A new group formed to provide members with information on how to begin making measurements; explain methods of double star measure; offer tips on having the measurements examined and published; provide an opportunity to meet other double star observers. Members receive the quarterly journal **Binary Star.**

★ **The Association of Lunar and Planetary Observers,** P.O. Box 16131, San Francisco, CA 94116. Contact John E. Westfall. The ALPO is an international group of astronomers who offer services primarily to amateur astronomers interested in the Solar System. Volunteer specialists supervise studies of the principal planets, the Moon, the Sun, asteroids, comets, and meteors. The ALPO publishes an annual **ALPO Solar System Ephemeris,** and a quarterly journal.

★ **The Astronomical League,** 6235 Omie Circle, Pensacola, FL 32504– 7625. Tel. (904) 477–8859. Contact Mrs. Merry Edenton-Wooten, Executive Secretary. Membership is $20 for members of affiliated societies with an additional $1.55 for individual members. The League has 10,800 members and serves as an umbrella group for many of the amateur societies in the country. It offers a variety of benefits, including book services, free pamphlets, tips on organizing amateur societies, observing guidelines and manuals, and slides, videos, audio tapes, and films that local member societies can borrow.

The League also publishes the newsletter **The Reflector,** plus provides a subscription to either the **Abram Star**

Chart, Griffith Observer, or **Star Dates News** from McDonald Observatory. The League also sponsors various regional meetings and an annual convention, and works with educators to promote astronomy.

★ **The Astronomical Society of the Pacific,** 390 Ashton Ave., San Francisco, CA 94112. Tel. (415) 337–1100. Contact Andrew Fraknoi, Executive Director. The Society has nearly 5,500 members worldwide, and works with scientists, educators, hobbyists, and others interested in astronomy. Regular dues are $29.50 in the U.S.; $37.50 outside the U.S. This includes a subscription to the ASP magazine, **Mercury,** plus monthly Sky Calendars. A technical membership, at a cost of $65 in the U.S. and $75 outside the U.S., includes the magazine **Publications.**

The ASP also supports a newsletter for astronomy educators, **The Universe in the Classroom,** donated free to primary and secondary schools. Other benefits include a catalog with listings of slides, posters, video tapes, computer software, gift items, and calendars.

Brochures include "How to Select Your First Telescope," "Computer Software for Astronomy, and "Astronomy Versus Astrology."

The ASP holds an annual meeting each year, in a different city. The meeting covers both professional and amateur topics.

★ **Astronomy Day** is an annual event, sponsored by 13 astronomy clubs. The Astronomy Day Headquarters is at the Chaffee Planetarium, 54 Jefferson S.E., Grand Rapids, MI 49053. Tel. (616) 456–3987. Contact Gary Tomlinson, coordinator. Astronomy Day is designed to introduce astronomy to the public through events such as public star parties, lectures, and mall displays. Astronomy Day is held each April.

★ **Aurora Alert Hotline,** 25 Manley Dr., Pascoag, RI 02859. Tel. (401) 568–9370. David Huestis, contact person. No dues for the 60–plus members who are primarily organized to alert each other of aurora, plus give each other tips on photographing the aurora. Members set up a telephone network to pass the word about aurora.

★ **Earthwatch,** 680 Mount Auburn St., Box 403, Watertown, MA 02272. This organization is devoted to a wide range of scientific endeavors, and occasionally works with astronomy-related research, drawing volunteers from among its 70,000 members world-wide. The organization's magazine describes projects, along with conditions at the site and the cost of participation. Annual dues are $25, and members receive the magazine **Earthwatch,** plus newsletters. Earthwatch also holds annual meetings, during which field representatives from around the world describe their research.

★ **Group 70,** 2331 American Ave., Hayward, CA 94545–1807. Tel. (415) 784–0391. The Group was formed to finance and build a 72–inch telescope, which will be time-shared with the professional community if possible. The Group has a mirror blank, and hopes to have the observatory operational by 1999. This project is the largest amateur telescope planned, and will be of a size comparable to the professional models. The observatory will be built on a site, yet to be determined, in central California. Group 70 seeks volunteers and members to work on the project and to help finance it. Membership dues start at $25, with a life membership of $1,000 and varying rates in between. Members receive a quarterly newsletter, **The Reflections,** have voting privileges, and will have equal access to the 72–inch telescope upon completion. There are 110 members.

★ **International Amateur-Professional Photoelectric Photometry,** A.J. Dyer Observatory, Box 1803 STA. B., Vanderbilt University, Nashville, TN 37235. The organization promotes cooperation between amateurs and professionals; accepts research papers from amateurs on photoelectric photometry with smaller instruments, equipment design and construction, field tests of software and equipment, and suggestions for observing programs of current scientific interest to professional astronomers. Dues are $15 annually, and the approximately 1,000 members receive the quarterly, **Com-**

munication, which contains articles on photoelectric-photometry by professionals and amateurs.

★ **International Dark-Sky Association,** 3545 N. Stewart, Tucson, AZ, 85716. Contact Dr. David L. Crawford, Executive Director. This 800–member organization is devoted to fighting the "light pollution" problem that threatens to eliminate dark skies from all but the most remote areas. Basic membership is a donation of $20, for which members receive a quarterly **International Dark-Sky** newsletter. Annual meetings are held every April. The association also sponsors a Star Watching Program.

★ **International Meteor Organization,** (North American Section), 181 Sifton Ave., Fort McMurray, Alberta, T9H 4V7, Canada. General Secretary, Paul Roggemans, Pijnboomstraat 25, B–2800, Mechelen, Belgium. Members receive six issues of **WGN,** and work together to coordinate and improve amateur observations of meteors, and to provide that data to professionals. The IMO maintains a Photographic Meteor Data Base and archive of amateur meteor photographs. Membership dues are 20 DEM, 400 FEF, or equivalent at the rate of the day in U.S. or Canadian dollars.

★ **International Occultation Timing Association,** 1177 SW Collins Ave., Topeka, KS

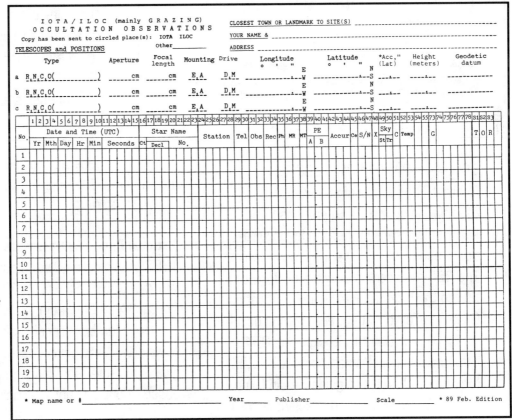

Form used by members of the International Occultation Timing Association to report grazing observations.

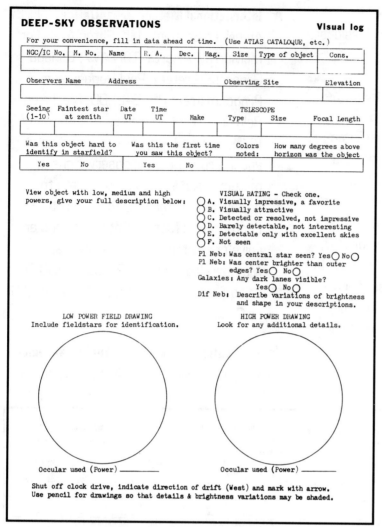

DEEP-SKY OBSERVATIONS   Visual log

For your convenience, fill in data ahead of time. (Use ATLAS CATALOGUE, etc.)

NGC/IC No.	M. No.	Name	R. A.	Dec.	Mag.	Size	Type of object	Cons.

Observers Name	Address	Observing Site	Elevation

Seeing (1-10)	Faintest star at zenith	Date UT	Time UT	Make	TELESCOPE Type	Size	Focal Length

Was this object hard to identify in starfield?		Was this the first time you saw this object?		Colors noted:	How many degrees above horizon was the object
Yes	No	Yes	No		

View object with low, medium and high powers, give your full description below:

VISUAL RATING - Check one.
○ A. Visually impressive, a favorite
○ B. Visually attractive
○ C. Detected or resolved, not impressive
○ D. Barely detectable, not interesting
○ E. Detectable only with excellent skies
○ F. Not seen

Pl Neb: Was central star seen? Yes○ No○
Pl Neb: Was center brighter than outer edges? Yes○ No○
Galaxies: Any dark lanes visible? Yes○ No○
Dif Neb: Describe variations of brightness and shape in your descriptions.

LOW POWER FIELD DRAWING
Include fieldstars for identification.

HIGH POWER DRAWING
Look for any additional details.

Occular used (Power) _____   Occular used (Power) _____

Shut off clock drive, indicate direction of drift (West) and mark with arrow.
Use pencil for drawings so that details & brightness variations may be shaded.

Visual log of the National Deep-Sky Observers Society

66604–1524. Tel. (913) 232–3693. Contact Terri and Craig McManus. The association sponsors expeditions to observe solar eclipses, asteroidal occultations, and grazes of stars by the Moon. The 350 members supply their information to the International Lunar Occultation Centre in Tokyo, Japan, and grazing occultation data to Don M. Stockbauer, 2846 Mayflower Landing, Webster, TX 77598. Members follow strict guidelines in filling out the forms to be used in scientific investigations by professionals. Membership costs $25 for full members in North America; $30 for members elsewhere. Subscription-only memberships cost $20 in North America; $25 elsewhere.

★ **The Meteoritical Society,** Meteoritics Office, Institute of Geophysics and Planetary Physics, Univ. of California, Los Angeles, CA 90024–1567. Formed in 1933, the Society is an international, non-profit organization that promotes the study of meteorites and other samples of extraterrestrial materials. There are approximately 865 members from 31 countries. The Society holds annual meetings, usually in Europe or North America. Annual dues are $30 for adults and $15 for students. Members receive the journal **METEORITICS.**

★ **National Deep-Sky Observers Society,** 1607 Washington Blvd., Louisville, KY 40242–3539. Tel. (502) 426–4399. Contact Alan Goldstein, National Coordinator. Members receive bimonthly newsletter **Betelgeuse,** participate in group projects, and contribute deep-sky observations or submit articles for

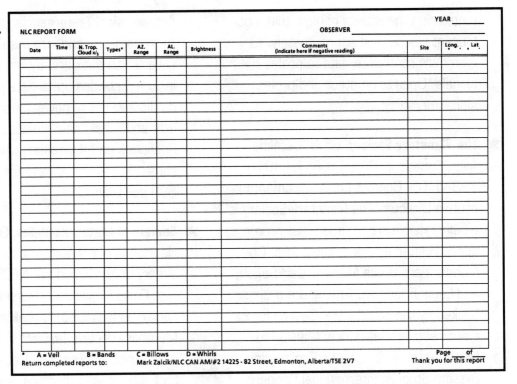

Form used by members of NLC CAN AM to report observations of noctilucent clouds

NLC REPORT FORM

YEAR _____

OBSERVER _____

Date	Time	N. Trop. Cloud x/s	Types*	AZ. Range	AL. Range	Brightness	Comments (indicate here if negative reading)	Site	Long. Lat.

* A = Veil   B = Bands   C = Billows   D = Whirls

Return completed reports to: Mark Zalcik/NLC CAN AM/#2 14225 - 82 Street, Edmonton, Alberta/T5E 2V7

Page ____ of ____

Thank you for this report

newsletter. Membership 85 to 100; sponsors some sessions, but not regularly. Members use a "Deep-Sky Observations" visual log to record their work. Dues are $8 per year.

★ **National Space Society,** 922 Pennsylvania Ave. SE, Washington, DC 20003–2140. Tel. (202) 543–1900. Contact David Brandt. A non-profit, educational membership organization dedicated to the creation of a spacefaring civilization. NSS has more than 30,000 members in the U.S. and foreign nations. Members receive **Ad Astra** (to the Stars), a monthly magazine that covers all aspects of space and space exploration. Also has a Space Hotline, NSS Dial-A-Shuttle, and Mir Watch. In addition, members may join the Society at Kennedy Space Center to view a live shuttle lift-off. NSS holds an annual conference over the Memorial Day weekend. NSS sponsors the **Oregon L5 Society** and its Moonbase Program in which crews work in an abandoned lava tube cave in Bend, Oregon, to simulate an actual Moonbase. NSS also includes **Spacecause,** a grassroots lobbying group, and **Spacepac,** a grassroots political action committee. Regular membership is $35 per year; $20 for students under 22 and senior citizens over 64.

★ **NLC CAN AM (Noctilucent Cloud Observers),** #2–14225 82 St., Edmonton, Alberta, T5E 2V7, Canada. Contact Mark Zalcik, Coordinator. This organization is under the guidance of the British Astronomical Association Aurora Section, and is an observing network interested in monitoring the activity of high, thin, noctilucent clouds. The approximately 30 members contribute data to professionals. Open to amateur and professional members.

★ **The Planetary Society,** 65 N. Catalina Ave., Pasadena, CA 91106. Tel. (818) 793–5100. Contact Louis Friedman, Executive Director. The Planetary Society is a highly visible organization that promotes space-related issues to the public. Cofounders are Bruce Murray, Carl Sagan, and Louis Friedman. Among the projects backed by the Society are: Search for Extraterrestrial Intelligence; Mission to Mars; Asteroid Discovery; Engineering-System Studies; International Cooperation; and Public Education. The Society sponsors a variety of conferences, seminars, lectures, meetings, and workshops. Dues are $25 annually, which include a subscription to **The Planetary Report.** Membership is open to the public.

★ **The Royal Astronomical Society of Canada,** 136 Dupont St., Toronto, Ontario, M5R 2V2, Canada. RASC is a nationwide organization with 3,000 amateur and professional members. The Society publishes **The Observer's Handbook,** plus the **Journal.** It hosts an annual three-day general assembly.

★ **Smithsonian Astrophysical Observatory,** Cambridge, MA 02138. Tel. (617) 495–7244. Has 720 members, with dues of $72 per year. The **Central Bureau for**

Astronomical Telegrams is located here. Astronomers send information on new discoveries to the Bureau, and the Bureau, in turn, provides up-to-date information on discoveries of novas, supernovas, comets, and other "new" objects in the sky. Publishes an **AV Circular,** which also comes in electronic form for an additional $90 per year.

★ **Society of Meteoritophiles,** 9 Airedale, Hadrian Lodge West, Wallsend, Tyne & Wear, United Kingdom, NE28 8TL. Contact Philip M. Bagnall, President. This society is for meteorite/tektite collectors. Members receive **Impact!** three times a year (April, August, and December), contact with other collectors, and free advertising. The Society has 152 members, 20 percent of whom are professional meteoriticists. Membership is 10 pounds in the United Kingdom; 11 pounds elsewhere.

★ **Spaceweek National Headquarters,** 1110 NASA Road One, #100, Houston, TX 77058. Contact Regina Kakadelis. Helps plan events related to space and astronomy. In 1990, more than 300 organizations sponsored events dealing with space awareness, aviation, aerospace, astronomy, and related topics in the U.S. and foreign countries. For an $8.50 registration fee, event planners receive materials as well as discounts on merchandise, annual posters, and promotional materials.

★ **United States Space Foundation,** P.O. Box 1838, Colorado Springs, CO 80901. Tel. (719) 550–1000. Contact Chuck Zimkas, Director of Operations. Promotes space policy alternatives to the government and public; fosters technological development and cooperation between space professionals. Sponsors educational programs for K–12 educators. The Space Foundation provides research, information, and computer telecommunications. Membership, which includes a subscription to the **Spacewatch** publication, is $35 for individuals, $29 for teachers, $20 for college students, $10 for high school and junior high school students, and $5 for elementary students.

LOCAL ASTRONOMY CLUBS AND GROUPS

Astronomy clubs range from informal groups with little or no dues, no formal meeting place, and only meager equipment, to clubs with a national reputation, slick publications, equipment to rival that of a college observatory, and, in some cases, personnel who, if not professional, fall just shy of that status. They provide a means of learning for newcomers, help in refining techniques and knowledge for the more advanced, and a social atmosphere for those who share a passion for the sky.

Some clubs, such as the Fremont Peak Observatory Association, run a public observatory; others simply publish a newsletter that chronicles the club meetings and routine business on a single page.

Joining a club exposes you to a variety of equipment— helpful if you're planning to buy but don't know exactly what you want—and gives you access to the club facilities. In today's light-polluted environment, just having a safe, dark sky site you can use can be a major benefit.

Some clubs do more than supply you with a viewing spot and equipment. They work with professionals, submitting meteor and variable star observations, for example, or even mounting letter-writing campaigns in support of a particular project.

Whatever your interest, the clubs will welcome your enthusiasm, expertise, and presence. For most, the only requirement for admittance is a love of the night sky.

Alabama

Huntsville

Van Braun Astronomical Society, Box 1142, Huntsville, AL 35807. Has 154 members, with annual dues of $10 for students; $20 for adults; $25 for families; and $500 for life membership. The club meets at a planetarium, built by members, that seats 90. Also has a 21–inch Cassegrain reflector, with dome, all member-built; a 16–inch Celestron housed in a roll-off roof building; a library, darkroom, conference room, 15 outdoor concrete observing pads, and a GOTO planetarium projector. The monthly meetings at the planetarium feature lectures, plus regular star parties, Messier Club, meteor observing, astronomy classes for the public, and special observing events. Members receive discounts on **Sky & Telescope, Astronomy, Telescope Making,** and **Odyssey.** Members of the club include several of the original members of the Van Braun rocket team who are still active in observing.

Alaska

Fairbanks

Astronomical Units, Box 82210, Fairbanks, AL 99708. Club has 15 members with access to an observatory located at the Poker Flat Research Rocket Range 30 miles Northeast of Fairbanks. This observatory has a 14–inch Celestron Schmidt-Cassegrain. Members own reflectors as large as 16 inches, and refractors up to 5 inches. Club not active from mid-April to August due to lack of darkness. In August, club members participate in a noctilucent cloud observing program.

Arizona

Tucson

Tucson Amateur Astronomy Association, P.O. Box 41254, Tucson, AZ 85717. Has 150 members, with annual dues of $20. Meets at 7:30 p.m. the first Friday of each month at the Steward Observatory lecture room. Holds a monthly star party outside Tucson. The club has a 16–inch f/6 Newtonian on equatorial mount, and is building a 30–inch Newtonian/Cassegrain telescope. Also has telescope-making facilities and a library. Holds an All-Arizona Star Party each fall, open to any amateur observer. Members receive discounts on **Sky & Telescope, Astronomy, Telescope Making, Odyssey,** and books, plus discounts at some local businesses.

Arkansas

Hardy

Northeast Arkansas Astronomical Society, P.O. Box 322, Hardy, AR 72542. Approximately 80 members; dues, family,

$15; adult, $10; student, $5. Club has a 12.5–inch Newtonian telescope in a 16–foot Ash Dome. Darkroom facilities and a library are part of the Leonard H. Holden Jr. Observatory. Meets first Tuesday of each month, sponsors star parties periodically, and invites civic groups to the observatory.

California

Costa Mesa

Orange County Astronomers, 2195 Raleigh Ave., Costa Mesa, CA 92627. Tel. (714) 722–7900. Has approximately 600 members, with dues set at $35 for regular members, and $20 for students and retirees. Meets at the Hashinger Science Hall, Chapman College, Orange County. Members receive discounts on **Sky & Telescope, Astronomy,** and other publications, plus astronomical calendar and RASC Annual. Members also receive a 12–page monthly newsletter, the **Sirius Astronomer.** The club has a 22–inch f/8–16 Cassegrain in a roll-off observatory near Anza, at 4,360 feet. This 20–acre site also has 30 observing pads, private observatories, and a room with computer, audio/video, darkroom, and small classroom, 300–volume library, video tapes, and software selections. Also has DS–16, 13.1 Odyssey, and Celestron 8 available for members at $5 per month. The Club co-sponsors, with the Ventura County Astronomical Society, an Astrophoto Seminar, and an Electronics

Oriented Astronomy seminar. Also produces the proceedings of the Riverside Telescope Makers Conference. Hosts star parties and invites speakers in for club meetings.

Idyllwild

Idyll-Gazers Astronomy Club, P.O. Box 1245, Idyllwild, CA 02349. Approximately 60 members, with annual dues of $10. Holds star parties in Idyllwild at Saunders Meadow Road Site, at an altitude of 5,400 feet. Club members have telescopes ranging from 2–inch to 24–inch, and an 8–inch Schmidt camera. Sends members a monthly newsletter, which includes a sky watch report.

Newhall

"Local Group" of Santa Clarita Valley, 25032 Walnut St., Newhall, CA 91321. Has 60 members, with annual dues of $12. Meets at the Placerita Canyon Nature Center, 19152 Placerita Canyon Road, Newall, CA.

Oakland

Astronomical Association of Northern California, 4917 Mountain Blvd., Oakland, CA 94619. An umbrella group of California astronomy clubs, the Association has 26 participating clubs and communities, with annual dues of $15. Meets at Lawrence Hall of Science, University of California, Berkeley, CA 94720. The organization annually coordinates a STAR-B-Q and conference, and also coordinates distribution of information to the public about astronomy.

Rancho Mirage

Astronomical Society of the Desert, P.O. Box 71, Rancho Mirage, CA 92270. Has 65 members, with annual dues of $15. Meets at the College of the Desert, Palm Desert. Has a monthly newsletter, holds monthly lectures, open to the public, and hosts star parties and special viewing sessions for such events as major conjunctions, comets, eclipses, etc. The Society estimates more than 5,000 people viewed Halley's Comet through sessions held by the members.

Ridgecrest

China Lake Astronomical Society, P.O. Box 1783, Ridgecrest, CA 93556. Has 70 members, with annual dues of $26. Meets at 7:30 p.m. the first Monday of each month at the East Kern Municipal Library. Holds a star party the Friday nearest to the new moon. Members receive discounts on **Sky & Telescope,** plus a monthly club newsletter.

Rocklin

Sacramento Valley Astronomical Society, P.O. Box 575, Rocklin, CA 95677. Has 153 members.

San Bernardino

San Bernardino Valley Amateur Astronomers, 1345 Garner Ave., San Bernardino, CA 92411. Contact David E. Garcia. Approximately 65 members, who meet the third Saturday each month at the California State University, Room 101 of the Biological Sciences Building. Dues are $25 per year, and members receive **Sky & Telescope,** a monthly newsletter, monthly sky charts, and Sky Publishing book and star chart discounts. The club has a 12.5–inch f/5 with Dobsonian mount, and a 200–book library. Members help with the annual Riverside Telescope Makers Conference, and hold yearly Messier Marathons, public star parties, and an Astronomy Day program.

San Jose

San Jose Astronomical Association, 3509 Calico Ave., San Jose, CA 95124. Tel. (408) 997–3347. Has 350 members; basic annual dues of $10. Meets at the Los Gatos Red Cross building, Monte Sereno, CA. Has loaner telescopes and holds monthly lectures plus observing sessions out of the city. Also hosts public observing sessions in the city park, and offers introductory astronomy classes, lectures, and star parties. Members receive group magazine subscriptions plus book discounts.

San Juan Bautista

Fremont Peak Observatory Association, Box 1110, San Juan Bautista, CA 95045. Tel. (408) 623–4255. Has 175 members. Dues, $10 annually. The Association provides astronomy education to Fremont Peak State Park visitors, in addition to club activities. The Association has a 30–inch telescope and holds star parties. Members receive a subscription to the quarterly publication, **Fremont Peak Observer,** and discounts on some items.

San Luis Obispo

Central Coast Astronomical Society, P.O. Box 1415, San Luis Obispo, CA 93406. Has 70 members, with annual dues of $12. Meets at the Senior Citizens Center in San Luis Obispo. The club has four telescopes, ranging in aperture from 4 inches to 6 inches, for free loan to members; slide and computer software; and a library. Holds monthly star parties, and two to three public observing sessions per year.

San Ramon

Tri-Valley Stargazers, 20 Cedar Point Loop, Apt. 213, San Ramon, CA 94583. Has 125 members. Dues $20. Meets at the Unitarian Fellowship Hall, 1893 N. Vasco Rd., Livermore, CA. Members receive a 10 percent discount on Lumicon products, and discount subscriptions to **Astronomy, Telescope Making,** and **Observers Guide.** Holds annual star parties at Yosemite, Sierras, and public programs at local schools. Members can use the Digger Pines Dark Sky Observing Site, and after one year, active members can pay $40 per year supplemental dues for use of the club observatory, which houses a 17–inch f/4.5 telescope.

Santa Cruz

Santa Cruz Astronomy Club, L–2 San Carlos Lane, Santa Cruz, CA 95065. Has 85 members, with dues of $10 per family per year. Meets at the recreation hall, 2500 Soqued Dr., Santa Cruz. Has three club telescopes and a video library with tapes of speakers from NASA, Lick Observatory, and Lockheed Corp. Holds one meeting and two star parties a month. Members receive discounts on **Sky & Telescope** and **Astronomy.** Once a year, at the invitation of the National Park Service, the club holds a star party at Glacier Point, Yosemite National Park, for campers.

Santa Rosa

Sonoma County Astronomical Society, P.O. Box 183, Santa Rosa, CA 95402. Has 175 members, with annual dues of $15. Meets at 7:30 p.m. on the second Wednesday of each month, at Proctor Terrace School, 4th & Brydon Lane. The club has an observing site with pads, telescope-making facilities, and a library. Hosts field trips. It also builds 10 to 12 Dobson telescopes per year, which are donated to area schools. This program, called "Striking Sparks," is meant to encourage young people to study science and astronomy. A monthly newsletter, **Sonoma Skies,** provides observing tips and includes a copy of the **Sky Calendar** from Abrams Planetarium. Members also receive discounts on **Sky & Telescope,** and **Astronomy.**

Vandenberg AFB

Vandenberg Amateur Astronomical Society, P.O. Box 5321, Vandenberg AFB, CA 93437. Has 31 members, with annual dues of $20 for a family. Meets the second Friday of every month at the Western Spaceport Museum and Science Center, Western Spaceport Park, Lompoc, CA. The club operates the Museum observatory, which is equipped with a 14-inch Celestron computer-controlled Schmidt Cassegrain. The unit is housed in a 3.2-meter Ash dome. The club also owns an 8-inch Newtonian. Members host public viewing sessions each Friday and Saturday, plus star parties on Figueroa Mountain in northern Santa Barbara County. New members receive a starter package, and a monthly newsletter. The club telescope is available to all members at no cost.

Whittier

Rio Hondo Astronomical Society, 14517 E. Broadway, Whittier, CA 90604–1313. Has more than 40 members, with annual dues of $24 for single membership; $36 for family; and $18 for students. Meets at 8 p.m. the first Friday night of each month,

except on holidays, at the Rio Hondo College, Room 232 in the Science Department. The club is building a 22–inch Dobson, and owns a 12–inch Springfield, trailer mounted, and smaller scopes in the 6–inch to 10–inch range. Also, the club is searching for a site to build an observatory. Holds a telescope users' clinic at the end of each year, and every other year tours the Knotts Berry Farm for a public star gazing show. Members receive discounts on astronomy books and publications. Members are involved in astrophotography, eclipse tours, variable star work, and photometer work.

Colorado

Colorado Springs

Colorado Springs Astronomical Society, P.O. Box 62022, Colorado Springs, CO 80962.

Rocky Mountain Astrophysical Group, 12815 Porcupine Lane, Colorado Springs, CO Zip 80908. Has 100 members.

Denver

Denver Astronomical Society, P.O. Box 10814, Denver, CO 80210.

Grand Junction

Western Colorado Astronomy Club, 2355 Teller Ct., #4, Grand Junction, CO 81505.

Longmont

Longmont Astronomical Society, P.O. Box 8029, Longmont, CO 80501. Has 30 members.

Pueblo

Southern Colorado Astronomical Society, 3 Sundance Ct, Pueblo, CO 81003. Has 30 members.

Connecticut

New Haven

Astronomical Society of New Haven, P.O. Box 3005, New Haven, CT 06515. Linda Rainey, President. Has 57 members, with annual dues of $20. Meets at the Foran High School Planetarium, Milford. The club has two 10–inch Odyssey Reflectors; one 7–inch f/9 refractor (AstroPhysics), housed at Yale University's Bethany Observatory, and has a small library of donated books. The club holds public sessions through the summer and fall, and is working on hosting a new event, the "Connecticut Star Party." Club members receive a monthly newsletter, and also have the use of club telescopes, plus a 10–inch Clark refractor at Yale University.

Waterbury

Mattatuck Astronomical Society, Mattatuck Community College, 750 Chase Parkway, Waterbury, CT 06708. Has 80 members, with annual dues of $20 for adults; $5 for students and seniors. Meets at 7:30 p.m. the third Thursday of each month, except July and August, at Room 440 of the UCONN Hall at the Higher Education Center, Mattatuck Community College. The Society operates and maintains a Celestron 14–inch telescope in a permanent observatory at UCONN Hall. The telescope is computer-assisted to locate deep-sky objects. Also has a CCD camera, hydrogen-alpha filter for solar viewing, and photometer for variable star work. The club library includes books, magazines, software, slide and video programs, open to members only. The Society holds free public viewing sessions two nights per month. Star parties are held at Black Rock State Park, with dark-sky viewing sessions held once per month at the White Memorial Nature Center, Litchefield, CT. Hosts an annual camping weekend. Members receive discounts on **Sky & Telescope** and **Astronomy,** plus discounts on astronomy books. The Society is a member of the "Astronomy Book Club." Society members also are members of the Astronomical League and the International Dark-Sky Association, receive a quarterly newsletter, **Mas Transit,** and take field trips to area observatories and planetariums.

Delaware

Wilmington

Delaware Astronomical Society, P.O. Box 652, Wilmington, DE 19899. Has 140 members.

Florida

Bradenton

Local Group of Deep Sky Observers, 2311 23rd Ave. W., Bradenton, FL 34205. Has 100 members, with annual dues of $10. Meets at the Myakka State Park for observing (monthly) and at the Bishop Planetarium for a quarterly business meeting. Members receive a discount on **Sky & Telescope,** discounts from Sky Publishing, and a newsletter, **New Horizons,** plus membership in the Astronomical League.

Cocoa

Brevard Astronomical Society, Box 1084, Cocoa, FL 32923. Barbara Smith, club president. Has 30 members, with annual dues of $10 per person, $15 per family. Meets at 2:30 p.m. the second Sunday of the month at the Cocoa Public Library, 308 Forrest Ave. Club has a mirror-grinding machine and is working to complete a 16-inch telescope. Holds star parties each Friday nearest the new moon. Members receive a monthly club publication, **The Sky Scanner.**

Fort Lauderdale

South Florida Amateur Astronomers Association, Robert Markham Park, 16000 W. State Road 84, Fort Lauderdale, FL 33326. Has approximately 70 members, with annual dues of $35. On the first Thursday of each month, meets at the Fox Observatory, which houses a 14-inch reflector and a 6.5-inch refractor. Members built the Fox Observatory and donated it to Broward County in 1976. Holds organized viewing sessions at two observing sites away from the observatory. Membership includes a subscription to **Sky & Telescope,** plus discounts on other magazines.

Pensacola

Escambia Amateur Astronomy Association, Physical Sciences, Pensacola Junior College, 1000 College Blvd., Pensacola, FL 32504-8998. Has 180 members with annual dues of $14. Meets at the E.G. Owens Planetarium, Pensacola Junior College. The club has a 16-inch Newtonian on a portable equatorial mount. The club participates in Astronomy Day, and provides sky interpretations. Members receive the **Reflector** and **Meteor.**

St. Petersburg

St. Petersburg Astronomy Club, 595-59th St. South, St. Petersburg, FL 33707. Has 140 members, with dues ranging from $15 to $39. Members meet at The Science Center of Pinellas County, 7701 22nd Ave.

North. The club also has an observing site at Hicky Hill. Hosts star parties and public lectures and observing displays in conjunction with local park systems. Members receive discounts on **Sky & Telescope, Astronomy,** and **Telescope Making,** plus a subscription to the regional **New Horizons** newsletter.

West Palm Beach

Gibson Observatory Astronomy Group, 4801 Dreher Trail North, West Palm Beach, FL 33405–3099. Tel. (407) 832–1988. Recently formed club dedicated to helping operate the Planetarium of the South Florida Science Museum. Annual dues of $30 include membership in the Science Museum. Family dues are $45. The Group uses a 15.5–inch Newtonian, three C–8s, two C–5s, and two 4–inch refractors, plus several 6–inch Newtonians; has access to the reference library and personal computers. Members also take part in the Gibson Observatory public viewing sessions, and have access to astronomy software at the Science Museum.

Georgia

Atlanta

Astronomical Society of the Atlantic, the Center for High Angular Resolution Astronomy, Georgia State University, Atlanta, GA 30303–3083. Tel. (404) 264–0451. Society is an adjunct organization of the Center for High Angular Resolution Astronomy. Membership includes 200 amateurs, 25 professionals. Yearly dues: individual, $15; family, $25; student, $10. Meets at 7:30 p.m. on the first Friday of the month at Ferbank Science Center. Society maintains a library with more than 100 volumes. Members have access to the Hard Labor Creek Observatory, which features a 16–inch Boller & Chivens Cassegrain; an antique 30–inch Fecker; complete darkroom; thermoelectrically cooled CCD system, intensified CCD video camera, photometer, and spectrography. Also is hoping to build an "equivalent aperture 54–inch telescope designed specifically for spectroscopy." The Society hosts the annual Georgia Star Party and members receive discount subscriptions to **Astronomy, Telescope Making, Odyssey,** and **Sky & Telescope.** Members also can receive the Society's **Journal of the Astronomical Society of the Atlantic.**

Atlanta Astronomy Club, P.O. Box 29631, Atlanta, GA 30359–0631. Has 150 members, with annual dues of $25 for students and $35 for families, which includes a subscription to **Sky & Telescope.** Meets at 8 p.m. the third Friday of the month at the Agnes Scott College Observatory. Club equipment includes an observatory west of Atlanta, a 20–inch reflector on a Dobsonian mount, a 10–inch reflector on an equatorial mount, and a library. Members receive discounts to Kalmbach publications, and the club newsletter, **The Focal Point,** plus the Astronomical League publication, **The Reflector.**

Auburn

Auburn Astronomical Society, Hillcrest Road, Box 113, West Point, GA 31833. Has 20 members, with annual dues of $15. Meets at Auburn University, Parker Hall, Room 126, Roosevelt Drive, Auburn. The club has 10–inch, 12–inch, and 14–inch reflectors, but most members have their own telescopes. An observatory is planned. Members hold a star party once a month, and teach continuing education courses in astronomy at Auburn University. Society members also receive a discount for **Astronomy Magazine,** and membership in the Astronomical League.

Macon

Middle Georgia Astronomical Society, Museum of Arts & Sciences, 4182 Forsyth Rd., Macon, GA 31210. Has 20 members, with annual dues of $12. Meets at the Museum of Arts & Sciences. The club owns a 10–inch Dobsonian for members. Club members also have access to the museum observatory, which has a 14–inch telescope, photometer, and other equipment. The club hosts the annual Astronomy Day in conjunction with the Museum. Members receive a club newsletter, membership in the Astronomical League, and discount subscriptions to **Astronomy.**

Savannah

Oglethorpe Astronomical Association, 4405 Paulsen St., Savannah, GA 31405. Has 20 members; annual dues are $25. Club meets on the first Saturday of each month at the Savannah Science Museum. Club hosts special events at local state parks and museums. Members receive a subscription to **Sky & Telescope.**

Hawaii

Captain Cook

Mauna Kea Astronomical Society, 84–5095 Hawaii Belt Rd., Captain Cook, HI 96704. Has 50 members.

Honolulu

Hawaiian Astronomical Society, P.O. Box 17671, Honolulu, HI 96817.

Puunene

Maui Astronomy Club, P.O. Box 1168, Puunene, HI 96784.

Idaho

Boise

Boise Astronomical Society, P.O. Box 8386, Boise, ID 83707. Has 70 members, with annual dues of $15; $10 for new members after July 1. Meets at the Discovery Center of Idaho, Boise. Hosts a star party at Brunead Sand Dunes State Park in August, and public star parties in September. Members also belong to the Astronomical League.

Idaho Falls

Idaho Falls Astronomical Society, 1710 Claremont Lane, Idaho Falls, ID 83404. Contact Jim Ruggiero. Has 15 members, with annual dues of $25. Meets in the public library or a member's home. Most members have their own instrument, but there is one club 13–inch reflector. Dues include a choice of **Sky & Telescope** or **Astronomy,** plus membership in the Astronomical League, which publishes the **Reflector.**

Illinois

Chicago

Chicago Astronomical Society, P.O. Box 48504, Chicago, IL 60648. Has 140 members, with annual dues of $36 for individuals, $26 for students. Meets at 7 p.m. the third Friday of the month, at the Adler Planetarium, 1300 S. Lake Shore Drive. Holds public observing sessions and deep sky sessions for members. Dues include subscription to **Sky & Telescope,** membership in the Astronomical League, and the club newsletter. The Society operates a loaner telescope program for members, and holds special classes for schools. The club bills itself as "The World's Oldest

Amateur Astronomical Society." It was founded in 1862 and members helped raise funds for the Dearborn Observatory at Northwestern University in the 1880s. The Society helped operate the observatory in conjunction with Northwestern until the stock market crash of 1929. Due to financial pressures of that time, the Society then transferred the telescope at the observatory to Northwestern.

Glenview

Skokie Valley Astronomers, and Space Science Explorers, 910 Glenwood Lane, Glenview, IL 60025. Has 22 members. Annual dues are $18. Meets at the Ryerson Nature Center, Deerfield. Club holds star parties, plus helps the Space Science Explorers, a club for youth, ages 14 to 21. Members also are in the Astronomical League.

Jacksonville

Central Illinois Astronomical Association, Illinois College, Jacksonville, IL 62650. Has 12 members, with annual dues of $20. Meets at the Crispin Science Hall, Illinois College. Members have access to the 14–inch and 10–inch Celestron telescopes of the Walter H. Blacke Observatory. The club library also has books and videotapes that members can check out. Members receive discounts on **Sky & Telescope** and belong to the Astronomical League.

Naperville

Naperville Astronomical Association, 205 N. Mill St., Naperville, IL 60540. Has 100 members. Annual dues, $16 individual, $22 family. Meets at 7:30 p.m. on the first Tuesday of every month in the basement of Fire Station 3, Diehl Road and Washington Street. Uses the "Glen D. Riley Observatory," with a 10–inch Newtonian; also has several loaner portable telescopes and a library of more than 300 books and 400 periodicals. Holds public star parties Wednesday evenings during the summer, plus parties for groups such as Scouts. Members receive a discount on **Astronomy** magazine and the **Observer's Handbook** each year, and membership in The Astronomical League.

Rock Island

Popular Astronomy Club, John Deere Planetarium, Augustana College, Rock Island, IL 61201. Has 65 members, with annual dues of $28. Meets at the planetarium. Has 10–inch, 8–inch, and 3.5–inch reflectors; a 5–inch refractor; astronomy book and video tape library; audio/visual equipment; and dark sky site at a local Girl Scout Camp. Hosts astronomy classes one to two times per year and a star party each month. Members receive **Sky & Telescope** with paid dues, plus discounts on other magazines and astronomy books. Members also belong to the Astronomical League.

Sleepy Hollow

Fox Valley Sky Watchers, 164 Hilltop Lane, Sleepy Hollow, IL 60118. Has 10 members, with annual dues of $10. Meets at the Elgin Planetarium. Members receive **Northern Lights** and the **Reflector.** Holds star parties in the summer.

Urbana

University of Illinois Astronomical Society, 103 Astronomy Bldg., 1002 W. Green, Urbana, IL 61801. Has 70 members, mostly students at the university, although some professors and alumni are members. Annual dues are $4. Meets every other Wednesday. Members receive the monthly newsletter, **The Sidereal Messenger;** instruction on the use of the club and university telescope; discounts on **Sky & Telescope** and **Astronomy;** access to a 12–inch reflector; and use of a darkroom, with black and white facilities only.

Indiana

Evansville

Evansville Astronomical Society, Inc., P.O. Box 3474, Evansville, IN 47733. Annual dues $24 for individuals, $30 for families. Founded in 1959, the Society has 60 members who meet at the Wahnsiedler Observatory, Lynnville. Members have access to the observatory, including a 14–inch Celestron telescope and a solar instrument. The observatory also has a lecture hall, darkroom, computer room, library, and restroom facilities. Members receive a subscription to **The Observer,** the Society's newsletter. A special subscription rate is available for **Sky & Telescope** magazine.

Griffith

Calumet Astronomical Society, Box 851, Griffith, IN 46319. Has 60 members with annual dues of $12; $13 per family. Meets at 7:30 on the second Monday of each month at the Griffith Public Library. Publishes a newsletter, holds three public shows per year, and has a 16–inch Deep Sky Newtonian. Members receive discounts on **Astronomy,** and **Telescope Making.**

South Bend

Michiana Astronomical Society, P.O. Box 262, South Bend, IN 46624. Has 24 members, with annual dues of $15. Meets the third Monday of each month at the Mishawaka Public Library. The club has a 4–inch Richfield, several eyepieces, a library, and mirror grinding machine. Holds special sessions for unusual events in the sky, and works with school classes, Scouts, etc. Club members receive a newsletter.

Warsaw

Warsaw Astronomical Society, RR 8, Box 236, Warsaw, IN 46580. Contact James D. Tague. Has 25 members. Membership dues are $20 for an individual, $25

for family. The club meets at the local library. It has an observatory at nearby Camp Crosely with a 16–foot Ash Dome that houses a 12.5–inch Meade reflector. Sponsors programs and observing sessions during the summer. Members receive a discount on subscriptions to **Astronomy** magazine.

Iowa

Ames

Ames Area Amateur Astronomers, 1208 Wilson Ave., Ames, IA 50010. Has 80 members, with annual dues of $15. Meets at the Iowa State University planetarium. The club has an observatory with a 12.5–inch Newtonian/Cassegrain. Hosts a monthly public star party April through October and monthly club star parties. Members receive a newsletter each month and belong to the Aurora Alert Network.

Burlington

Catfish Bend Astronomy Club, 610 Walnut, Burlington, IA 52601–5902. Contact Jim Blair. Has 31 members, with dues of $20 annually. Meets at 8 p.m. the first Friday of each month at the Big Hollow Creek Recreation Park. Club members can set up telescopes and use electrical power free, plus have free use of the park and meeting room. Members also help with public programs at the park, and may subscribe to **Sky & Telescope** and **Northern Lights.**

Southeastern Astronomy Club, 610 Walnut, Burlington, IA 52601–5902. Contact Jim Blair. Has 91 members, with annual dues of $12 for standard membership, $6 for students, and $18 for families. Meets at 7 p.m. the third Friday of each month at the John H. Witte Observatory. Members may use the observatory telescope, a 12–inch f/15 Alvan Clark refracting telescope; a 8–inch f/7 Fecker refracting telescope, CCD camera with Amiga computer and related software, slide projector, VCR, and classroom. Members also have access to observing pads on the observatory grounds and use of electrical power. The first Friday of each month is public night at the observatory, and members host shows there, plus give talks at schools and camps. Members may subscribe, at a discount, to **Astronomy, Odyssey,** and **Telescope Making.** Also receive a discount on the **Astronomical Calendar.**

Davenport

Quad Cities Astronomical Society, P.O. Box 3706, Davenport, IA 52808. Has 40 members, with annual dues of $15 for individuals, $20 for families. Meets at 7:30 p.m. the third Monday of every month, except July and August, at the Deere-Wiman Carriage House, 817 11th Ave., Moline, Illinois. The club has a 20–inch reflecting telescope at Sherman Park, Clinton County, Iowa. Also has an 8–inch refractor yet to be housed, and a 6–inch reflector that members may use at home. Also has a small

library of astronomy books and videos. Sponsors two star parties per month from May through October for the public, and hosts the annual Eastern Iowa Star Party in the late summer or early fall. Club members receive monthly newsletter, **The Meridian,** as well as the Astronomical League's **Reflector.** Discounts given for **Astronomy, Telescope Making,** and **Odyssey.**

Kansas

Kansas City

Astronomical Society of Kansas City, 5424 W. 101st Terrace, Overland Park, KS 66207. Has 200 members with annual dues of $27 for family or individual; $22 for junior or senior. Meets at 7:30 p.m. the fourth Saturday of each month, except December, in Lecture Room 103, Royal Hall, University of Missouri at Kansas City. The Society owns and operates Powell Observatory near Louisburg. The observatory has a 22–foot dome with a 30–inch, f/4.5 Newtonian telescope, fork-mounted and computer controlled. Also has a 4–inch f/15 refractor nearby. The observatory has a 25–seat classroom, kitchen, darkroom, restrooms, and television monitors plus computer equipment. The observatory is open to the public two Saturday nights each month. Membership benefits include access to the observatory; access to the club book and slide libraries; subscription discounts to **Astronomy, Sky & Telescope, Tele-**

scope Making, and **Odyssey** magazines; membership in the Astronomical League; a club newsletter, the **Cosmic Messenger;** and various club parties and picnics.

Topeka

Northeast Kansas Amateur Astronomical League, P.O. Box 951, Topeka, KS 66601. Has 50 members, with annual dues of $20 for families; $15 for individuals. Meets at Washburn University, Stoffer Science Hall, Room 103, 1700 College Ave. The club is building an observatory and has five acres under dark skies in the Kansas Flint Hills. The club has an extensive library, a 6–inch reflector, and a CCD camera. Members own several types of telescopes. The club promotes Astronomy Day each year and helps local schools with open houses. Members receive reduced rates for **Astronomy,** and access to the dark-sky site. Club members also conduct research.

Kentucky

Fort Wright

Midwestern Astronomers, 1643 Elder Ct., Fort Wright, KY 41011. Has 20 members, admitted by invitation only. No annual dues; meetings held at members' homes. All equipment owned by individual members. Members receive **Sky & Telescope** and membership in the Astronomical League.

Lexington

Blue Grass Amateur Astronomy Club, 1016 Della Dr., Lexington, KY 40504. Has 22 members, with annual dues of $10. Meets at 8 p.m. the second Friday of the month in Room 179 of the Chemistry-Physics Building on the University of Kentucky campus. The club has an 8–inch homebuilt telescope and holds star parties on an irregular basis. Members receive subscription discounts to **Sky & Telescope.**

Louisville

The Louisville Astronomical Society, Inc., P.O. Box 20742, Louisville, KY 40250–0001. Established in 1933, the club has 75 members with annual dues of $20 for single, $25 for family, $12 for friends and seniors. Meets in Room 102, Strickler Hall, University of Louisville, Belknap Campus. The Society owns two 8–inch Dobsonians, a 10–inch Dobsonian, a 12–inch Dobsonian, and an 8–inch SCT. The club also is completing a 16–inch Newtonian and a 23–inch Newtonian and is working on an observatory. The club has an extensive collection of books, magazines, and computer software. The Society conducts Boy Scout merit badge classes, and public observations at state and public parks. Each year the Society invites approximately six professional astronomers, physicists, and scientists to speak at club meetings. Members receive discount subscriptions to **Sky & Telescope, Astronomy, Telescope Making, and Observers Guide,** and **Observers Hand-**

book. Club members have been active in the Astronomical League, and member Virginia C. Lipphard was awarded the 1991 Astronomical League Award. The Society also is sponsoring a national award, the "National Outstanding Junior Astronomers Award," which will be given annually.

Paducah

West Kentucky Amateur Astronomers, 4360 Stonewall Dr., Paducah, KY 42001. Has 25 members, with annual dues of $12. Meets at the Golden Pond Observatory. The observatory has an Ash Dome, 12.5–inch reflector, and a 4.5–inch refractor. The Gold Pond Planetarium has a 40–foot dome, seats 82 people, and has a Spitz 512 projector. The club hosts the Twin Lakes Star Party at the planetarium in the fall.

Louisiana

Westwego

Pontchartrain Astronomy Society, 948 Ave. "E", Westwego, LA 70094. Has 130 members with annual dues of $14. Meets at the Science Building at the University of New Orleans. Has a public observatory with a 14–inch telescope with computer system; a 10–inch Dobsonian telescope for loans; and a library. This club was one of the founding members of the Deep South Regional Stargaze. The club also holds monthly star parties at a member's home, and members

receive discounts on astronomy publications.

Maine

Eliot

Astronomy Society of Northern New England, 80 Goodwin Rd, Eliot, ME 03903. Has 53 members.

Maryland

Arnold

Anne Arundel Association of Amateur Astronomers, Anne Arundel Community College, 101 College Parkway, Arnold, MD 21012. Has about 10 members, with no annual dues. Meets at the observatory at Anne Arundel Community College. The club has a 14–inch telescope and three 6–inch reflectors.

Baltimore

Baltimore Astronomical Society, meets at the Maryland Academy of Sciences/Maryland Science Center, 601 Light St., Baltimore, MD 21230. Tel. (301) 685–2370. Founded in 1881, the club has 140 members, with annual dues of $30. The club has an 8–inch Clark refractor and the center has a 140–seat planetarium. Monthly business meetings and lectures are held the second Tuesday of each month and star parties are scheduled monthly. Discounts given on **Astronomy.**

Bel Air

Harford County Astronomical Society, P.O. Box 906, Bel Air, MD 21014. Richard E. Hagenston, President. The club has 65 members, with annual dues of $18. Meets at the Harford Community College, either at the club's observatory on the campus, or in a classroom. The society has an observatory with a 16–inch Cassegrain. The observatory has a meeting room, a library with extensive back issues of astronomy magazines, and a computing room nearby. The society also has access to the darkroom facilities at the college. Meets once a month, with a speaker, and has a dinner once a month at a local restaurant and one or two star parties a month. The club also conducts courses in learning the sky, free to members and as a non-credit course through the college for non-members. A public observatory open house is held each month, as well as an "Astronomy Expo" at the college or at a local shopping mall. Displays include exhibits on loan from NASA, including a Moon rock. Members receive discount subscriptions to **Astronomy** and **Sky & Telescope** magazines.

Westminster

Westminster Astronomical Society, 3481 Salem Bottom Rd., Westminster, MD 21157. Has more than 70 members, with annual dues of $13 to $15. Meets in Room 111 of Lewis Hall of Science, Western Maryland College. Holds monthly star parties, semi- annual public star parties, and Astronomy Day displays. Members receive a monthly journal, the **Mason-Dixon Astronomer,** plus membership in the Astronomical League.

Massachusetts

West Springfield

Springfield Stars Club, 107 Lower Beverly Hills, West Springfield, MA 01089. Has 78 members, with annual dues of $29. Meets at the Springfield Museum of Science. Monthly meetings the fourth Tuesday of the month, September through June. The club has a Unitron refractor, 4–inch f/15, with alt-azimuth mounting on a tripod. Holds star parties on varying dates. Members receive subscriptions to **Sky & Telescope** and membership in the Astronomical League.

Michigan

Alpena

Huron Amateur Astronomers, 491 Johnson St., Alpena, MI 49707. Has 19 members, with annual dues of $25. Meets at a local planetarium or at a member's home. An observatory is in the design stages. Club members receive **Sky & Tele-**

scope and the Astronomical League quarterly, **Reflector.**

Dexter

University Lowbrow Astronomers, 9287 Chestnut Circle, Dexter, MI 48130. Contact Frederick Schebor, Tel. (313) 426-2363. Has 45 members, with annual dues of $20 for individuals or families; $12 for students. Meets at 7:30 p.m. the third Friday of each month, September through May, at the Detroit Observatory in Ann Arbor. Meets at the Peach Mount Observatory, Dexter, in June, July, and August. The club operates a 24-inch McMath telescope at Peach Mountain. Club members may reserve the telescope for exclusive use during the week. The club maintains a library of books and astronomical software. Members also receive a monthly newsletter, **Reflections,** as well as discounts on material advertised in **Sky & Telescope.**

East Lansing

Capital Area Astronomy Club, Abrams Planetarium, Michigan State University, East Lansing, MI 48824. Club has 60 members; dues are $7 per year. Meets at Abrams Planetarium, and members have access to planetarium facilities. The club holds monthly public observing sessions. Also publishes the popular **Sky Calendar,** which is mailed to observers nationwide. Members receive a newsletter, and membership in the Astronomical League.

Grand Rapids

Grand Rapids Amateur Astronomical Association, c/o Ronald J. Vander Werff, GRAAA Treasurer, 3333 Bradford NE, Grand Rapids, MI 49506. Tel. (616) 949-1749. Dues are $25 for 18 and older, $10 for 8 to 17 years, and $30 for families. Members receive discounts to **Sky & Telescope** and **Astronomy,** plus use of the club's James C. Veen Observatory, a quarterly journal, **Inside Orbit,** a monthly newsletter, and automatic membership in the Astronomical League. The observatory has four fully-equipped optical telescopes, a meeting room, library, and darkroom. The observatory is open to the public twice a month from April through October. The club offers a 24-hour information service at (616) 897-7065 for upcoming club activities, current sky highlights, and visitors' night status.

Warren

Warren Astronomical Society, P.O. Box 1505, Warren, MI 48090-1505. Dues are: family, $25; senior citizen and college student, $15; individual, $20; student, $10. General meetings on the first Thursday of the month at the Cranbrook Institute of Science, 500 Lone Pine Road, Bloomfield Mills, Michigan. Business meeting the third Thursday at the Macomb Community College, South Campus, Building B, Room 216, 14500 Twelve Mile Road, Warren. Club owns the Stargate Observatory, in conjunction with the Rotary International.

The observatory features a 12.5–inch Cassegrain telescope. It is open to all club members. Sub-groups include solar, lunar/planetary, cosmology, deep sky, and computer. Benefits include discounts on magazine subscriptions, membership in the Astronomical League, and use of the club library.

Minnesota

St. Paul

Minnesota Astronomical Society, 30 E. 10th St., St. Paul, MN 55101. Has 170 members, with annual dues of $33 per year; student membership, $9. Meets at 7:30 p.m. the first Tuesday of each month at the Science Museum of Minnesota. Has two observing sites: Metcalf Nature Center, which has a warming house and telescope piers, and Baylor Regional Park. The club is trying to raise funds for an observatory at Baylor Park. The club has two 16–inch telescopes, in storage until an observatory is built, and a library. Star parties are held two weekends a month, except in winter. Also holds mirror-making classes about once a year. All regular members receive a subscription to **Sky & Telescope** and the club's bimonthly newsletter, **Gemini.** The society also is in the Astronomical League. Discounts are offered on other astronomy publications.

Mississippi

French Camp

Rainwater Astronomers Association, French Camp, MS 39745. Has 40 members, with dues of $12 per year. Meets at 7 p.m. the first Thursday of the month at the Hill Music Building on the campus of the French Camp Academy. Book discounts and membership in the Astronomical League come with membership. Publishes the monthly newsletter, **The Rainwater Observer,** and holds monthly star parties and open houses. Also hosts the Mid-South Messier Star Party at the end of March.

Jackson

Jackson Astronomical Association, 6207 Winthrop Circle, Jackson, MS 39206. Tel. (601) 982–2317. Contact Walter Rebmann. Has approximately 40 members, with annual dues of $18. Holds meetings the first Friday of each month at 7:30 p.m. at the Salvation Army Building, Riverside Drive, Jackson. Has an observatory with an 8–inch Celestron and a 13–inch Dobson. Members may use these telescopes once they are "tested" on them. Club library has books, videos, and slides. Club meetings feature talks by amateur and professional astronomers. Members also receive discounts on **Astronomy** magazine and other publications.

Missouri

Blue Springs

Astronomical Society of Kansas City, P.O. Box 400, Blue Springs, MO 64013. Has 200 members with annual dues of $27. Meets at 7:30 p.m. the fourth Saturday of the month at Room 103, Royal Hall, on the University of Missouri, Kansas City campus. The society has an extensive library and collection of photographic slides, which can be checked out by members. The society also owns and operates Powell Observatory, near Louisburg, Kansas. The observatory has a 30–inch Newtonian which is computer controlled, and a 4–inch refractor. Membership in the society includes membership in the Astronomical League. Members receive a monthly newsletter, **The Cosmic Messenger,** and are eligible for discount subscriptions to astronomy publications.

Dawn

North Central Missouri Amateur Astronomers, Route 1, Box 111, Dawn, MO 64638. Has three members with annual dues of $10. Meets at members' homes. Has a telescope and black and white darkroom. Holds special sessions for events such as Halley's Comet and eclipses. Members receive a monthly newsletter.

Hazelwood

Rural Astronomers of Missouri, 209C Chapel Ridge, Hazelwood, MO 63042. Has 15 members, with annual dues of $10. Business meetings and observation sessions held monthly at the White Wildlife Area, Troy. The club has a 6–inch f/8 reflector to lend to members. Holds one to two public star parties per year. Members also belong to the Astronomical League.

St. Louis

St. Louis Astronomical Society, 10965 Whitehall Dr., Apt. 2, Bridgeton, MO 63044. The club has 270 members and meets at 7:45 p.m. the third Friday of the month at the St. Louis Science Center. The club has four telescopes ranging in size from 4 inches to 12 inches and a library with 900+ books. Members receive discount subscriptions to **Sky & Telescope.**

Nebraska

Lincoln

Prairie Astronomy Club, P.O. Box 80553, Lincoln, NE 68501. Has 65 members.

Omaha

Omaha Astronomical Society, 5025 S. 163 St., Omaha, NE 68135. Has 85 members.

Nevada

Reno

Astronomical Society of Nevada, 825 Wilkinson Ave., Reno, NV 89502. Has 65 members; dues are $26 per year, which includes subscription to **Sky & Telescope.** Meets in room 203 of the Leifson Physics Building, University of Nevada. Frequently holds star parties for local schools, and works with the Fleischmann Planetarium. Shares an observing site at Blue Canyon with the Sacramento Valley Astronomical Society. Has a portable 24–inch Dobsonian telescope.

New Hampshire

Penacook

New Hampshire Astronomical Society, 22 Center St., Penacook, NH 03303. Has 30 members.

New Jersey

Cranford

Amateur Astronomers Inc., William Miller Sperry Observatory, 1033 Springfield Ave., Cranford, NJ 07016. Tel. (908) 549–0615. George Chaplenko, Correspondence Secretary. Founded in 1949, the association has 375 members. Members receive a subscription to **Sky & Tele-scope** for their $25 annual fee. Also, AAI publishes a club newsletter, **Asterism,** from September through May, which includes updated schedules, bulletins, and monthly sky reports. The club boasts two large telescopes (a 10–inch f/15 refractor and a 24–inch Cassegrain reflector) plus darkroom facilities, a computer room, machine shop, and optical shop for amateur telescope making, all at the Sperry Observatory. There are various astronomical classes offered, plus seminars on how to use and buy telescopes.

Holmdel

STAR Astronomy Society Inc., P.O. Box 547, Holmdel, NJ 07733. Has 50 members, with annual dues of $25. Meets at the Holmdel Park Activity Center, Longstreet Road. The club has an equipment loan program of telescopes in the 2–inch to 8–inch range; a library with books and magazines, including **Sky & Telescope** from 1960 to the present. There are four observing nights per month at Huber Woods Park and special observing sessions for public and school groups. Members receive **Sky & Telescope** with their dues, plus discounts on **Astronomy Telescope Making,** and on purchases from Edmund Scientific Co.

Princeton

Amateur Astronomers Association of Princeton, Box 96, Princeton, NJ 08550. Has 100 members; dues of $40 per year include **Sky & Telescope** or **Astronomy** magazine subscriptions. Meets at Peyton Hall, Princeton University, on the second Tuesday of each month except during July and August. Monthly meetings usually include a lecture by a leading researcher in astronomy. Uses observatory at Washington's Crossing State Park; has a 12.5-inch Newtonian and a 6-inch refractor. Publishes **The Sidereal Times** 11 times a year.

Toms River

Astronomical Society of the Toms River Area (ASTRA), Novins Planetarium, Ocean County College, Toms River, NJ 08754-2001. Has 70 members who meet at 8 p.m. the second Friday of each month (except August) at the Robert J. Novins Planetarium, Ocean County College. Members have access to the planetarium library, receive the monthly newsletter (**Astral Projections**), membership in the Astronomical League, and student rates at planetarium shows. ASTRA hosts monthly star parties for members, plus an annual star party open to the public.

New Mexico

Albuquerque

Albuquerque Astronomical Society, P.O. Box 54072, Albuquerque, NM 87153. Has 230 members, with annual dues of $20 plus $1.75 for membership packet for first-time members. Meets at Regener Hall, University of New Mexico, Albuquerque. The club has a 16-inch f/6 Newtonian on an equatorial mount, an observatory, and a library. Holds public star parties, helps at University of New Mexico observatory open houses, and holds instructional sessions for public schools. Members receive discounts on **Sky & Telescope, Astronomy, Odyssey, Telescope Making** and **Observer's Guide** publications. The society publishes a monthly newsletter, **Sidereal Times.** Membership includes professional and amateur astronomers.

Clovis

Clovis Astronomy Club, 216 Sandzen, Clovis, NM 88101. The club has 11 members, with annual dues of $3. Meets at members' homes.

Los Alamos

Pajarito Astronomers, P.O. Box 1092, Los Alamos, NM 87544. Has 45 members, with annual dues of $7. Meets at the Fuller Lodge, Los Alamos, generally every other month. The club has a wide field 6-inch refractor and a small library of books and charts. Schedules star parties and members receive a monthly sky calendar.

New York

Chappaqua

Westchester Amateur Astronomers, P.O. Box 111, Chappaqua, NY 10514. Has 75 members with annual dues of $25. Meets at the Andrus Planetarium & Chappaqua Observatory. The club has a 10–inch Newtonian, a 6–inch Clark, two 8–inch Schmidt-Cassegrains, two 10 x 80 binoculars, and access to a 24–inch Cassegrain at Harriman Observatory. The club holds special planetarium shows, public observing and lectures, and publishes a monthly four-page newsletter.

Frewsburg

Marshal Martz Astronomical Association, 176 Robin Hill Road, Frewsburg, NY 14738. Has 55 members, with annual dues ranging from $15 to $50 per year. Life membership, $150. Meets at the Martz Observatory. The club has a 30–inch, 17.5–inch, and 8–inch Newtonians; a library; 50–seat meeting room; and a planetarium projector. Members receive discounts on astronomy magazines and equipment, use of club discounts, discount film processing, and mirror- and telescope-making classes, plus Astronomical League membership.

Getzville

Association of Observational Astronomers of Western New York, 1955 Hopkins Rd., Getzville, NY 14068. Has 65 members, with annual dues of $15. Meets at 7:30 p.m. on full moon Saturdays at Room 114, Hochstetter Hall on the University of Buffalo's Amherst Campus. Tel. (716) 688–4869. The club was formed in 1989, and is testing sites for a club observatory complex. When complete, the club plans to have a club room, and three or more observatories. The club hosts public nights, star parties, field trips, and public displays, and attends conventions, such as Steelafane, Star Fest, Hidden Hollow, and Martz. Club members have scopes as large as 26–inch, 25–inch, 22.5–inch and 20–inch, several homemade. There also is an 8–inch loaner telescope, and a library. Club members are involved in astrophotography, computer, research, and theory. They observe variable stars, double stars, aurora, meteors, supernovas, solar eclipses, comets, and deep sky objects. Members receive the newsletter **Light Minutes** monthly.

Lake Placid

Tri-Lakes Astronomical Society, 100 Sentinel Road, Lake Placid, NY 12946. Has 20 members, with annual dues of $15. Meetings held the Thursday of each month that is closest to the full moon. Meets at 7:30 p.m. at the North Country Community College. The club owns an 8–inch f/9, 8–inch f/6 (Newtonians), and 11 x 80 binoculars. Sponsors star parties for the general public during the summer, and holds lectures. Members receive **Astronomy** at a discount, and also may order astronomy books at a discount. Several members are involved with astrophotography and use cold cameras and/or hypered film, as well as CCD cameras. Two members also are involved in astronomy-related computer work.

Lindenhurst

Amateur Observers Society of New York, Inc., P.O. Box 838, Lindenhurst, NY 11757. Has 52 members with annual dues of $15 for individuals, $20 for families. Meets at 1 p.m. the first Sunday of each month in Room 5 of the Freeport Memorial Library, Freeport. Holds an evening program the second Thursday of each month at the Lindenhurst Rainbow Center. Also holds at least two observing sessions a month at the Robert Moses State Park. Club members have a variety of telescopes and computer equipment. Members receive discounts on subscriptions to **Sky & Telescope** and **Astronomy,** plus book discounts.

Pearl River

Rockland Astronomy Club, 110 Pascak Road, Pearl River, NY 10965. Approximately 230 members. Dues, $15 per year. Meetings held at Lake Sebago Harriman State Park. Club operates a 24-inch Cassegrain, and the observatory has a library, meeting area, and darkroom. Publishes a monthly calendar with dates to view objects in the sky.

North Carolina

Albemarle

Stanly County Astronomical Society, P.O. Box 1269, Albemarle, NC 28002. Has 15 members with annual dues of $20 for students, $25 for adults, $30 for couples, and $30 for families plus $2 for each child. Meets at Morrow Mountain State Park and at various locations in Richfield, North Carolina. The club owns a 6-inch Newtonian and members share telescopes of various sizes. Members have access to various local college libraries and NASA publications. Classes are offered in basic astronomy, observational techniques, and telescope making. Holds observing sessions for campers and the public. Members receive a monthly club newsletter and discount subscriptions to **Sky & Telescope.**

Castle Hayne

Cape Fear Astronomical Society, 110 Linville Dr., Castle Hayne, NC 28429. Has 30 members with annual dues of $20. Meets at 7 p.m. the first Sunday of every month at the Bryan Auditorium of Morton Hall on the campus of the University of North Carolina at Wilmington. The Society has two 8-inch and a 10-inch telescope and a library with books and tapes of astronomical subjects. The Society holds star parties, group observing sessions, and exhibits at schools. Members may receive **Astronomy** magazine at a discount. The Society publishes a monthly newsletter.

Greensboro

Greensboro Astronomy Club, Natural Science Center, 4301 Lawndale Dr., Greensboro, NC 27408. Has 51 members, with annual dues of $10. Meets at the Natural Science Center. Members have three club telescopes and other astronomy equipment. Meetings held monthly September through May, with observing sessions and meteor watches monthly. Members receive discounts on magazine subscriptions and membership in the American Youth Hostel Association.

Matthews

Charlotte Amateur Astronomers Club, 245 Timber Lane, Matthews, NC 28105. Has 100 members, with annual dues of $35. Meets at 7:30 p.m. the fourth Friday of the month September through May, at the Piedmont Natural Gas Co. Has a 16–inch Cassegrain, a 17.5–inch Newtonian, a 4–inch Quantum, and a 6–inch Newtonian, in a remote observatory. Sponsors an annual convention, "Southern Star," and holds festivals. Members receive a free subscription to **Sky & Telescope,** plus discounts on other publications.

Raleigh

Raleigh Astronomy Club, P.O. Box 10643, Raleigh, Raleigh, NC 27605. Tel. (919) 460–7900. Has between 55 and 65 members. Regular membership is $15 annually; $10 for junior members; $20 for families; and $7 for subscribing members. Meets the second and fourth Friday of each month at Hunter Hall on the campus of Meredith College. One meeting is devoted to observing, while a presentation is given at the other. Members receive the quarterly RAC newsletter and postcard reminders of upcoming events. Club members take part in the Messier Marathon and Astronomy Day, and organize camping trips to observe in remote, dark-sky locations. Meetings often feature talks by astronomers and astrophotographers, plus sessions on telescope making, observing techniques, and current astronomical theories and events.

Winston-Salem

Forsyth Astronomical Society, Route 9, Box 414–E Clodfelter Rd., Winston-Salem, NC 27107. Has 40 members, with annual dues of $15. Meets the third Wednesday of each month at the Polo Park Recreation Center. Beginner/novice class at 7 p.m.; general meeting at 7:30 p.m. Club equipment includes an 11–inch Celestron Schmidt-Cassegrain, 12–inch and 7–inch Newtownians, 13–inch Dobsonian, 4–inch refractor, and a library of astronomy books, star charts, slides, and videos. Hosts monthly star parties, generally within a week of the new moon. Occasional school and private shows. Members receive a monthly newsletter, and discounts for subscriptions to **Sky & Telescope** and **Astronomy.** The Society was founded in 1939.

North Dakota

Bismarck

Dakota Astronomical Society, P.O. Box 2539, Bismarck, ND 58502–2539. Has 50 members with annual dues of $10; $5 for students. The club meets at the local chapter sites throughout the state. The Society has a 12.5–inch Newtonian, and is building an observatory. The annual meetings are combined with the Dakota Star Watch in July or August. Members receive the bi-monthly newsletter, **The Stellar Messenger,** and membership certificates; novices receive astronomy lessons.

Ohio

Akron

Astronomy Club of Akron, Inc., P.O. Box 1881, Akron, OH 44309. Has 115 members, with annual dues of $35. Club meetings held the fourth Friday of the month in Room 19, Ayer Hall, on the campus of the University of Akron. The club has an observatory with 12.5 reflector, a 5–inch refractor, two 8–inch and three 6–inch reflectors, and a library. The club holds at least one star party per month. Members receive a one-year subscription to **Sky &**

Telescope and discounts for **Astronomy** magazine and publications from Sky Publishing Co.

Cleveland

Cuyahoga Astronomical Association, Box 29089, Cleveland, OH 44129–0089. Has 76 members, with dues of $15 per year for adults and $8 for juniors. Meets at the Rocky River Nature Center in the Cleveland Metro Park system. Uses Leatha Horse Park in Medina County for observing. Has 200 books in the library, and members receive discounts to **Astronomy, Telescope Making,** and **Sky & Telescope,** plus discounts from Sky Publications. Produces **The Observer,** a newsletter.

Columbus

Columbus Astronomical Association, P.O. Box 16209, Columbus, OH 43216. Tel. (614) 459–7742. Has 140 members, and frequently holds visiting sessions at the Perkins Observatory in Delaware, Ohio.

Dayton

Miami Valley Astronomical Society, 2629 Ridge Ave., Dayton, OH 45414. Headquarters in the Apollo Observatory. Tel. (513) 275–7433 or 275–7431. Has 90 members, with annual dues of $35. Meets at the Dayton Museum of Natural History. The Apollo Observatory site has a 50–cm Cassegrain plus eight other telescopes, and a library with more than 500 books. Members also use the John Bryan State Park Observatory, which has a dome and a 12-inch and 16-inch reflector, plus a darkroom and telescope-building room. The club holds a "Camper's Stargaze" each odd-numbered Saturday from Memorial Day to Labor Day. A slide show is followed by public star gazing. The club also holds classes for the public and hosts the Apollo Rendezvous, a meeting of Midwest amateurs, which is held the second Saturday in June. Members receive a subscription to **Sky & Telescope** and a 30 percent discount for **Astronomy.**

Mansfield

Richland Astronomical Society, P.O. Box 1118, Mansfield, OH 44901. Tel. (419) 468-3542. Has 45 members. The club operates the Warren Rupp Observatory, has a meeting room, and hosts an annual conference.

Toledo

Toledo Astronomical Association, 21601 Pemberville Road, Luckey, OH 43443. Has 40 members with annual dues of $25. Meets at McMaster Hall on the campus of the University of Toledo. The club uses two observatories—one with a 25-inch Newtonian, and one with a 12-inch catadioptric. Holds a "Chili, Chilly Observing Party" in the fall and spring. Members receive discounts on **Astronomy** magazine, plus membership in the Astronomical League.

Wilmot

Wilderness Center Astronomy Club, P.O. Box 202, Wilmot, OH 44689. Has 50 members, with annual dues of $6, plus membership in the Wilderness Center. The club uses a 6-inch f/8 refractor and a 16-inch f/11 Cassegrain, and has plans to build an observatory. The club has a small library and access to darkrooms. Holds monthly public star watches, a quarterly "Starfest-Starwatch and Lecture," and general backyard astronomy workshops for amateurs, students, and teachers.

Youngstown

Mahoning Valley Astronomical Society, P.O. Box 6445, Youngstown, OH 44501. Has 35 members.

Oklahoma

Oklahoma City

Oklahoma City Astronomy Club, 2100 N.E. 52nd St., Oklahoma City, Oklahoma 73111. Tel. (404) 424-5545 (Kirkpatrick Planetarium). Has approximately 100 members, with annual dues of $18. Meets at 7:30 p.m. the second Friday of each month, at the Kirkpatrick Planetarium. Has an observatory site with 25 concrete pads, warm-up building, and electric power, and classroom with an observatory housing a 12.5-inch Newtonian. The club has five telescopes: a 5-inch Schmidt-Newtonian, two 8-inch Newtonians, and a 10-inch and

12.5–inch Newtonian. Hosts the Okie-Tex Star Party annually during the October new moon. Members receive the club newsletter and discounts to **Astronomy,** and **Telescope Making.**

Oregon

Portland

Rose City Astronomers, Oregon Museum of Science and Industry, 4015 S.W. Canyon Rd., Portland, OR 97221. Has 104 members.

Pennsylvania

Philadelphia

Rittenhouse Astronomical Society, 216 Elbow Lane, Haverford, PA 19041–1806. Contact Nancy Tucker Blossom, treasurer. Has 90 members with annual dues of $24. Meets at the Planetarium of the Franklin Institute, Philadelphia. Members observe with a 10–inch Zeiss refractor following meetings, or attend a planetarium show at the Institute. Members receive a one-year subscription to **Sky & Telescope** and other discounts from Sky Publishing; reduced-rate subscriptions to **Astronomy, Telescope Making,** and **Odyssey.** Club members also belong to the Astronomical League and receive **The Reflector.** The club was formed in 1888, and is named after David Rittenhouse, a surveyor and clock maker who studied astronomy in the 1700s.

Pittsburgh

Amateur Astronomers Association of Pittsburgh, Inc., P.O. Box 314, Glenshaw, PA 15116. Tel. (412) 224–2510. Has 240 members with annual dues of $25. Meets on the second Friday of each month at either Buhl Science Center or Allegheny Observatory. The Association owns and operates the Nicholas E. Wagman Observatory, Deer Lakes Park, which houses a 12.5–inch Newtonian. Plans are to add a classroom, a permanently mounted 10–inch Schiefspiegler, and a 11–inch Brashear refractor. Members receive **Sky & Telescope** as a benefit.

Wyomissing

Berks County Amateur Astronomical Society, 1211 Parkside Drive South, Wyomissing, PA 19610. Tel. (215) 371–5854 (Reading School District Planetarium). Annual dues, $10 for 16 and up; $5 under 16. The Society meets at the Planetarium at 7:30 p.m. the second Thursday of each month from October through May. Informal meetings held June through September. Members receive bimonthly newsletter **Pegasus** and membership in the Astronomical League. Members also may use the Society's telescopes—a 12.5–inch reflector, a 10–inch f/6 Newtonian reflector, and a 4–inch f/15 refractor.

Rhode Island

Newport

Celestial Observers of Rhode Island, 10 Redcross Terrace, Newport, RI 02840. Has 45 members.

North Scituate

Skyscrapers, Inc., 47 Peeptoad Road, North Scituate, RI 02857. Has 127 members.

South Carolina

Greenville

Roger Mountain Astronomers, 209 Chapman Road, Greenville, SC 29605. Has 105 members.

Rock Hill

Carolina Skygazers Astronomy Club, Museum of York County, 4621 Gallant Rd., Rock Hill, SC 29730. Has 75 members.

Tennessee

Brentwood

Barnard-Seyfert Astronomical Society, 1000 Oman Dr., Brentwood, TN 37027. Has 75 members, with annual dues of $7. Meets at the Dyer Observatory, Vanderbilt University, or at the Cumberland Science Museum. The club has a 10–inch reflector (co-owned with Cumberland Museum), and holds monthly meetings and three to four star parties per year at local and state parks. Members receive discounted subscriptions to **Sky & Telescope** and **Astronomy** magazines.

Bristol

Bristol Astronomy Club, 940 Reedy Creek Rd., Bristol, TN 24201. Has 22 members, with annual dues of $22. Meets at King College, at the Burke Observatory. The club has a 12.5–inch f/5 reflector with observatory, a 3–inch refractor, a 10–inch reflector on a mobile trailer, an observatory darkroom, classroom, electronics lab, and photo-electric photometry room. Holds public star parties. Members receive discounts on **Sky & Telescope.** Astronomical League membership and book and other magazine discounts.

Kingsport

Bays Mountain Amateur Astronomers, 853 Bays Mountain Park Rd., Kingsport, TN 37660. Has 50 members, with annual dues of $5. Meets at the Bays Mountain Nature Center & Planetarium. The club uses a 16–foot domed observatory with an 8–inch refractor, and has concrete pads for additional telescopes. Takes part in public star parties. Members receive group rates for **Astronomy, Telescope Making,** and **Odyssey.**

Knoxville

Orion, 4412 Damas Rd., Knoxville, TN 37921. Has 35 members, with annual dues of $10. The club has an observatory with several 8–inch and 6–inch telescopes, a radio telescope (80 percent complete), computers, and two-way radio equipment. Holds one public meeting a month, plus star parties and special event sessions. Receives group rates for **Astronomy** and Guy Ottwell's publications.

Manchester

Middle Tennessee Astronomical Society, 1305 Sycamore Dr., Manchester, TN 37355. Has 15 members, with annual dues of $18. Meeting place varies. Hosts some special sky event sessions. Members receive discounts to **Sky & Telescope.**

Memphis

Society of Low-Energy Observers, Memphis Chapter of the Astronomical League, 4277 Park Forest Drive, Memphis, TN 38141. Attn: Kathey J. Nix. Has 21 members, with annual dues of $15 for individuals; $25 for two persons at the same address; and $30 for three or more at the same address. The club is part of the Astronomical League, and receives the Astronomical League newsletter, **The Reflector,** full discounts on books, and subscriptions to **Sky & Telescope.**

Texas

Brazosport

Brazosport Astronomy Society, Brazosport Nature Center and Planetarium, 400 College Dr., Lake Jackson, TX 77566. Tel. (713) 483–9218. Meets at 7 p.m. on the second Thursday of each month in the Planetarium of the Fine Arts Center at Brazosport College.

Fort Bend

Fort Bend Astronomy Club, P.O. Box 942, Stafford, TX 77497. Tel. (713) 499–4993. Meets on the second Friday at 8 p.m. at George Observatory.

Georgetown

Williamson County Astronomy Club, 901 S. Church St., Georgetown, TX 78626. Has 40 members, with no annual dues. Meets at 7:30 p.m. the second Thursday of each month, at Bank One in Round Rock. Holds monthly star parties and occasional special outings to view meteor showers, eclipses, etc. Members receive a discount subscription to **Astronomy.**

Houston

Houston Astronomical Society, P.O. Box 20332, Houston, TX 77225–0332. Has 365 members, with annual dues of $45 for regular members; $22 for students; and

$3 for associates. Meets on the first Friday of each month in Room 117 of the Science and Research Building, University of Houston. The society observatory, located near Columbus, has a 12–inch f/5 Newtonian, a 12–inch f/7 Newtonian, and a 14–inch Celestron SCT; a library; and a meeting room. The club holds an open house one Saturday each month at the observatory. Members receive discount subscriptions to **Sky & Telescope** and the Society newsletter, **Guidestar,** plus a subscription to the Astronomical League newsletter, **Reflector.** Also available are access to special interest groups, including groups focusing on astrophotography, planetary observing, amateur telescope-making, occultations & grazes, and advanced astro imaging.

Lubbock

South Plains Astronomy Club, 1920 46th St., Lubbock, TX 79412. Contact Wayne Lewis. Has 25 to 30 members, with annual dues of $22. Meets at 7 p.m. the third Thursday of each month at the Garden & Arts Center, 44th Street and University, Lubbock. Club members will have access to a 16–inch f/4.5 Newtonian which is being installed at Texas Tech University. The club has a number of portable telescopes and a small library. Hosts public star parties in the spring and fall. Members receive a subscription to **Sky & Telescope** with payment of dues, plus membership in the Astronomical League. Members also receive discounts on astronomy publications through

the Astronomical League and Sky Publishing. A newsletter is under development.

Utah

Salt Lake City

Salt Lake Astronomical Society, 15 S. State St., Salt Lake City, UT 84111. Has approximately 140 members, with annual dues of $23. Meets at 7 p.m. on the third Thursday of each month at the Hansen Planetarium. The club has an observatory with a 40–cm Newtonian. Membership includes a subscription to **Sky & Telescope,** and special discounts for **Astronomy, Odyssey,** and **Telescope Making** magazines as well as all Sky Publishing Corp. publications. Members also receive the club newsletter, **Nova.**

Vermont

Williston

Vermont Astronomical Society, P.O. Box 782, Williston, VT 05495. Has 45 members.

Virginia

Charlottesville

Charlottesville Astronomical Society, 2717 Northfield Road, Charlottesville, VA 22901. Has 40 members, with annual dues of $20. Club meets at the McCormick Observatory and other sites. Holds public star parties and light pollution seminars. Members receive discount subscriptions to astronomy magazines.

Portsmouth

Astronomical Society of Tidewater, 4205 Faigle Road, Portsmouth, VA 23703. Has 20 members, with annual dues of $10. Meets at 7:30 p.m. on the second Monday of each month at the 9th floor, faculty lounge, Arts & Letters Building, Old Dominion University, Norfolk, VA. Club uses a 10–foot, circular, moveable-domed observatory, with a 10–inch Newtonian reflector. Hosts two star parties each month on moonless Saturday nights.

Washington

Centralia

S.W. Washington Astronomical Society, 2421 Leisure Lane, Centralia, WA 98531. Contact Carl M. Newton. Has 30 members, with annual dues of $10. Meets in Olympia. The club has access to three observatories, and members have telescopes of various sizes, including one 24.5–inch Cassegrain. The club holds fair and mall displays, star parties, and slide shows for schools and senior centers. Dues include membership in the Astronomical League. Members also publish a monthly newsletter, **Tell-A-Scoop.**

Wisconsin

Beloit

Rock Valley Astronomical Society, 2220 E. Ridge Road, Beloit, WI 53511. Has 15 members, with annual dues of $25. Meets at the University of Wisconsin, Janesville. The club mostly does field observations in remote areas, but meets monthly for business matters. Also holds a Moon watch for the public. Dues include a subscription to **Sky & Telescope.**

Franklin

Wehr Astronomical Society, Wehr Nature Center, 9701 W. College Ave., Franklin, WI 53132. Has 117 members, with annual dues of $22 for a single membership and $27 for family. Monthly meetings held at the Nature Center include basic instruction and viewing with the club's 12–inch telescope. Members also receive the club newsletter, discounts to **Astronomy** magazine, discounts on astronomy items at a local store, and access to the Society equipment and library.

Grafton

Northern Science Foundation, 1327 11th Ave., Grafton, WI 53024. Contact William L. Fisher. Has approximately 50 members, with annual dues of $16. The club has a 17.5–inch Newtonian telescope housed in an observatory six miles west of Cedarburg, and is polishing the mirror of a 20–

inch research–grade telescope which will have a Newtonian focus, a Cassegrain focus, and a Coude focus, and will be computerized. The club is searching for land for an observatory. The club holds sessions with local schools and offers mirror–grinding classes. Members take an active role in building telescopes and teaching others. The club is a member of the Astronomical League.

Green Bay

Neville Museum Astronomical Society, 161 Rosemont Dr., Green Bay, WI 54301. Contact Ron Parmentier. Tel. (414) 336–5878. Has 45 members, with annual dues of $12. Meets at the Neville Museum, 210 Museum Place. Members' telescopes range in size from 6–inches to 30–inches. A dark site and observatory are available to club members. Members receive discount subscriptions to **Astronomy,** and **Telescope Making.**

LaCrosse

LaCrosse Area Astronomical Society, P.O. Box 2041, LaCrosse, WI 54602–2041. Contact Robert Allen. The club has 30 members, with annual dues of $12. Meets several times a year, in a classroom at the University of Wisconsin–LaCrosse science building. The club has a 13–inch Coulter Odyssey Dobsonian. Club members also have membership in the Astronomical League, and receive the club newsletter, plus the League's **Reflector.**

Madison

Madison Astronomical Society, 404 Prospect Road, Waunakee, WI 53597. Has 85 members, with annual dues of $25 for student; $35 for regular; $20 for observers. Meets at the M&I Bank, 5250 Verona Road, Madison. The Yanna Research Station, near Brooklyn, has three permanently mounted telescopes: a 16–inch Cassegrain, fork–mounted; an 11–inch f/10 Schmidt–Cassegrain; and a 17.5–inch Dobsonian. Also has observing pads for private telescopes, with access to electricity. The YRS has a meeting room, library, and records of observations by members. Schedules star parties near each new moon and sponsors public viewings in the spring and fall at area parks. Membership dues include a subscription to **Sky & Telescope,** plus reduced rates on **Astronomy, Deep Sky,** and **Odyssey.** Astronomical League membership is included with dues, and the club produces a quarterly newsletter, **The Capitol Skies.** The Society was founded in 1930, and members have taken part in observations of variable stars, transient luna phenomena, lunar grazes, and occultations, as well as in astrophotography and telescope making. The Society is a member of the Association of Lunar and Planetary Observations and the International Occultation Timing Association.

Milwaukee

Milwaukee Astronomical Society, W248 S7040 Sugar Maple Drive, Waukesha, WI 53186. Has 360 members, with annual dues of $40 for adults, $20 for non–residents, and $25 for juniors. Meets at 9201 West Watertown Plank Road. The club has a 25–inch Cassegrain, two 12.5–inch reflectors, twelve 10–inch portable Newtonians, three 8–inch Dobsonians, and a library. Holds open houses during the summer, telescope–making classes in the winter, and classes in telescope use and observing during the spring and fall. Members receive **Sky & Telescope,** membership in the Astronomical League, and discounts on **Astronomy, Telescope Making,** and **Odyssey.** Members also receive discounts on purchases at the American Science Center, Milwaukee, and discounts on the Ottewell Calendar and the Royal Astronomical Society handbooks. The club publishes a monthly newsletter.

Racine

Racine Astronomical Society, Inc., P.O. Box 085694, Racine, WI 53408. Has 71 voting members, with annual dues of $16 for ages 16 and over, $8 for students and seniors, $32 for Patrons, $400 for life

members, and $4 for associate members. Meets the third Monday of every month at the J.I. Case High School. The Society owns the Modine–Benstead Observatory, which houses a 16–inch Cassegrain/Newtonian, a 14–inch Schmidt–Cassegrain, a 12.5–inch Newtonian, an 8–inch Schmidt Camera, a 6–inch refractor, and a 4–inch Schmidt–Cassegrain. The observatory features a meeting room, a small library, a rudimentary workshop, and a darkroom. The observatory is open to the public every clear Thursday from May through September. Also holds special sessions for events such as the 1990 Mars opposition and Comet Halley. Members may reserve instruments. Members belong to the Astronomical League and the International Dark Sky Association, and receive the **Reflector** and **Northern Lights.** Members receive either **Astronomy** or **Sky & Telescope** at discounted rates.

Wyoming

Cheyenne

Cheyenne Astronomical Society, 3409 Frontier St., Cheyenne, WY 82001. Has 40 members.

PROFESSIONAL ORGANIZATIONS

★ **American Astronomical Society,** 2000 Florida Ave., NW, Suite 300, Washington, DC 20009. Tel. (202) 328–2010. The Society is the major organization of professional astronomers in the United States, Canada, and Mexico. Its objective is to promote astronomy, and its 5,100 members include astronomers, physicists, mathematicians, geologists, and engineers. Membership dues include subscriptions to the **AAS Newsletter** and **Physics Today** and each member receives the annual AAS Membership Directory. Members also receive discounts on Hertz rental cars and access to life and accident insurance through the American Physical Society.

Membership categories include: Junior, $25 annually, (first year free) for students under 28 years old; Junior/Society of Physics Students, $33; Associate, $75; and Full Member, $75. Two Full Members of the Society must sign your nomination when you apply for membership.

Society Publications include the **Bulletin of the AAS,** $20 for members, $50 for non–members, and $30 for foreign members; the **Astronomical Journal,** $75 for members, $280 for non–members, and $105 for foreign members; and the **Astrophysical Journal,** $135 for members, $600 for non–members, and $261 for foreign members. Five times annually, the Society also publishes the **AAS Newsletter,** which includes information about federal agencies and other news of interest to astronomers.

Other publications include: **Understanding the Universe: A Career in Astronomy,** and the **Job Register,** a newsletter that advertises open positions in astronomy.

The Society awards five prizes annually for outstanding contributions to astronomical research; four divisions of the AAS also award prizes. In addition, the AAS operates three grant programs—the Small Research Grant Program, which helps unsupported astronomers cover some costs of research; the International Travel Grant Program, which helps American astronomers with travel expenses; and the Chretien Awards, which promote observational astronomy on an international basis.

The Society holds two general meetings each year, with the location varying. Specialized groups include Planetary Sciences, Solar Physics, Dynamical Astronomy, High Energy Astrophysics, and Historical Astronomy.

Each year the Society sponsors 100 Harlow Shapley Visiting Lectureships for astronomers to visit colleges that do not have professional astronomers on staff.

★ **The Association of Astronomy Educators,** Physics Department, University of Wisconsin, LaCrosse, WI 54601. Contact Chaz E. Hafey, Science Museum of VA. The AAE encourages improvements in the curriculum of astronomy courses, publishes a newsletter with teaching tips and resources, and has an **Astronomy Education Material Resource Guide,** which lists curricula and resources available for cost.

★ **Association of Universities for Research in Astronomy,** 1625 Massachusetts Ave. N.W., Suite 701, Washington, DC 20036. Tel. (202) 483–2101. This organization, formed in 1957, brings together universities across the country interested in astronomy research. The organization operates the National Optical Astronomy Observatories, headquartered at Tucson, Arizona. AURA works with the National Science Foundation and the National Aeronautics and Space Administration. AURA also oversees The Space Telescope Science Institute, which operates the Hubble Space Telescope. AURA is primarily an administrative group that allocates much of the resources of the various universities involved in astronomy research.

★ **Society for Scientific Exploration,** Office of the Secretary, P.O. Box 3818, Charlottesville, VA 22903–0818. Dues are $45 annually, with 384 members involved in active astronomy research. Members usually are PhDs. The Society holds an annual meeting and publishes the **Journal of Scientific Exploration** and a newsletter, **The Explorer.**

AMATEURS CAN MAKE A DIFFERENCE

In earlier centuries, amateur astronomers made many of the important discoveries that expanded our knowledge of the heavens. William Herschel, for example, was not formally trained in astronomy (his formal education was in music), but he nevertheless discovered the planet Uranus and demonstrated that the galaxies are made up of stars. Neither was Percival Lowell formally educated as an astronomer; still, his planetary studies added volumes to our knowledge of Mars and the other planets.

Today, professional astronomers use expensive, complex instruments and advanced mathematical concepts to study remote galaxies, pulsars, black holes, and missing "dark matter." But to assume that only professionals with the most technologically advanced equipment can contribute to the science of astronomy would be a mistake. Although amateurs are unlikely to make major scientific advances in an area such as settling the dispute over distances to quasars, the heavens are open to anyone. It is sometimes humbling to remember that Galileo, with equipment that would be inferior to even modest telescopes available today, found new worlds to explore and forever changed the way we look at our Universe. For those with a little guidance, desire, and persistence, the opportunities are still there. There are many organizations that serve as a conduit, partner, and teacher for amateur astronomers who want to collect scientifically useful data.

Some scientists, such as Steve Edberg, an astronomer who works at the Jet Propulsion Laboratory, actively promote and encourage amateur contributions. Edberg coordinated the Comet Halley watch in 1986 and frequently speaks to amateur associations around the country, spreading the word that professionals often can use the long-term observations that only amateurs, without restrictions on their time at the telescope, can provide. Variable star work is a prime candidate for amateur work, he says. Furthermore, Edberg points out that many professionals list amateurs as co-authors of papers if the amateurs provide substantial observational data.

Accuracy and consistency, however, are essential. Recording your data requires much more than just noting that you "saw something odd" in the sky. Unfortunately, as Brian Marsden, director of the Central Bureau for Astronomical Telegrams, lamented in an article in the November 1988 issue of **Sky & Telescope,** there is a lack of "scientific literacy" among North American amateurs. Marsden recommends amateurs learn to calculate orbits, make astrometric observations, and, at the least, learn how to provide coordinates of objects in the sky. That might mean hitting the books again if you want to really contribute to one of the many groups willing and eager to work with amateurs.

The following areas are accessible to "serious" amateurs who demonstrate a level of professionalism. For additional ideas about a wide variety of amateur projects, see the November 1988 issue of **Sky & Telescope.** A series of articles in this issue explain the numerous contributions possible for amateur astronomers, even those with modest equipment.

Variable Star Observing

The American Association of Variable Star Observers, a long-time amateur-professional link, continually seeks new members, even those with modest equipment. Data from a number of observers can help scientists determine the long-time history of a variable star; a primary source of data for professionals who need to test a theory based on actual observations. All that is required is an ability to judge the brightness of a variable star, even via naked-eye or small telescope estimations, and to record the data on a consistent, accurate basis. The AAVSO can provide information on observing techniques; David Levy's book, **Observing Variable Stars,** also offers useful tips. (See Chapter 4).

The data compiled by the thousands of observations in a year may not immediately be included in the lead article of a major astronomy publication, but for scientists who need to trace a history of light variations from a star, the data can be invaluable.

Meteor Observing

During the early days of the space program, the U.S. was concerned that space debris might harm instruments and rockets and eagerly sought information from the amateur organizations dedicated to timing and counting meteor showers. Although the 1950s and 1960s were the heyday of NASA funding for such projects, the information still is needed, and groups such as the American Meteor Society and the International Meteor Organization still compile data on meteors. Once again, these observations can be made with a minimum of equipment. Naked eye observations and the ability to keep accurate records are the primary tools.

The American Meteor Society provides new members with tips on observing. It

also asks you to submit some observations so the Society can determine if they are of professional quality. See the **National and Special Interest Groups** section above for the addresses of the meteor societies.

Solar Observations

Although professional astronomers turn their instruments toward the Sun constantly, amateurs can still contribute by filling in gaps in information that might have been missed by the solar patrols of the professionals. For instance, a short-term change in a flare or sunspot might not catch the professionals' attention unless you notice it, and report it. You can also give exact timings or trackings of solar flares, sunspots, or other eruptive events. You should be aware, however, that in contrast to variable star and meteor observations, solar observations require more equipment, such as filters, telescopes, and photo techniques.

Two groups, the AAVSO and the Association of Lunar and Planetary Observers, regularly mount programs for amateur contributions to solar observations. See the **National and Special Interest Groups** section above for addresses of these organizations.

Photoelectric Photometry

Amateurs today have access to photoelectric photometers to measure the brightness of variable stars or other objects that capture their fancy. Basically, the work requires long hours at the telescope, with a photoelectric photometer attached to the telescope to measure the brightness of a star. The readings often are downloaded into a computer, but that is not necessary if you want to transfer them to a log book by hand.

One group, International Amateur-Professional Photoelectric Photometry, serves as a link between professional astronomers and amateurs who can or want to do photoelectric photometry. The IAPP reports that more than two hundred research papers have been written or co-written by amateurs involved in such work. For information about the association, write to the IAPP at the address in the **National and Special Interest Groups** section above.

Nova and Supernova Searches

Predicting where a nova will appear is impossible, so scientists eagerly seek all the help they can get in detecting the sudden outburst of a star. That help often comes from amateurs, as this is yet another field in which amateurs can contribute without having expensive equipment. A good atlas such as Wil Tirion's **Sky Atlas 2000.0** and a pair of binoculars are your major tools. One key for amateurs hoping to discover a nova is to study constellations on a regular basis to memorize star fields. That way, if a new star suddenly appears, you can recognize it. Knowing the star fields is essential if you don't want the chagrin of "finding" a new object that has been on even the most basic star chart for the last one hundred years. The AAVSO has a Nova

What to Do If You Find a New Object

First, wait at least one day, if you can contain your excitement, and double check your observations. Then prepare to break your observations down to numbers. For example, you'll need to know the coordinates; date; time, in Universal time; right ascension; declination; magnitude. Detail all this information in a telegram, adding a few comments about the appearance of the object. Be brief. The last lines of the notification should include your name, address, and telephone number. Send your telegram to:

Central Bureau for Astronomical Telegrams
Smithsonian Astrophysical Observatory
60 Garden St.
Cambridge, MA 02138.

If you're interested in scanning the skies for new objects, the Astrophysical Observatory will, upon written request, send information on astronomical projects for amateurs.

Search Division through which amateurs can notify scientists of an early find, enabling them to quickly turn instruments on the nova or supernova.

Planetary Studies

Although spacecraft have flown by, over, around, and even landed on some planets, ground-based observations still are needed. By carefully observing the planets, an amateur can spot sudden changes that may be of interest to professionals, who seldom can devote hours of telescope time to the planets. Two amateurs, for example, were the first to note the appearance of a large white spot on Saturn. On September 24, 1990, Stuart Wilber of Las Cruces, New Mexico, detected the Great White Spot with a homemade, 10–inch, F/7 reflector and immediately reported the discovery. Alberto Montalovo of Burbank, California, also spotted it, but delayed his report one day so he could verify his finding with a second night's observation.

Dust storms on Mars and changes in the atmosphere of Jupiter are prime targets of study for amateur astronomers. Amateurs who spend time at the telescope learn to detect subtle changes in the upper atmosphere of the planets, and can alert professionals to turn their instruments there in the event of a significant occurrence. In recent years professionals have sought the assistance of amateurs for a number of projects, such as monitoring the dust storms on Mars or searching for the Ashen Light of Venus.

Further areas of study for amateurs include timing occultations of stars by the planets; lunar observations, especially for examples of Transient Lunar Phenomena (flashes of light in some craters); orbit computations of the minor planets; and comet discoveries.

Comets

Although professional astronomers remain interested in the comets, the time it takes for them to conduct a search makes it impractical, if not impossible, for large instruments to be committed to such research. Consequently, searching for comets today is almost exclusively the realm of the amateurs. Searchers such as David Levy, who has discovered sixteen comets, scan the skies for small fuzzy patches of light and compare those patches against charts of known deep sky objects. (See the interview with David Levy, "On the Trail of Comets," in Chapter 4.) Some of the important comet discoveries made by amateurs in recent years include Comet Levy, Comet West, Comet Ikeya-Seki, and Comet IRAS-Araki-Alcock.

Associations

The following associations work closely with amateurs. For more information on each group, see the **National and Special Interest Groups** section above.

★ **American Association of Variable Star Observers,** 25 Birch St., Cambridge, MA 02138. Tel. (617) 354–0484. Contact Janet A. Mattei.

★ **American Lunar Society,** P.O. Box 209, East Pittsburgh, PA 15112. Tel. (412) 829–2627. Contact Francis G. Graham.

★ **The American Meteor Society,** Dept. of Physics and Astronomy, SUNY, Geneseo, NY 14454.

★ **The Association of Lunar and Planetary Observers,** P.O. Box 16131, San Francisco, CA 94116. Contact John E. Westfall.

★ **International Amateur-Professional Photoelectric Photometry,** A.J. Dyer Observatory, Box 1803 STA. B., Vanderbilt University, Nashville, TN 37235.

★ **International Meteor Organization,** (North American Section), 181 Sifton Ave., Fort McMurray, Alberta T9H 4V7, Canada.

Comet West, photographed March 8, 1976, with the Kitt Peak National Observatory/Case Western Reserve Burrell-Schmidt telescope. (National Optical Astronomy Observatories)

General Secretary, Paul Roggemans, Pijnboomstraat 25, B–2800, Mechelen, Belgium.

★ **International Occultation Timing Association,** 1177 SW Collins Ave., Topeka, KS 66604–1524. Tel. (913) 232–3693. Contact Terri and Craig McManus.

★ **The Meteoritical Society.** Contact at Meteoritics Office, Institute of Geophysics and Planetary Physics, Univ. of California, Los Angeles, CA 90024–1567.

TELESCOPES AND ACCESSORIES

BUYING A TELESCOPE

Today's amateur astronomers need not resort to building a telescope—unless, of course, they want the pleasure of doing so. There are many high quality instruments on the market. The key is to wind your way through the galaxy of advertising claims, avoiding the pitfalls of cheaply made "toys" that promise much and deliver little. Take promotional literature with a grain of salt, bearing in mind that slick advertising often promotes even low quality telescopes as capable of showing details in objects such as the Orion Nebula that, in reality, are visible only in large instruments or in long-exposure photographs.

The basic telescope designs are: Refractor; Newtonian; and Catadioptric. Each has special attractions; each also has drawbacks. Since most of your purchases will probably be via mail-order, it's a good idea to at least visit a local club's star party before you buy. That way you get a chance to look at different instruments and ask questions of the instruments' owners. (See the **Local Astronomy Clubs** section in Chapter 2 to locate a group in your area.)

The refractor is probably the easiest to use, and the one most familiar to non-astronomers. The telescope consists of a tube with a lens (objective) through which light passes and is focused at an eyepiece at the rear of the instrument. It is durable and seldom needs adjustments. A refractor is an excellent choice for those who don't have much time, or the inclination, to tinker with their telescope. A major drawback, however, is that refractors cost more than other designs per inch of aperture. A good quality, large telescope, 6 inches or more, is bulky and expensive. The cheap refractors sold at department stores are to be avoided at all costs. All too often they leave budding astronomers frustrated when they discover that the poor optics and even poorer mountings reveal little of the beauty and grandeur of the Universe.

The best buy, when you consider size and dollars spent, remains the Newtonian reflector. These instruments have a mirror at the bottom of the tube which reflects light back to an elliptical flat, and into an eyepiece located near the top. Nearly all amateur telescopes are of the Newtonian design. Many of the large "light buckets" from manufacturers such as Coulter, Jupiter, JMI, and Obession are Newtonians, as are the majority of large instruments at the world's major observatories.

Despite their cost and size advantages, Newtonians have their drawbacks. The optical system is more temperamental than those of either the refractor or the catadioptric, and must constantly be adjusted, especially if the instrument is moved frequently. Furthermore, reflectors can be sensitive to temperature changes and dust on the mirrors, and instruments with larger apertures can be bulky to move about.

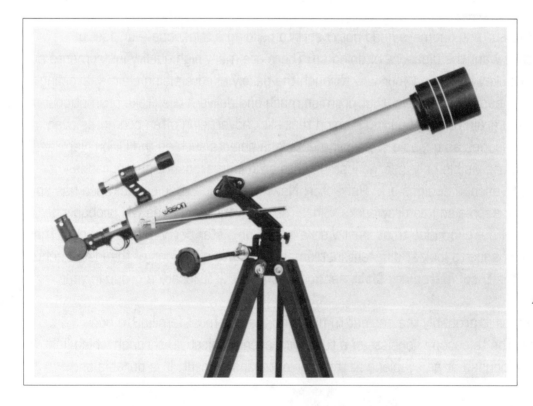

A basic, 60mm refractor from Jason (model 407). (Courtesy of Jason)

A Newtonian from Celestron (model SP—C6). (Courtesy of Celestron)

The catadioptrics are popular for astrophotography, and are easily portable. These telescopes enable you to obtain greater focal lengths by essentially "folding" the light back through mirrors inside the tube. In the popular Schmidt-Cassegrain design, light passes through a Schmidt correcting lens, then strikes a spherical primary mirror. It then is reflected back up the tube to a small secondary mirror, which reflects the light out an opening in the rear of the instrument where the eyepiece is located. Another catadioptric design similar to the Schmidt-Cassegrain, the Maksutov, provides

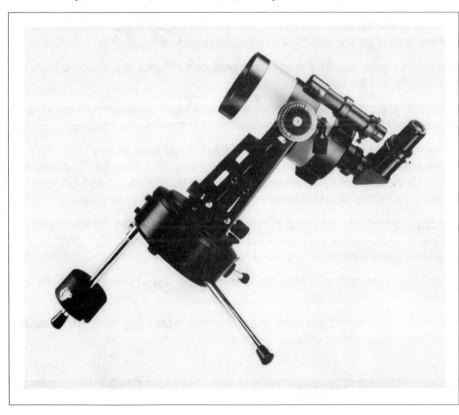

A Cassegrain catadioptric from Swift Instruments (model 854). (Courtesy of Swift Instruments)

excellent wide field views of the sky at a somewhat higher price. The major manufac-turers—Meade, Celestron, and Questar—produce excellent instruments that are durable, portable, and less temperamental than Newtonians. Catadioptrics, however, cost more per inch of aperture than Newtonians.

Ultimately, your choice of instrument should depend on what you want to observe and where you live. If you plan to observe galaxies and other deep sky objects, you should generally go for the largest instrument you can afford—the "light buckets" are superior for this kind of observing. But unless you live under dark skies and have a permanent observing site, you must also factor portability into the equation. If you live in the city, you may need

Telescope Terms

Aperture—The diameter of the lens or mirror. The aperture is given in either inches or millimeters. The larger the aperture, the more light the telescope collects. As a rule, a larger aperture will give you a better image.

Astigmatism—The aberration of a lens which elongates images. It is associated with poorly made optics or collimation errors.

Chromatic Aberration—The failure of a lens to bring light of different wavelengths to a common focus. It produces a faint colored halo around the bright stars, the planets, and the Moon.

Coma—Affects parabolic reflector telescopes. The images seen produce a v-shaped appearance; distortion is more pronounced near the edges of the field of view.

Diffraction Pattern—The optical effect caused by the interference of light waves passing around or through an opening. The angular diameter of a diffraction disk becomes smaller as the lens size increases.

Exit Pupil—The circular beam of light that leaves the eyepiece. The size should never be larger than the diameter of the pupil of the human eye (about 1/6 of an inch) or smaller than 1/64 of an inch. To determine the size of the exit pupil, divide the aperture by the power of the eyepiece being used. You also can deter-mine the exit pupil by dividing the focal length of the eyepiece by the focal ratio of the telescope.

Eyepiece or Ocular—The eyepiece magnifies the image formed by the main optical system (a lens or mir-ror). There are several designs on the market. A variety of eyepieces, from low power to high power, allow you to change views, and see either a wider field of the sky or focus in on a detail.

Finderscope—A small, low-power telescope mounted on the main telescope. It is used to help you point to and find objects.

Field Curvature—Occurs when not all the light rays come to a sharp focus in the same plane. The center of the field may be sharp, while the edges are out of focus, or the opposite may occur.

to drive long distances to set up your instruments, and should therefore make sure you will be able to wrestle your telescope into and out of your car without too much trouble. If you plan to specialize in the planets and the Moon, a smaller refractor may give you more than adequate views, even if you live in a light-polluted city. A small refractor or catadioptric may also be the best choice for those with limited storage space.

Telescope Manufacturers

★ **Astro-Physics,** 11250 Forest Hills Rd, Rockford, IL 61111. Tel. (815) 282–1513. Builds refractors starting at 4.7– inch and up. Recently revamped product line.

★ **AutoScope Corporation,** P.O. Box 2560, Mesa, AZ, 85214–2560. Tel. (602) 497–6882. Fax (602) 497–9501. These

---

Field of View—The amount of sky you can see through a telescope. It is measured in degrees of arc. The larger the view, the larger the area of sky you can see.

Focal Length—The distance from the lens or primary mirror to the point where the telescope is in focus (the focal point). The longer the focal length of the telescope, the more power it has, and the larger the image. The formula to calculate focal length is aperture times the focal ratio. A 6-inch aperture with a focal ratio of f/7 would have a focal length of 42 inches.

Focal Ratio—The ratio of the focal length of the telescope to its aperture. To determine the focal ratio, divide the focal length by the aperture.

Light Power—Determined by the objective diameter—the bigger the lens or mirror, the more light it will pick up.

Limiting Magnitude—The faintest star you can see with a telescope under the best viewing conditions. This limit is directly related to aperture, as larger apertures allow you to see fainter stars.

Magnification—Magnification, or power, often is touted as a selling point for cheap telescopes. Magnification is determined by dividing the focal length of the telescope by the focal length of the eyepiece you are using. As a rule, the maximum usable power is about 60 times the aperture of the telescope. For example, a six-inch telescope has a maximum usable power of 50 x 6 = 300. After 50x, the image begins to distort, although some optics can reach powers of 60 times the aperture. Generally, you should use the highest power that enables you to pick out highlights or details of the object under study. If you jump to higher powers, you tend to destroy the definition of an image rather than improve it.

Resolution—The ability of a telescope to render detail. The higher the resolution, the better the detail.

Resolving Power (Dawes Limit)—The ability of a telescope to separate two closely-spaced double stars into two distinct images, measured in seconds of arc. The theoretical limits are determined by dividing the aperture of the telescope into 4.56. The larger the aperture, the better the resolving power.

Spherical Aberration—Causes light rays passing through a lens or reflected from a mirror to come to focus at different points. This creates a blurred image rather than a sharp point of a star.

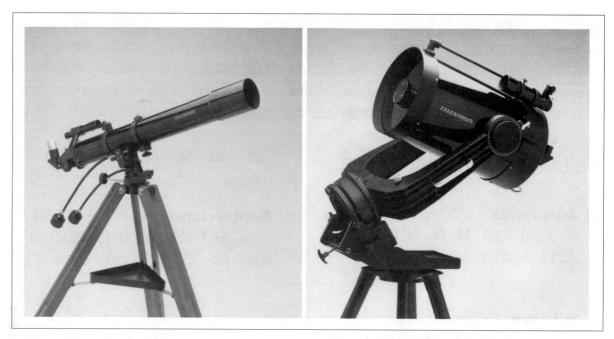

The Celestron Firstscope 80 refractor, left, and the Celestron Ultima 11 catadioptric, right. (Courtesy of Celestron)

robotic observatories are designed for serious researchers who need automatic telescopes that work without direct human intervention. Many can be operated, via computers and telephone lines, from hundreds and thousands of miles away. The automatic telescopes work well for photometric and variable star observations, CCD photometry, and narrow-split spectroscopy. Larger robotic telescopes cost in the hundreds of thousands of dollars, but the equipment is designed to accomplish, with minimal human oversight, the study of objects that require volumes of information that often cannot be obtained on larger telescopes where many competing astronomers with different projects are vying for time.

AutoScope generally requires a 40 percent deposit with each order, with additional payments at various stages of development. Delivery on the smaller models is within six to 10 months; delivery on larger models may take up to two years. Write for catalog.

★ **Celestron International,** 2835 Columbia St., Torrance, CA 90503. Tel. (213) 328–9560. Toll-free 1–800–421–1526. Fax (213) 212–5835. Celestron is one of the leaders in marketing portable Schmidt-Cassegrains. These telescopes are used as teaching tools at many colleges and universities, and are attractive to amateurs, especially those interested in astrophotography. They also serve well observers who don't have a permanent observing site. The telescopes can come with a number of extras, including photog-

raphy adapters, drive motors, hand controller, wedge with latitude adjuster, and a wide variety of other items. The telescopes often are sold at a discount by dealers, but primarily are available through the company, through mail-order houses such as camera dealers, and through astronomy-related businesses across the country.

The company has an excellent brochure describing telescopes in general, plus tips on viewing, optical terms, definitions of telescope parts, etc.

★ **Chicago Optical & Supply Co.,** 9114 N. Waukegan Rd., P.O. Box 1361, Morton Grove, IL 60053. Tel. (708) 827–4846. Supplies telescope-making materials as well as complete telescopes. View finders, eyepieces, slow motion heads, camera adapters, color filters, ring mounts, and pre-figured and aluminized mirrors available.

★ **Coulter Optical,** P.O. Box K, Idyllwild, CA 92349. Tel. (714) 659–4621. A company built on the concepts of John Dobson, who developed the style in the 1950s. The telescopes are designed for viewing, with minimal "extra" equipment. You can add an equatorial "Dobson" mount. The scopes range from 8–inch to

17.5–inch, and range in price from $275 for an 8–inch to $1,150 for a 17.5–inch scope. These popular "light buckets" paved the way for the bigger scopes used by amateurs today. The telescopes come standard with an alt-azimuth mount, 1¼–inch focuser, 27mm eyepiece, and tube with paraboloidal mirror and matching elliptical flat, aluminized and overcoated. Most Coulter products are sold factory-direct.

★ **DFM Engineering Inc.,** 1035 Delaware Ave., Longmont, CO 80501. Tel. (303) 678–8143. Telescope instrumentation and research- grade telescopes.

★ **Great Lakes Instruments,** P.O. Box 610, Haslett, MI 48840–0610. Tel. (517) 349–4180. Builds kits and complete tele-

scopes in the modest range, 6–inch to 10–inch. The company bills its products as functional, low-cost equatorial mount Newtonian reflectors. Write for a brochure.

★ **Jason,** Jason Empire Inc., 9200 Cody, Box 14930, Overland Park, KS 66214. Tel. (913) 888–0220. Toll-free orders at 1–800–255–6366. Fax ordering, (913) 888–0222. Sells mostly smaller, 60mm refractors and smaller reflectors, along with binoculars.

★ **Jim's Mobile Industries (JMI),** 1960 County Road 23, Evergreen, CO 80439. Tel. (303) 277–0304. Toll-free orders at 1–800–247–0304. Fax (303) 526–9140. Builds large telescopes, 16–inches and up, with equatorial mounts. Also sup-

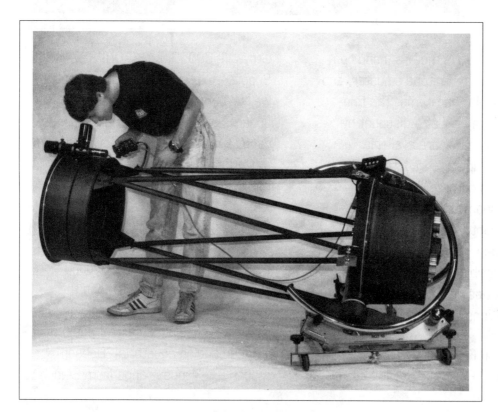

The JMI NGT–18.
(Courtesy of JMI)

plies accessories, such as computer data bases, motor focus, motor drive, digital setting circles, computerized sky charts and accessories, and retrofit equipment for Schmidt-Cassegrains and Newtonians. The NGT telescopes come in three models, a 16–inch, 18–inch, and 25–inch. Prices range from $7,400 to more than $20,000. These telescopes are for serious amateurs, and the electronic accessories are designed with the astrophotographer in mind. Charges $2 for general catalog and $3 for detailed information on the NGT telescope.

★ **Jupiter Telescope Company,** 815 S. U.S. 1, Suite 4–237, Jupiter, FL 33477. Tel. (407) 881–1365. Another Dobson telescope manufacturer, Jupiter features telescopes with heavier mirrors than in some Dobsons, which come with a standard mount that creates an equatorial mount based on a Dobson design. The mount is the D'Autumen Equatorial Table, which permits observers to add a drive system. One model comes equipped with the drive. Jupiter uses Novak mirror cells, spiders and focuser, a Telrad "bulls eye in the sky" sight, and optional Lumicon Sky Vector II computer setting circles. Terms: 50 percent down; remainder prior to delivery. Prices start at $2,695 for a Juno–14 Dobsonian. Sold only through manufacturer.

★ **Lorraine Precision Optics,** 1319 Libby Lane, New Richmond, OH 45157. Tel.

(513) 553–4999. Catalog $2. Schiefspieglers optics.

★ **Lumicon,** 2111 Research Dr., Livermore, CA 94550. Catalog $3. Tel. (415) 447–9570. Telescopes, binoculars, mirrors and lenses, filters, photo equipment, astrophotography aids.

★ **Meade Instruments Corporation,** 1675 Toronto Way, Costa Mesa, CA 92626. Tel. (714) 556–2291. For list of dealers and assistance, call 1–800–854–7485. Fax (714) 556–2291. Sells Schmidt-Cassegrains and other telescope accessories, Newtonians, and binoculars. Catalog package $3.

★ **Obession,** 923 Stony Rd., Lake Mills, WI 53551. Tel. (414) 648– 2328 or (414) 648–8284. Newcomers to the marketplace, the Obession telescopes of Dave Krieg are basic Dobsons with some interesting variations. The 20–inch and 25–inch f/5 scopes are built with consideration for the observer who must transport the telescope to a dark-sky site. A "wheelbarrow" setup allows you to easily move the scopes, which weight from 150 to 250 pounds, into position. The design also permits easy on-site assembly, without the need for numerous tools. It has an open tube arrangement, but optional covers or light shrouds are available. The optics are from Galaxy Optics. All orders must include a 50 percent check or money order deposit, with the balance due prior to shipment. Costs are

Model 826C eight-inch Newtonian by Meade. (Courtesy of Meade Instruments)

$4,495 for the 20–inch; $8,896 for the 25–inch. Shipping and crating are extra.

★ **Optical Guidance Systems,** 2450 Huntingdon Pike, Huntingdon Valley, PA 19006. Tel. (215) 947–5571. The company offers research-quality telescopes using Ritchey-Chretien optical designs, custom made by Star Instruments. Optical Guidance also can supply Newtonian,

Classical Cassegrain, Wright-Schmidt, Maksutov, and refracting telescopes, plus mountings. These mounts and telescopes, along with Schmidt cameras, are for serious amateurs. The company also custom builds to specifications supplied by clients. The guidance systems—which include mountings, digital guides, and coordinate and motor systems—are outside the range of many if not most amateurs, with prices for mounts ranging from $3,850 up to $42,000. The telescope system, with all the equipment, is designed for observatories. Optical Guidance Systems also serves as a dealer for several companies, including Asko, Lumicon, Meade, Mikage, Parks, Takahashi, and Tele Vue.

Full payment or a deposit is required with each order. A 50 percent deposit is required on complete telescopes, and a 30 percent deposit on standard mountings. Shipping date is one to five months from receipt of payment on mountings; complete telescopes will be shipped in two to eight months. The firm suggests calling for current availability.

★ **Optical Research Corporation,** 3009 E. Forest, Appleton, WI 54915. Tel. (414) 734-5006. Optical equipment.

★ **Parks,** 270 Easy St., Simi Valley, CA 93065. For information and orders, call (805) 522-6722. Toll-free, in California, 1-800-43-PARKS. Elsewhere, 1-800-44-PARKS. One of the early telescope companies serving amateurs. Established in 1954, Parks features a variety of telescopes, binoculars, mounts, drives, accessories, etc. Newtonian telescopes range in size from 6-inch to the 16-inch Observatory styles. Refractors, spotting scopes, giant binoculars also are offered, as are telescope-making components, including tubes, primary mirrors, secondary mirrors, focuser, mirror blanks, mirror cells, spiders, mounting rings, setting circles, finderscopes, guidescopes, mounts, eyepieces, filters, camera adapters, drivers, and drive correctors. To order, send check or money order, or use a credit card. Larger orders are shipped freight collect. Write for catalog.

★ **Questar Corporation,** P.O. Box 59, New Hope, PA 18938. Tel. (215) 862-5277. Fax (215) 862-0512. Regional Office, 101 Progress Dr., West Bend, WI 53095. Tel. (414) 338-3389. Fax (414) 338-3798. A portable telescope with a big price. The company features desktop models as well as the Questar 12 with a German equatorial mount. Model extras include powerguides, various mirror coatings, rapid focus, and accessories for astrophotography. Also offers various camera lenses. Provides product literature on request, and arranges extended payment plans. Accepts credit card purchases. Write for catalog.

★ **Safari Telescopes,** 110 Pascack Rd., Pearl River, NY 10965. (212) 621-9199. Designed for "serious amateur astronomers," Safari Telescopes are

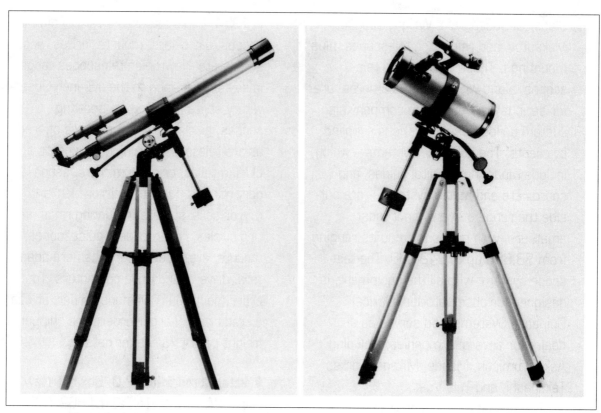

The Swift 859R 60mm refractor, left, and the Swift 856 catadioptric. (Courtesy of Swift Instruments)

basic Dobson designs, with fiberglass and aluminum used in place of the traditional plywood of Dobson mounts. The telescopes can be transported in small cars and assembled within minutes without using tools. The scope comes with a ground board, base, mirror box, secondary cage, primary mirror cell, mirror, secondary flat, secondary holder and spider, focusers, and truss supports. The basic components are purchased from manufacturers such as Galaxy Optics for the mirrors, Novak for the holder and spider, Tectron for the focuser. Accepts Visa/Master/American Express/Optima Card. Requires 25 percent down with

order; balance before delivery date. Write for catalog.

★ **Sky Designs,** 4100 Felps, #C, Colleyville, TX, 76034. Tel. (817) 656–4326. Manufactures large Dobson mount telescopes.

★ **Star-Liner Co.,** 1106 S. Columbus, Tucson, AZ 85711. Tel. (602) 795–3361. Offers telescopes ranging from backyard models to research models. Catalog $5.

★ **Swift Instruments Inc.,** 952 Dorchester Ave., Boston, MA 02125. Or, P.O. Box 562, San Jose, CA 95106. Toll-free to Boston: 1–800–446–1116; to San Jose:

1–800–523–4544. Offers binoculars, telescopes, spotting scopes, weather and marine instruments, specialty optics, and rifle scopes.

★ **Takahashi,** sold in the U.S. by Texas Nautical Repair Company, 3119 S. Shepherd, Houston, Texas, 77098. Tel. (713) 529–8480. Fax (713) 529–3108. Offers refractors, including beginner and advanced models, ranging in price from a little more than $300 to more than $14,000. Also sells telescope assembly parts, tripods, filters and astrophotography accessories, equatorial mounts, and astrographs.

★ **Tectron Telescopes,** 2111 Whitfield Park Ave., Sarasota, FL, 34243. Tel. (813) 758–9890. A builder of giant Dobsonian telescopes in sizes of 15–inch, 20–inch, 25–inch, and 30–inch. Prices range from $2,250 to $9,500, plus shipping. Also sells focusers for the scopes. The company sells to the "top end" of the amateur astronomy market. Brochures cost $1.

★ **Tele Vue Optics,** 20 Dexter Plaza, Pearl River, NY 10965. Tel. (914) 735–4044. Free information. Telescopes and accessories.

Building a Telescope

For many years, the best way for amateurs to own a telescope of any size was to build it themselves. Today, many amateurs skip that route, but glass pushers still abound. Many companies, in addition to selling you a complete telescope, will supply you with parts to assemble an instrument and the materials to grind and polish your own mirror. Or, as an alternative, you can buy a mirror already figured for you, or even special-order a mirror to your specifications.

Grinding a mirror is one of those chores that can give you a supreme sense of satisfaction once the job is done, but during the process can leave you wondering what bit of insanity forced you into this obsession. Grinding and polishing a mirror to the correct figure or paraboloid requires patience, patience, and more patience.

You begin with a mirror blank and tool. Starting with coarse grains of grinding materials and switching to progressively finer and finer materials, you gradually remove bits of glass. Little by little, you wear down the glass to a figure that will reflect rays of light to a single point back up the tube of the Newtonian. Finally, you reach the stage where you need a tester, such as a Foucault tester, to measure the paraboloid that is your ultimate goal.

Once you've finished grinding, polishing, and perhaps cursing, your mirror, it's time to send it off for the finish reflective coating. Aluminizing, especially enhanced, is a popular, and long-lasting final step in preparing your mirror for use. Silvering, although of high quality and reflecting qualities, tends to deteriorate quickly in today's polluted atmosphere.

Before sending your mirror off to be aluminized, most dealers recommend you follow a few precautions:

- The mirror should be packed face up, wrapped in soft material such as tissue paper or cotton balls, then placed in a box large enough to provide a minimum of two inches of space all around the mirror. The outer box should be sturdy and clearly marked as containing a breakable object. It's best to be a little on the safe side with extra wrapping and crating. It's hard to imagine the agony of working for months to get the mirror figured just right, only to have it damaged while en route to an aluminizing company.

- Chances of losing a mirror are probably slim, but if you write or scratch your name and address on the back of the mirror, it may help in the off chance there is a mix-up somewhere along the line.

- The time it takes for the mirror to be returned to you depends on the company, its workload, and the size of the mirror, but two to three weeks appears normal.

The following companies provide mirror services, aluminizing, refiguring, or a combination of services. Many also offer mirror blanks, grinding and polishing materials, and other telescope-making supplies.

Mirror Services & Telescope-Making Supplies

★ **Augen Optics,** 947 Parkside Lane, Lancaster, PA 17601. Tel. (717) 295–4679. Will aluminize, test, and refigure or rework your mirror. Also sells mirror blanks, including Zerodur mirror blanks up to 16 inches; secondaries; and mirror grinding/polishing materials.

★ **Cascade Optical Coating, Inc.,** 1225 E. Hunter Ave., Santa Ana, CA 92705. Tel. (714) 543–9777. Fax (714) 543–4394. Primarily does high quality work for large observatories. Has done work for the observatories in Hawaii and Arizona, plus some work for Cal Tech and JPL.

★ **Denton Vacuum, Inc.,** Cherry Hill Industrial Center, 2 Pin Oak Ave., Cherry Hill, NJ 08003–4072. Tel. (609) 424–1012. Telex (910) 380–9894. Fax (609) 424–0395. Offers aluminum and silver coatings. Prices start at $30 for 3–inch aluminized mirror and $75 for protected silver, and rise to $300 for 24–inch

aluminized and $600 for silvered mirror. Mirrors above 12 inches are quoted FOB. Denton strips the old surface and cleans it before aluminizing. The company does not polish or improve the glass surface. Both silver and aluminum coatings are protected by hard dielectric overcoats. Suggested cleaning methods are by careful wiping with a clean cotton cloth and alcohol. Allow two to four weeks for delivery. Denton does not check mirrors, or determine the accuracy of your blank.

★ **Edmund Scientific Co.,** Dept. 11B1, N937, Edscorp Bldg., Barrington, NJ 08007. Tel. (609) 573–6250. Fax (609) 573–6295. Optical equipment, including mirrors and lenses. Also a wide variety of other scientific and technical materials. Free catalog.

★ **Galaxy Optics,** P.O. Box 2045, Buena Vista, CO 81211. Tel. (719) 395–8242. Optics for Newtonians. Catalogs available for $1.

★ **Lumicon,** 2111 Research Drive, Suite 5, Livermore, CA 94550. Tel. (415) 447–9570. Fax (415) 447–9589. Telescopes, filters and other telescope accessories, guides, and astrophotography accessories.

★ **Midwest Optical Systems,** 701 N. State St., Elgin, IL 60123. Tel. (708) 695–4150. Fax (708) 695–4191. Surplus mirrors and lenses, flats. Custom fabrication available.

★ **Newport Glass Works, Ltd.,** 2044–D Placentia Ave., Costa Mesa, CA 92627. Tel. (714) 642–9980. Fax (714) 642–4832. Mirror blanks, diagonals, and lenses made from pyrex; optical glasses. Free catalog.

★ **Ohara Corporation,** 50 Columbia Rd., Branchburg Township, Somerville, New Jersey 08876–3519. Tel. (908) 281–0100. Fax (908) 218–1685. Supplies telescope mirror blanks. Write for catalog.

★ **Optica b/c,** 4100 MacArthur Blvd., Oakland, CA 94619–1990. Supplies telescopes, plus amateur telescope-making supplies, including mirror blanks and tools, grinding/finishing/polishing compounds, aluminizing, refractor optics, kits, finished mirrors, various parts to build your own telescope. Also offers extensive selection of telescope-making books and brochures. Write for catalog.

★ **Optico Glass Fabrication Inc.,** 3164 El Camino Real, Atascadero, CA 93422. Tel. (805) 461–9402. Fax (805) 461–0420. Supplier of achromatic telescope objectives. Payment required in full before delivery. Delivery time is six to eight weeks.

★ **Palomar Optical Supply,** P.O. Box 1310, Wildomar, CA 92395. Tel. (714) 678–5393. Supplies mirror blanks, tools, abrasives, polishing agents, and elliptical flats, plus lenses for refractors, kits for

reflectors, and refractor optics. Discounts available for volume purchases. Also sells glass blanks and grinding/polishing compounds separately. Write for price quotes.

★ **P.A.P. Coating Services,** 1112 Chateau Ave., Anaheim, CA 92802. Tel. (714) 778–2525. Fax (714) 778–2470. Provides regular aluminizing and enhanced aluminizing for mirrors. For regular aluminizing, charges $3.25 per inch of diameter for sizes up to 12.5-inch; larger sizes up to 18 inches, $5.75 per inch for regular aluminizing. Enhanced aluminizing charges are $8.50 per inch of diameter up to 12½ inches; $14.25 per inch for sizes up to 18 inches. Charges $5 to remove old coatings; but diagonals coated free when supplied with matching primary. Refractor optics and windows coated with magnesium fluoride. The turnaround time is approximately 20 working days. The company marks mirrors for identification when it receives them.

★ **Parks,** 270 Easy St., Simi Valley, CA 93065. For information and orders, call (805) 522–6722. Toll-free, in California, 1–800–43–PARKS. Elsewhere, 1–800–44–PARKS. Telescope-making components, telescopes, mounts, drives, accessories. Catalog available. See listing under **Telescope Manufacturers,** above.

★ **Pegasus Optics,** 2301 W. Corrine Drive, Phoenix, AZ 85029. Tel. (602) 943–

3279. Mirrors and optical equipment. Brochure for $2.

★ **Telescopics,** P.O. Box 98, La Canada, CA 91011. Tel. (818) 341– 8178. Custom optics, tube assemblies, elliptical optical flats, aluminizing services. Catalog for $2.

★ **Roger W. Tuthill Inc.,** Box 1086, Mountainside, NJ, 07092–0086. Tel. (201) 232–1786; 1–800–223–1063. Fax (201) 232–3804. Offers a variety of telescopes, astro-video equipment, and accessories, such as filters, drives, tripods, finderscopes. Also markets books and videos for observers.

★ **Universal Photonics,** 495 West John St., Hicksville, NY 11801. Supplies polishing pitches, grinding abrasives, etc., for telescope makers.

★ **University Optics, Inc.,** P.O. Box 1205, Ann Arbor, MI 48106. Toll-free orders, 1–800–521–2828. Fax (313) 663–1156. Offers a variety of books, accessories, and eyepieces for the telescope.

★ **Willmann-Bell Inc.,** P.O. Box 35025, Richmond, VA 23235. Sells mirrors, tools, polishing compounds, and grinding abrasives for telescope makers.

Telescope-Making Books

★ **Advanced Telescope Making Techniques,** edited by Allan Mackintosh. Available from Willmann-Bell, P.O. Box 35025, Richmond, VA 23235. $19.95 per volume. Volume 1 deals with optics; Volume 2 with the mechanical aspects of building a telescope. The books contain a compilation of 143 articles from the publication **Circulars** for the now-defunct Maksutov Club.

★ **All About Telescopes,** by Sam Brown. Available from Edmund Scientific, Dept. 11B1, N937, Edscorp Bldg., Barrington, NJ 08007. Tel. (609) 573–6250. Fax (609) 573–6295. An easy-to-follow source for the newcomer to telescope building. The material is somewhat dated (no mention of Dobson mounts, for example), but the information still is useful, especially in mirror grinding and polishing. Includes simple formulas for calculating focal length, etc.

★ **Amateur Telescope Making,** books 1, 2 & 3. Available from Willmann-Bell, P.O. Box 35025, Richmond, VA 23235. $13.95 each.

★ **Build Your Own Telescope,** by Richard Berry. Available from Macmillan Publishing Co., 866 3rd Ave., New York, NY 10022, as well as many bookstores. An excellent guide for the amateur with plenty of desire but not a lot of money. Berry demonstrates several innovative ways to build a telescope using ordinary hand tools, scrap materials, and a little hard work. Does not go into great detail about mirror grinding, polishing, and figuring, but still an excellent work.

★ **Construction of a Maksutov Telescope,** by Warren I. Fillmore. Available from Sky Publishing Corporation, 49 Bay State Rd., Cambridge, MA 02138. Tel. (617) 864–7360. A large-format booklet that describes how the author ordered, ground, tested, and assembled the optical and mechanical parts for an award-winning 6–inch Gregory-Maksutov f/15.

★ **How to Make a Telescope,** 2nd edition, by Jean Texereau. Available from Willmann-Bell, P.O. Box 35025, Richmond, VA 23235. A classic, with tips for the telescope builder who wants a complete, and even complex, telescope. Goes beyond the simple designs and explains optics from theory to practice.

★ **Making Your Own Telescope,** revised edition, by Allyn J. Thompson. Available from Sky Publishing Corporation, 49 Bay State Rd., Cambridge, MA 02138. Tel. (617) 864–7360. This has been a favorite among amateurs for more than four decades. The author details the construction of a six-inch reflector, procedures which also apply to larger mirrors.

★ **Telescope Optics: Evaluation and Design,** by Harie Rutten & Martin van Venrooij. Available from Willmann-Bell, P.O. Box 35025, Richmond, VA 23235. $24.95. Detailed information on designing a telescope.

MOUNTS AND DRIVES

No matter what your choice of optics, the right mount is essential. Otherwise, years of potential viewing pleasure can be cut short by nights of frustrating, hair-pulling anger as images bounce about like dancing fleas. Shaky mounts, such as those sold with most department store telescopes, bounce at a touch, and continue shaking for what seems like an eternity. A sturdy mount, on the other hand, reduces vibration in the telescope, even when a drive is used. The sidebar on the next page describes the types of mounts commercially available. You can also make a homemade mount out of scrap materials if you have the skills and equipment to work with metal. Or you can make a basic Dobson mount out of plywood, a few nails, bolts, and Teflon for the "gears," plus a little paint to dress it up. These mounts, named after their original designer, John Dobson, are simple to construct and work smoothly when used purely for observation. They cannot, however, follow the motion of the stars or planets and must be pushed along by the observer. There are variations of the Dobson mount which include motor drives and can be adjusted to follow the motions of the stars.

Common Mounts and Drives

Alt-Azimuth—A simple type of mount with two motions: Altitude, or up and down; Azimuth, or side-to-side or horizontal motions. Primarily used as an observing mount. Is impractical for astrophotography.

Clock Drive—A system of gears and motors used with an equatorial mount to compensate for the Earth's rotation during observing sessions when it is important to keep celestial objects centered in the field of view. Essential for good astrophotography.

Equatorial—A mount that rotates on one axis (polar/right ascension) adjusted to your latitude, and so that axis is parallel to the Earth's axis. If that axis is turned at the same speed as the Earth, but in the opposite direction, objects appear to remain stationary in the telescope view.

Forked Mount—As its name suggests, this mount has the telescope mounted between the tines of a fork. It is used with shorter optical tubes. The mount is stable, works well for catadioptrics telescopes, and is an excellent astrophotography mount.

German Mount—This equatorial mount features a large counterweight to balance the weight of the optical tube. A popular mount, especially for refractors and reflectors with long tubes.

A Newtonian with an equatorial mount (Swift model 853)
(Courtesy of Swift Instruments)

Setting Circles—Circles on a mount which show right ascension on one circle and declination on the other and allow you to locate celestial objects easily from their coordinates.

Wedge—A wedge is used with a fork mount so you can tilt your telescope toward the celestial pole at an angle equal to your latitude. This allows a clock drive to function properly, and gives you an accurate reading on setting circles. The wedge goes between the bottom of the fork mount and the tripod.

The majority of companies that sell telescopes also sell mounts or tripods to go with their instruments. The following companies, however, can supply you with mounts and drives ranging from simple alt-azimuth mounts, to substantial ones requiring a permanent observing site and electrical power lines.

★ **Edward R. Byers Company,** 29001 West Highway 58, Barstow, CA 92311. Tel. (619) 256–2377. Precision telescope driving systems.

★ **DFM Engineering Inc.,** 1035 Delaware Ave., Longmont, CO 80501. Tel. (303) 678–8143. Telescope instrumentation and research- grade telescopes.

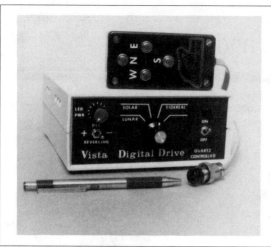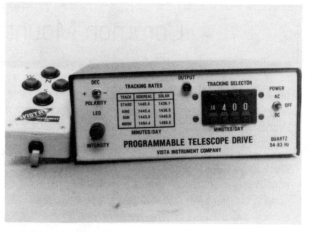

Two drives available from Vista Instrument Company: the Digital Drive, left, and the Programmable drive, right.
(Courtesy of Vista Instrument Co.)

★ **Losmandy, (Hollywood General Machining),** 1033 N. Sycamore Ave., Los Angeles, CA 90038. Tel. (213) 462–2855. Builds precision equatorial mounts and secondary systems for use in astrophotography, drive systems, and Schmidt and Wright camera systems. Can order by telephone or mail. Accepts Visa/Master Card. Available direct, or through dealers. Will work with sketches to design mounts to fit your system.

★ **Lumicon,** 2111 Research Dr., Suites 4–5, Livermore, CA 94550. Tel. (415) 447–9570. Fax (415) 447–9589. Telescope accessories, including mounts.

★ **Optic-Craft Machining,** 33918 Macomb, Farmington, MI 48024. Tel. (313) 476–5893. Builds precision clock drives and equatorial mountings. Designed for professionals or serious amateurs.

★ **Parks Optical,** 270 Easy St., Simi Valley, CA 93065. Tel. (805) 522–6722. Sells a variety of mounts and other astronomy items. See **Telescope Manufacturers,** above.

★ **Frederick Stager,** P.O. Box 61, Birchrunville, PA 19421. Tel. (215) 827–7026. Plans for a worm wheel clock drive you can build yourself. Also sells completed worm wheel clock drives.

★ **Tech2000,** 82 State St., Norwalk, OH 44857. Tel. (419) 663–6041. Fax (419) 668–4039. Manufactures dual axis clock drive systems for telescope mounts.

★ **Telerad,** 7092 Betty Dr., Huntingon Beach, CA 92647. Tel. (714) 847–8903. An aiming device used to point a telescope.

★ **Tele Vue Optics, Inc.,** 20 Dexter Plaza, Pearl River, NY 10965. Tel. (914) 735–

4044. Dealer in telescopes, mounts, eyepieces. Catalog for $3.

★ **Vista Instrument Company,** P.O. Box 1919, Santa Maria, CA 93456. Tel. (805) 925–1240. Sells camera tracking devices for astrophotography. Also sells binocular guides, batteries and power converters for the tracking devices, tripods designed for use as astrophotography mounts, and programmable drive correctors.

★ **Vogel Enterprises, Inc.,** 38W150 Hickory Court, Batavia, IL 60510. Tel. (708) 879–TRAK or 1–800–457–TRAK. Sells drive correctors. Call or write for free information.

Computer Controls

★ **Astro-Computer Control,** RD 1, Alexandria, PA 16611. (814) 669–4483. This system works with your personal computer to control your telescope. It provides position read-out, coordinate conversion, motor control, and the ability to slew to the position of a given time. You also can add on other systems, such as maps and charts, and put the telescope on "automatic" to move from star to star on a preprogrammed viewing schedule.

★ **Opto-Data,** 600 Mariners Island Blvd., Suite #36, San Mateo, CA 94404. Tel. (415) 377–0211. A portable computer

sky atlas that shows more than 40,000 stars and 10,000 deep-sky objects. Cost: $895. Write for more information.

★ **Software Bisque,** 912 12th St., Suite A, Golden, CO 80401. Tel. (303) 278–4478. Sells software designed to guide telescopes, with a few hardware additions. Also see listing in **Software** section of Chapter 1.

Domes

★ **Ace Dome,** 3186 Juanita, Las Vegas, NV, 89102. Tel. (702) 873– 5790. Portable domes. Free brochure.

★ **Ash Manufacturing Company,** Box 312, Plainfield, IL 60544. Tel. (815) 436–9403. Fax (815) 436–1032. Sells domes to professionals and amateurs. Dome sizes advertised range from 8 to 36.5 feet. All domes are sold from the factory. Technical help is available for buyers. Truck delivery possible for most sites in the U.S. and Canada. Interested customers receive a formal proposal covering the requirements. A 50 percent deposit is required before construction begins, with the balance due prior to delivery. Most smaller models are available within 90 days, with larger units taking from 120 to 150 days. Free brochures.

★ **Learning Technologies Inc.,** 59 Walden St., Cambridge, MA 02140. Tel. (617)

647–5364. Toll-free at 1–800–537–8703. Fax (617) 547–2686. A portable planetarium system that includes a projector and accessories.

★ **Observa-Dome Laboratories, Inc.,** 371 Commerce Park Dr., Jackson, MS,

39213. Tel. (601) 982–3333. Toll-free at 1–800–647–5364. Fax (601) 982–3335. Specializes in domes for amateurs and for professional activities such as tracking, research, communications, and defense systems. Free information.

RETAILERS AND WHOLESALERS OF EQUIPMENT

Buying astronomy equipment mostly means mail-order for all but a few of us who live near a dealer or manufacturer. Fortunately, the majority of companies that sell telescopes, filters, mounts, drives, and other astronomical equipment have developed and maintained good reputations for service and quality products. Nearly all offer some kind of catalog, usually for little or no cost, which makes it easy to comparison shop.

In deciding among similar products offered by different companies, there are several factors to keep in mind. First, when comparing prices, make sure you understand what accessories are included in the base price. Sometimes one company may offer a more attractive package of equipment than another. Second, consider delivery time. Deliveries sometimes can be slow; a buyer in Mississippi reportedly waited two years for a telescope ordered through one of the big dealers. Usually, when you order a larger telescope, a wait of six months or more is common, and—truthfully, probably to be expected—since we all want precision optics and drives rather than a hurried job. Finally, consider shipping costs; many companies expect the buyer to pay the transportation fees, but charges can vary widely.

The following companies offer an alternative to buying directly from the manufacturer. Most sell several makes of telescopes, filters, mounts, and other accessories. If you are interested in acquiring used equipment, you might also consider a subscription to **The Starry Messenger.** (See the **Periodicals** section in Chapter 1.)

★ **Ad-Libs Astronomics,** 2401 Tee Circle, Suite 106, Norman, OK 73069. Tel. (405) 364–0858. Toll-free, 1–800–422–7876. Telescopes and accessories, binoculars, photo equipment, mounts, lenses, filters, eyepieces, star maps, books.

★ **Adorama Camera,** 42 West 18th St., New York, NY 10011. Tel. 1–800–223–2500. Free information. Telescopes and accessories, binoculars, telescope-making supplies, cameras and photographic equipment, astronomy audio-visual aids, mounts, lenses, filters, eyepieces, charts, and star maps, books.

★ **Advance Camera Corporation,** 15 West 46th St., New York, NY 10036. Tel. (212) 944–1410. Free information. Telescopes, telescope-making equipment, astronomy audio-visual aids, cameras and photographic equipment, lenses, filters, eyepieces, charts, and star maps.

★ **Analytical Scientific,** 11049 Bandera Rd., Helotes, TX 78023–0198.

★ **Aries Optics,** Rt. 1, Box 1436, Palouse, WA 99161. Tel. (509) 878–1713. Dealer in Questar, Brandon, Tele Vue, and Celestron.

★ **Astro-Physics,** 7470 Forest Hills Rd., Loves Park, IL 61111. Tel. (815) 282–1513. Telescopes and accessories.

★ **Astro-Tech,** 101 West Main, P.O. Box 2001, Ardmore, OK 73402. Tel. (405) 226–3068. Free catalog. Telescopes and

accessories, binoculars, filters, telescope mounts, star maps, and atlases.

★ **Astro Track Engineering,** 3900 "B" East Mira Loma Ave., Anaheim, CA 92807. Tel. (714) 630–7381.

★ **Astro Works Corp.,** P.O. Box 86, Highway 244, Cloudcroft, NM 88317. Tel. (505) 682–2218. Telescopes and accessories.

★ **Astro World,** 5126 Belair Rd., Baltimore, MD 21206. Tel. (301) 483–5100. Free price list with long SASE. Telescopes and accessories, telescope-making supplies, audio-visual aids, photographic equipment, charts and star maps, and books. Also used equipment.

★ **Berger Brothers Camera Exchange,** 209 Broadway, Rt. 110, Amityville, NY 11701. Tel. (516) 264–4160. Free information. All major brands of telescopes and accessories, telescope-making supplies, photographic equipment, eyepieces, charts, and star maps.

★ **Black Forest Observatory,** 12815 Porcupine Lane, Colorado Springs, CO 80908. Tel. (719) 495–3828. Free information with long SASE. Telescopes, binoculars, books, cameras, film processing, computer software, mirrors and lenses, star maps, and atlases.

★ **Bushnell, Division of Bausch & Lomb,** 300 North Lone Hill Ave., San Dimas, CA 91773. Free literature about binoculars.

★ **Edward R. Byers Company,** 29001 West Highway 58, Barstow, CA 92311. Tel. (619) 256–2377. Precision telescope-driving systems.

★ **California Telescope Company,** P.O. Box 1338, Burbank CA 91507. Tel. 1–800–843–4780; (818) 505–8424 (in CA). Free information. Telescopes and accessories, telescope-making supplies, audio-visual aids, photographic equipment, computer software, lenses, filters, eyepieces, charts, and star maps.

★ **Camera Shop,** 60 East Broadway, Muskegon, MI 49444. Tel. (616) 733–1286. Free information with long SASE. Telescopes, binoculars, books, cameras, film processing, computers and software, eyepieces and filters, mirrors, and lenses.

★ **Camera Wholesalers,** 2770 Summer St., Stamford, CT 06905. Free information with long SASE. Tel. (203) 328–9560. Telescopes, binoculars, cameras, eyepieces, film processing, and filters.

★ **Celestial Systems,** 2428 Jefferson St., Napa, CA 94558. Tel. (707) 224–3195.

★ **Century Telescope Co.,** 12555 Harbor Blvd., Garden Grove, CA 92640. Free information. Tel. (714) 530–3861. Telescopes and accessories, binoculars, telescope-making supplies, mounts, photographic equipment and accessories, eyepieces, charts, star maps, and books.

★ **Cheshire Instrument Co.,** Box 65, Mableton, GA 30059.

★ **City Camera,** 15336 W. Warren, Dearborn, MI 48126. Tel. (313) 846–3922.

★ **Colonial Photo,** 634 N. Mills Ave., Orlando, FL 32803. Tel. (407) 841–1485.

★ **Company Seven,** 14300–117 Cherry Lane Ct., Laurel, MD 20707. Tel. (301) 953–2000.

★ **Cosmic Connections, Inc.,** 1460 North Farnsworth Ave., Aurora, IL 60505. Tel. 1–800–634–7702; (708) 851–5353 (in IL). Catalog, $2. Telescopes and accessories, binoculars, telescope-making supplies, photographic equipment and accessories, eyepieces, charts and star maps, domes, books.

★ **Danville Camera & Sound,** 201 North Hartz Ave., Danville, CA 94526. Tel. (415) 837–0222. Free information. Telescopes, telescope-making equipment, mirrors and lenses, filters, electronic optical equipment, books, binoculars, cameras, film and photo processing.

★ **Dexter's Camera,** 484 E. Main St., Ventura, CA 93001. Tel. (805) 643–2172.

★ **Eagle Optics,** 6109 Odana Rd., Madison, WI 53719. Tel. (608) 271–4751. Free price list. Telescopes and accessories, binoculars, photographic equipment.

★ **Eastern Tele-Optics,** 446 Kent Rd., Springfield, PA 19064. Tel. (215) 543–3998.

★ **Edelman's,** 465 Rt. 46, Wayne, NJ 07470. Tel. (609) 663–3196. Free information. Telescopes and accessories, binoculars, filters, eyepieces, charts and star maps, domes, books.

★ **Edmund Scientific Company,** 7782 Edscorp Building, Barrington, NJ 08007. Free catalog. Tel. (609) 573–6260. Optical equipment, including telescopes, telescope-making supplies, astronomy audio-visual aids, photographic equipment, eyepieces, charts and star maps, domes, books.

★ **Effonscience, Inc.,** 3350 Dufferin St., Toronto, Ontario, Canada. M6A 3A4. Tel. (416) 787–4581. Free information with long SASE. Telescopes, telescope-making supplies and equipment, mounts, binoculars, audio-visual aids, books, cameras, computers and software, mirrors and lenses, planetariums.

★ **Faraday & Wheatstone,** 194 Main St., Marlborough, MA 01752. Tel. (508) 485–1144. Free information with long SASE. Telescopes, binoculars, telescope-making equipment and supplies, books, computers and software, mirrors and lenses, star maps and atlases, film processing.

★ **Focus Camera,** 4419 13th Ave., Brooklyn, NY 11219. 1–800–221–0828; (718) 436–6262 (in NY). Catalog, $3. Telescopes and accessories, astronomy audio-visual aids, cameras, and darkroom equipment and supplies.

★ **Focus Scientific Ltd.,** 596 Rideau St., Ottawa, Ontario, Canada. K1N 6A2. Tel. (613) 236–7767. Free information with long SASE. Telescopes, binoculars, books, cameras, computers and software, mirrors and lenses, planetariums, science equipment, and supplies.

★ **Galleria Optics,** 59 The Circle, East Hampton, NY 11937. Tel. (516) 822–4691. Free information with long SASE. Refractor telescopes and accessories, mounts, binoculars, more.

★ **Green Mountain Tropical Fish,** Ripley Rd., Rutland, VT 05701. Tel. (802) 775–2320.

★ **Guild Camera Shop Inc.,** 737 West Camelback Rd., Phoenix, AZ 85013–2294. Tel. (602) 264–5808.

★ **Edwin Hirsch,** 168 Lakeview Dr., Tomkins Cove, NY 10986. Tel. (914) 786–3738. Free information. Meade and Celestron telescopes and accessories.

★ **Hooper Camera & Video Centers,** 5059 Lankershim Blvd., North Hollywood, CA 91601. Tel. (818) 762–2846. Free information with long SASE. Telescopes, mirrors and lenses, mounts, star maps and atlases, books, binoculars, cameras.

★ **Hopkins Phoenix Observatory,** 7812 West Clayton Drive, Phoenix, AZ 85033. Tel. (602) 849–5889. Free information. Photoelectric photometry equipment.

★ **Image Point,** 831 North Swan, Tucson, AZ, 85711. Tel. (602) 327–6643. Catalog $2. Telescopes and accessories.

★ **John's Photo & Video,** 615–4th Ave. North, Birmingham, AL 35203. Tel. (205) 251–1600.

★ **Kenmore Camera,** P.O. Box 82467, Kenmore, WA 98028. Tel. (206) 485–7447. Free information with long SASE. Telescopes, binoculars, cameras and photo equipment, mirrors, and lenses.

★ **Khan Scope Center,** 3243 Dufferin St., Toronto, Ontario, Canada, M6A 2T2. Tel. (416) 783–4140. Catalog $3. Telescopes, telescope-making supplies and equipment, binoculars, cameras, computers and software, mirrors, and lenses.

★ **Krauth Precision Instruments,** 530 Main St., South Weymouth, MA 02190. Tel. (617) 331–3795. Free catalog. Astronomy equipment and accessories, binoculars, books, mirrors, lenses, star maps, and atlases.

★ **La Maison De L'Astronomie,** 8056 ST-Hubert, Montreal, Quebec, Canada, H2R 2P3. (514) 279–0063.

★ **Land, Sea & Sky,** 3110 South Shepherd, Houston, TX 77098.

★ **Los Angeles Optical,** 12129 Magnolia Blvd., P.O. Box 4868, North Hollywood, CA 91607–0868. Tel. (818) 762–2206. Free information. Meade, Celestron, Bausch & Lomb, Bushnell, Edmund, Tele Vue, Lumicon, Zeiss, Leitz, etc. Also books, maps and charts, and filters.

★ **Lumicon,** 2111 Research Dr., Livermore, CA 94550. Catalog $3. Tel. (415) 447–9570. Telescopes, binoculars, mirrors and lenses, filters, photo equipment, astrophotography aids.

★ **Mardiron Optics,** 4 Spartan Circle, Stoneham, MA 02180. Tel. (617) 938–8155. Brochure for two first-class stamps. Telescopes and other astronomy equipment.

★ **Martin's Star Tracker,** 633 South Broadway, Boulder, CO 80303. Tel. (303) 449–3350. Free information. Telescopes, telescope-making supplies, accessories. Also antique instruments, photo equipment, charts, star maps, meteorites, lenses, filters, science supplies.

★ **F.C. Meischsner,** 182 Lincoln St., Boston, MA 02111. Tel. (617) 426–7092. Free information. Telescopes, antique instruments, photographic equipment, filters, eyepieces, star maps, books. Also has a repair service.

★ **National Camera Exchange,** 9300 Olson Highway, Golden Valley, MN 55427. Tel. 1–800–624–8107 or (612) 546–6831. Free information. Telescopes and accessories, binoculars, astronomy audio-visual aids, cameras, lenses, filters, eyepieces, charts and star maps, books.

★ **New England Astro Optics,** 2 Gordon St., Simsbury, CT 06070. Tel. (203) 658–0701. Catalog $2. Telescopes, binoculars, photo equipment, and books.

★ **New Jersey Telescope Headquarters,** 770 Route 17 North, Paramus, NJ 07652. Tel. 1–800–631–7111 or (201) 444–7367. Free information. Optics and optical equipment at discount prices; general astronomy equipment.

★ **Northern Sky Telescopes, Inc.,** 5667 Duluth St., Golden Valley, MN 55422. Tel. 1–800–345–4202 or (612) 545–6786. Fax (612) 545–9297. Free information. Telescopes and accessories, telescope-making supplies, binoculars, photographic equipment and accessories, mounts, charts, lenses, filters, books.

★ **Kenneth F. Novak & Company,** Box 69, Ladysmith, WI 54848. Tel. (715) 532–5102. Free catalog. Telescopes and accessories, research-quality accessories, books, and more.

★ **Oceanside Photo,** 1024 Mission Ave., Oceanside, CA 92054. Tel. (619) 722–3348.

★ **Odd Assortment,** 4980 Pacheco Blvd. Pacheco, CA 94553. Tel. (415) 447–9570. Telescopes, including Coulter Optics.

★ **Optica b/c Company,** 4100 MacArthur Blvd., Oakland, CA 94619. Tel. (415) 530–1234. Catalog $5. Telescopes and telescope-making supplies and equipment, binoculars, film processing, computers and software, mirrors, and lenses.

★ **Optical Guidance Systems,** 2450 Huntingdon Pike, Huntingdon Valley, PA 19006. (215) 947–5571.

★ **Orion Telescopes,** 2450 17th Ave., Box 1158–S, Santa Cruz, CA 95061. Tel. (408) 464–0446. Toll-free, 1–800–447–1001; 1–800–443–1001 (in CA). Free catalog. Telescopes, accessories, photo equipment, binoculars, eyepieces.

★ **Pauli's Discount Optics,** 29 Kingswood Rd., Danbury, CT 06811. Tel. (203) 746–3579. Catalog $3. Telescopes and accessories, telescope-making supplies, cameras and photo equipment, computer software, general science products.

★ **Perceptor,** Brownsville Junction Plaza, Box 38, #103, Schomberg, Ontario, Canada, LOG 1TO. Tel. (416) 939–2313. Free information with long SASE. Telescopes, telescope-making supplies and equipment, binoculars, books, cameras, eyepieces, mirrors and lenses, filters.

★ **Quasar Optics, Inc.,** 7220 Fairmount Dr. S.E., Calgary, Alberta, Canada, T2H OX7. Tel. (403) 255–7633. Catalog $4. Telescopes and accessories, telescope-making supplies, photographic equipment, lenses, filters, binoculars, books, repair service.

★ **Questar Corporation,** Route 202, New Hope, PA 18938. Tel. (215) 862–5277. Telescopes and accessories. See listing under Telescope Manufacturers, above.

★ **Redlich Optical,** 711 West Broad St., Falls Church, VA 22046. Tel. (703) 527–5151. Free information with long SASE. Telescopes, telescope-making equipment and supplies, binoculars, cameras, computers and software, eyepieces, filters, mirrors, lenses, star maps, and atlases.

★ **Roseville Hardware,** 203 Harding Rd., Roseville, CA 95678. Tel. (916) 782–8402. Filters, accessories.

★ **Rowlab Science Center, Inc.,** 1650 Art Museum Drive, Jacksonville, FL 32207. Tel. (904) 399–8036. Free information with long SASE. Telescopes, telescope-making supplies and equipment, binoculars, mounts, electro-optical equipment, mirrors and lenses, computers, and software.

★ **Ruby Optics,** P.O. Box 2136, Kingston, Ontario, Canada, K7L 5J9. Tel. (613) 544–5857. Catalog $1. Astronomy equipment and accessories.

★ **S & S Optika Ltd.,** 5174 S. Broadway Englewood, CO 80110. Tel. (303) 789–1089. Filters and accessories.

★ **St. Michael's Video & Photo Center,** 413 Talbot St., Box 887, St. Michaels, MD 21663. Tel. (301) 745–2595. Free information. Telescopes and accessories, binoculars, cameras, star maps, and atlases.

★ **Science Education Center,** 125 South Hillside, Wichita, KS 67211. Tel. (316) 682–1921. Free information with long SASE. Telescopes, binoculars, star maps and atlases, eyepieces, filters, and more.

★ **Scientific Wizardry,** 9925 Fairview Ave., Boise, ID 83704. Tel. (208) 377–8575. Free information with long SASE. Telescopes and accessories, mirrors and lenses, binoculars, books.

★ **Scope City,** 679 Easy St., Simi Valley, CA 93065. Tel. (805) 522–6646. Order line, 1–800–235–3344. Free information. Telescopes, telescope-making supplies, cameras, mounts, lenses, filters, eyepieces, binoculars, more. Also has offices in Sherman Oaks, CA; Torrance, CA; Costa Mesa, CA; Riverside, CA; San Diego, CA; Las Vegas, NV.

★ **Scope Source,** 222 West Main, Ardmore, OK 73402. Tel. (405)226– 3068.

★ **Sharpshooters,** 1034 W. Hillsborough Ave., Tampa, FL 33603. Tel. (813) 237–2289.

★ **Shutan Camera & Video,** 312 West Randolph, Chicago, IL 60606. Tel. 1–800–621–2248; (312) 332–2000 (in IL). Free catalog. Telescopes, telescope-making supplies, cameras, charts and star maps, books, binoculars.

★ **Sky Designs,** 4100 Felps St., Colleyville, TX 76034. Tel. (817) 581–9878. Free information. Portable telescopes.

★ **Sky Opticals,** 12428 Gladstone St., Sylmar, CA 91342. Tel. (818) 361–6576. Catalog $1. Precision primary mirrors, elliptical mirrors, professional oculars, precision flats, aluminum and enhanced coatings.

★ **Sky Scientific,** P.O. Box 184, Sky Forest, CA 92385. Tel. (714) 337–3440. Catalog $1. Telescopes and accessories.

★ **Spectra Astro Systems,** 6631 Wilburn Ave., #30, Reseda, CA 91331. Tel. (818) 343–1352. Fax (818) 996–7698. Free catalog.

★ **Spectra Research Group,** 762 Madison Ave., New York, NY, 10021. Tel. (212) 744–2255.

★ **Star-Liner Company,** 1106 South Columbus, Tucson, AZ 85711. Tel. (602) 795–3361. Catalog $5. All sizes of telescopes.

★ **Stellar Vision,** 1835 S. Alvernon, #208, Tucson, AZ 85711. Tel. (602) 571–0877.

★ **Steve's Pro Shop,** 5606–B S.E. 15th St., Midwest City, OK 73110. Tel. (405) 732–1350. Telescopes and accessories.

★ **Tele Vue Optics,** 20 Dexter Plaza, Pearl River, NY 10965. Tel. (914) 735–4044. Free information. Telescopes and accessories.

★ **Telescopics,** P.O. Box 98, La Canada, CA 91011. Tel. (818) 341– 8178. Catalog $2. Custom optics, tube assemblies, elliptical optical flats, aluminizing services.

★ **Texas Nautical Repair Company,** 2129 Westheimer, Houston, TX 77098. Tel. (713) 529–3551. Free catalog. Telescopes, eyepieces, filters, mirrors and lenses, star maps, atlases.

★ **Thousand Oaks Optical,** P.O. Box 248098, Farmington, MI 48024. Tel. (313) 353–6825. Free brochure. Solar filters and astronomical equipment and accessories.

★ **Roger W. Tuthill Inc.,** P.O. Box 1086, Mountainside, NJ 07092. Tel. 1–800–223–1063; (908) 232–1786 (in NJ). Fax (908) 232–3804. Free catalog. Telescopes and accessories, astronomy audio-visual aids, telescope-making supplies, photographic equipment, binoculars, lenses, filters, eyepieces, books, and more.

★ **Tymer Inc.,** 1601 Broadway, Vancouver, WA 98663. Filters and accessories.

★ **University Optics,** P.O. Box 1205, Ann Arbor, MI 48106. Tel. 1–800–521–

2828; (313) 665–3575 (in MI). Free catalog. Telescopes and accessories, filters, eyepieces, more.

★ **VERNONscope & Co.,** 5 Ithaca Road, Candor, NY 13743. Tel. (607) 659–7000. Fax (607) 659–4000. Sells a variety of telescopes and accessories, including Brandon, Jena, used equipment, mounts, tripods, filters, objectives, and eyepieces.

★ **Ward's Natural Science,** P.O. Box 92912, Rochester, NY 14692. Tel. (716) 359–2502. Free information. Telescopes and telescope-making equipment, binoculars, computers and software, filters, meteorites.

★ **Robert Waxman Inc.,** 1514 Curtis St., Denver, CO 80202. Tel. (303) 623–1200. Free information. Telescopes, binoculars, electro-optical equipment, computers, and software.

★ **Bill Weaver Sporting Goods,** 3515 West Vickery, Fort Worth, TX 76107. Tel.

(817) 731–0804. Free information with long SASE. Telescopes, filters, audiovisual equipment, computers, and software.

★ **Wholesale Optics of Pennsylvania,** RR 6, Box 6329, Moscow, PA 18444. Tel. (717) 842–1500. Free information. Astronomy equipment and accessories, binoculars, telescope-making supplies, charts and star maps, books, and more.

★ **Willmann-Bell Inc.,** P.O. Box 23235, Richmond, VA 23235. Tel. (804) 320–7016. Catalog $1. Telescopes, accessories, books, telescope-making supplies, and more.

★ **Wilson's Camera Sales,** 3144 East Camelback Rd., Phoenix, AZ 85016. Tel. (602) 955–6773. Free information with long SASE. Telescopes, telescope-making equipment and supplies, mirrors and lenses, filters, mounts, star maps and atlases, books, cameras, film, and photo processing services.

OLD ASTRONOMY EQUIPMENT

★ **The Gemmary Inc.,** P.O. Box 816, Redondo Beach, CA 90277. Tel. (213) 372–5969. Sells 18th- and 19th-century mathematical and optical instruments, including telescopes, globes, orreries, and

navigation instruments. Also buys and sells old science and mineralogy books. Science books catalogs are updated twice a year and cost $2; scientific instruments catalogs are published once a year and cost $5.

★ **Historical Technology Inc.,** 6 Mugford Street, Marblehead, MA 01945. Established in 1970, the company deals in antique scientific instruments, including astronomy items.

★ **Paul MacAlister & Associates,** 280 Arden Shore Rd., Lake Bluff, IL 60044. Sells kits for building replicas of old scientific instruments, including a mariner's astrolabe, time instruments, graphometer, and planispheric astrolabe.

★ **Martin's Star Tracker,** 633 South Broadway, Boulder, CO 80303. Tel. (303) 449–3350. Antique instruments, as well as telescopes, telescope-making supplies, accessories, and photo equipment.

★ **F.C. Meischsner,** 182 Lincoln St., Boston, MA 02111. Tel. (617) 426–7092. Antique instruments, telescopes, photographic equipment, accessories, books.

★ **Tesseract,** Box 151, Hastings-on-Hudson, NY 10706. Tel. (914) 478–2594. Fax (914) 478–5473. Publishes a catalog listing early scientific and medical instruments for sale. The cost is $5 per single issue, or $18 for a full year of four issues. Also publishes **Rittenhouse,** a quarterly publication that carries articles about old scientific instruments. Subscription is $25 annually.

4

FINDING
YOUR WAY
IN THE SKY

ATLASES, CATALOGUES
AND OBSERVING GUIDES

The millions upon millions of stars in the sky may seem a daunting target. Some objects are difficult to find with even the best of directions and huge telescopes, while others are only visible in long-exposure photographs. But with patience, knowledge, and a good guide, you can travel through the Universe and glimpse stars in the making, galaxies on the move, and globular clusters sparkling light years away.

Atlases and maps provide you with a "road map" to the sky to help you find specific objects, or to pinpoint a comet or nova that may appear. An atlas or map generally tries to represent, on paper, the night sky. In contrast, a catalogue usually provides data about the objects without attempting to show where they are in the sky. Catalogues list such data as the spectral type of a star, its variable period, the make-up of a nebula or cluster, the number of estimated stars in a cluster, the galaxy type, and an object's right ascension and declination. An observing guide combines elements of both the atlas and catalogue, with short descriptions of objects, plus small maps showing their location. Unlike the typical atlas, map, or catalogue, an observing guide also offers observing tips. For example, an observing guide may tell you the size of telescope needed to observe a particular galaxy or other object. Used together, a good atlas or map, catalogue, and observing guide can provide you many years of observing pleasure.

For addresses of the companies that offer the maps and atlases listed here, see the **Books** section in Chapter 1.

ATLASES

★ **AAVSO Star Atlas,** by Charles E. Scovill. Available from the AAVSO and Willmann-Bell. $49.95.

★ **Astro Cards,** P.O. Box 35, Natrona Heights, PA 15065. Tel. (412) 295–4128. $7.50 per set. These handy, index-sized cards come in five sets: the Messier Objects, Double Stars, NGC Ob-

jects (two parts), and NGC objects for larger scopes. Easy to use at the telescope. (See **Observer's Guide** in the **Periodicals** section of Chapter 1 for information about AstroCards publishing).

★ **Atlas of Deep Sky Splendors,** by Hans Vehrenberg. Available from Sky Publishing and Willmann-Bell. $39.95. A

The Andromeda Galaxy (M31, NGC 224), the most easily visible and nearest spiral galaxy. (National Optical Astronomy Observatories)

photographic atlas that contains 175 photographs of deep-sky objects such as galaxies, star clusters, and nebulae, and including all the Messier objects. Also contains data on the objects pictured. For advanced observers and professionals.

★ **Atlas of Galactic Nebulae,** by Thorsten Neckel and Hans Vehrenberg. Available from Sky Publishing. Part 1, $68; Part 2, $82. This three-volume set consists of black-and-white reproductions from the Palomar Observatory Sky Survey, plus other sources. A booklet comes with the book and gives explanations and data tables of the nebulae.

★ **Atlas Stellarum,** by Hans Vehrenberg. Available from Sky Publishing. **Stellarum North,** $145; **Stellarum South,** $80. A photographic atlas of the sky to at least photographic magnitude +14. Comes in two versions, **Atlas Stellarum North,** which covers declinations +90 degrees to −25 degrees in 315 charts; and **Atlas Stellarum South,** which has 171 charts from −15 degrees to −90 degrees. The packages include a booklet, grids, and conversion tables. Shipped from Germany, for the advanced user or professional.

★ **Bright Star Atlas 2000.0,** by Wil Tirion. Available from Willmann-Bell. $9.95. Contains 10 maps, each 9 inches by 12 inches high. Features more than 9,100 stars and includes more than 600 deep-sky objects and all the Messier Objects.

★ **Burnham's Celestial Handbook—An Observer's Guide to the Universe Beyond the Solar System,** by Robert Burnham, Jr. Dover Publications, 31 E. Second St., Mineola, NY 11501. Three volume set, $34.85; Vol 1: $11.95; Vol. 2 & 3, $12.95 each. Available in three volumes grouped by constellations, the guide lists double and multiple stars; variable stars; star clusters, nebulae, and galaxies; and descriptive notes. Designed as an observing guide, it works best when used with an atlas such as the **Sky Atlas 2000.0.**

★ **The Cambridge Atlas of Astronomy,** edited by Jean Audouze, Guy Israel, and Jean-Claude Falque. Published by Cambridge University Press, 40 W. 20th St., New York, NY 10011. $72.00. Contains excellent photos and descriptions of astronomical objects.

★ **The Color Atlas of Galaxies,** by James D. Wray. Published by Cambridge University Press, 40 W. 20th St., New York, NY 10011. $63.60. Presents color images of more than 600 galaxies. An interesting publication for the observer who wants to examine images from large telescopes.

★ **Deen Publications,** Dept. ST, P.O. Box 831991, Richardson, TX 75083. Tel. (214) 517–8485. Sells microfiche reproductions of 936 Palomar Sky Survey Images for $250. Write for more information.

★ **The Edmund Mag 6 Star Atlas,** by T. Dickinson, V. Costanzo, and G. Chaple. Available from Sky Publishing or Edmund Scientific, Dept. 11B1, N937, Edscorp Bldg., Barrington, NJ 08007. Tel. (609) 573–6250. Fax (609) 573–6295. Identifies all stars to magnitude 6.2 and gives data on more than 1,000 celestial objects. Designed for use by beginners equipped with small- to medium-size telescopes.

★ **The Greenwich Guide to Astronomy.** Available from Cambridge University Press and Sky Publishing. $7.95 per issue. A series of guides for the beginner, written by experts from the Old Royal Observatory at Greenwich. The series includes **The Greenwich Guide to Stars, Galaxies and Nebulae; The Greenwich Guide to Stargazing; The Greenwich Guide to Astronomy in Action;** and **The Greenwich Guide to the Planets.**

★ **Handbook of the Constellations,** by Hans Vehrenberg and Dieter Blank. Available from Sky Publishing. $39.95. A combination of astronomical charts and catalogues. A chart and corresponding data are given for each object visible in a medium-sized telescope. Displays stars down to magnitude 6 and deep-sky objects. Comes in a 11–by–8–inch format. Suitable for beginners to intermediate.

★ **Hubble Atlas of Galaxies,** based on plates taken by Dr. Edwin Hubble from 1919 to 1948 with the Mount Wilson 60–inch and

100–inch telescopes. Available from Sky Publishing. $29.95. The full detail of most of the galaxies is beyond the reach of most amateur equipment.

★ **The Monthly Sky Guide,** by Ian Ridpath and Wil Tirion. Cambridge University Press, 40 W. 20th St., New York, NY 10011. $8.75. A guide for the general observer. Contains naked eye stars, shows which constellations are visible, and has notes on meteor showers and the positions of the planets for a five-year period.

★ **Nearby Galaxies Atlas,** by R. Brent Tully and J. Richard Fisher. Cambridge University Press, 40 W. 20th St., New York, NY 10011. $50.00. Although not really an observing aid, the book provides excellent color photos and explanations of the galaxies near the Milky Way.

★ **Norton's 2000.0 Star Atlas and Reference Book,** edited by Ian Ridpath. Available from Longman Scientific & Technical, 605 Third Ave., New York, NY 10158. $34.95. This classic guide to the heavens appeals to almost anyone with an appreciation for the beauty of the night sky. The sky maps cover from pole to pole, and show more than 8,400 stars to a magnitude limit of 6.49 visual, as well as 600 deep-sky objects.

★ **The Observers Sky Atlas,** by E. Karkoschka. Available from Springer-Verlag New York, Inc., Attn.: K. Quinn/Dept. S 782, 175 Fifth Ave., New York, NY

In 1888, British astronomer J.L.E. Dreyer published an extensive catalogue of the skies called **A New General Catalogue of Nebulae and Clusters of Stars,** or the **NGC.** He later published two supplementary **Index Catalogues.** Astronomers often refer to objects in the sky by their NGC number or their Messier number. For example, the Great Nebula in Andromeda is called either M31 or NGC 224.

10010. Tel. 1–800–777–4643; (201) 348–4033 (in New Jersey). Contains 50 star charts.

★ **Opto-Data,** 600 Mariners Island Blvd., Suite 36, San Mateo, CA 94404. Tel. (415) 377–0211. $895. A portable computer sky atlas that shows more than 40,000 stars and 10,000 deep-sky objects. Write for more information.

★ **Photographic Star Atlas—The Falkau Atlas,** by Hans Vehrenberg. Available from Sky Publishing. Edition A, North, $48; Edition B, North, $68; Edition A, South, $30; Edition B, South, $40. For the professional or advanced amateur. Comes in four sections, covering the Northern and Southern skies. Also, two editions for each section: Edition A is photo-offset with black stars on a white background; B is photo-printed with white stars on a black background.

★ **Sarna Deep Sky Atlas.** Available from Willmann-Bell. $29.95.

★ **Sky Atlas 2000.0,** by Wil Tirion. Published by Sky Publishing Corporation. Field edition, $15.95; deluxe color edition, $39.95. Comes in two formats, a field edition with white stars on black background, and desk edition, with colors and black stars and a white background. This popular and useful atlas has 26 star charts covering both hemispheres, and contains 43,000 stars to visual magnitude 8.1 and about 2,500 deep-sky objects.

★ **Sky Calendar,** produced by Abrams Planetarium, Michigan State University, East Lansing, MI 48824. This popular calendar, at an annual cost of $6, lets you know "what's up" and gives tips on photography, viewing, and locating interesting sky objects. The calendar is mailed monthly. (See Chapter 7 for information about Abrams Planetarium.)

★ **Uranometria 2000.0,** by Wil Tirion, Barry Rappaport, and George Lovi. Available from Willmann-Bell, Inc. Uranometria 1, $39.95; Uranometria 2, $39.95. This in-depth atlas continues Tirion's penchant for developing usable atlases. Available in two volumes, one covering the Northern Hemisphere and one covering the Southern Hemisphere. Each volume has 259 charts, with more than 332,000 stars and 10,300 deep-sky objects.

CATALOGUES

★ **Nearby Galaxies Catalog,** by R. Brent Tully. Cambridge University Press, 40 W. 20th St., New York, NY 10011. $39.60. A companion to **Nearby Galaxies Atlas,** it provides information on the 2,367 galaxies mapped in the atlas.

★ **NGC 2000.0—The Complete New General Catalogue (NGC) and Index Catalogue (IC) of Nebulae and Clusters of Stars,** edited by Roger W. Sinnott. Available from Sky Publishing and Cambridge University Press. $19.95. An update of the J.L.E. Dreyer directory. The catalogue gives modern positions, sizes, brightness, and object types. Also includes visual descriptions collected by Dreyer.

★ **The Revised New General Catalogue of Nonstellar Astronomical Objects (Epoch 1975.0),** by J.W. Sulentic and W.G. Tifft. Available from Sky Publishing and Cambridge University Press. $35.00. Compiled at the University of Arizona, this catalogue contains information on the type of object, its right ascension and declination, galactic longitude and latitude, coordinates of the object on plates of the National Geographic Society-Palomar Observatory Sky Survey, photographic magnitude, and a statement by the authors on how the object appears visually on the Sky Survey prints.

★ **Sky Catalogue 2000.0,** edited by Alan Hirshfeld and Roger Sinnott. Cambridge University Press and Sky Publishing. Comes in two volumes. Volume 1, paper, $29.95; Volume 2, paper, $29.95; cloth, $49.95. Volume 1: Stars to Magnitude 8.0; Volume 2: Double Stars, Variable Stars and Nonstellar Objects. Contains data such as the Henry Draper Number; Smithsonian Astrophysical Observatory Number; star name, right ascension and declination, proper motions in right ascension and declination per year; apparent visual magnitude; color index; absolute visual magnitude; spectral type, luminosity class, and peculiarity code; radial velocity; distance; and notes.

OBSERVING GUIDES

★ **The Astronomical Almanac,** a publication of the U.S. Naval Observatory and the H.M. Nautical Almanac Office, Royal Greenwich Observatory. Available from Superintendent of Documents, U.S. Government Printing Office, Washington, DC 20402. Tel. (202) 783–3238. Contains data on planets, moon phases, sunsets, star magnitudes, etc.

★ **The Astronomical Companion,** by Guy Ottewell. Available from the Astronomical Workshop, Furman University, Greenville, SC 29613. Ottwell also compiles an **Astronomical Calendar** for each year. The **Astronomical Companion** costs $12; the **Calendar** $15.

★ **Astronomy with Binoculars,** by James Muirden. Available from Sky Publishing. $7.95. A beginners' guide.

★ **The Deep-Sky Field Plan,** by John Vickers. Available from Sky Publishing. $24.95. The work is a guide to objects visible photographically to advanced amateurs. It is based on photos taken by amateur astronomer John Vickers from his home in Duxbury, Massachusetts.

★ **Exploring the Night Sky with Binoculars,** by Patrick Moore. Cambridge University

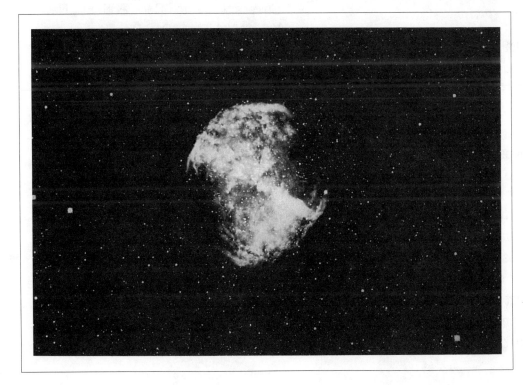

The Dumbbell Nebula (M27, NGC 6853) a planetary nebula in Vulpecula. (National Optical Astronomy Observatories/W. Schoening/N. Sharp)

Press, 40 W. 20th St., New York, NY 10011. $14.95. This book covers the night sky, season by season, and gives the observer tips on using binoculars and spotting celestial objects in the constellations.

★ **A Field Guide to the Stars and Planets,** by Donald H. Menzel and Jay M. Pasachoff. A handy pocket guide published by the National Audubon Society/Peterson Field Guide Series. It features short explanations on the lore and seasons for the constellations; maps of the sky by Wil Tirion; charts and short explanations of objects ranging from galaxies to nebulae; and a section on lunar observing, complete with maps. The maps are on the small side, but the book is handy for those who like to take a guide along on a camping trip or for a quick reference. Available in most book stores.

★ **Handbook for Visual Meteor Observations,** by Paul Roggemans. Sky Publishing Corporation. $19.95. This handbook contains instructions and report forms for observing and reporting meteors. Included are 20 star maps for plotting meteor paths.

★ **The Messier Album,** by John Mallas and Evered Kreimer. Sky Publishing Corporation and Cambridge University Press. $14.95. This guide to Charles Messier's catalogue of deep-sky objects is based on a series that ran in **Sky & Telescope.** It contains a finder chart for each object, plus descriptions and photos.

★ **The Moon Observer's Handbook,** by Fred W. Price. Available from Sky Publishing. $27.60. Price, a founding member of the American Lunar Society, outlines everything an amateur astronomer needs to know for lunar observations. Price even discusses transient phenomena. Charts and photographs support the text.

★ **Observing Handbook and Catalogue of Deep-Sky Objects,** by Christian B. Luginbuhl and Brian A. Skiff. $39.60. Published by Cambridge University Press, 40 W. 20th St., New York, NY 10011. This volume describes more than 2,000 galaxies, nebulae, and star clusters. Each object is described as it would appear in telescopes of various sizes.

★ **Observing Variable Stars: A Guide for the Beginner.,** by David H. Levy. Cambridge University Press, 40 W. 20th St., New York, NY 10011. $19.95. This volume discusses ways amateurs can make contributions to the science of astronomy using a small telescope, binoculars, or the naked eye. Levy discusses how to buy a telescope or binoculars, and gives information on known variables.

★ **1000+: The Amateur Astronomer's Field Guide to Deep-Sky Observing,** by Tom Lorenzin. Sky Publishing Corporation. $39.95. This star atlas and observing guide has only 83 pages, but it lists more than 1,000 deep-sky objects as they appeared to Lorenzin in his 8–inch Schmidt-Cassegrain.

★ **The Universe from Your Backyard: An Atlas of Deep Sky Objects,** by David J. Eicher. Published by Cambridge University Press, 40 W. 20th St., New York, NY 10011, and Kalmbach Publishing, 21027 Crossroads Circle, P.O. Box 1612, Waukesha, WI 53187. $19.95. This volume explores double and multiple stars, variable stars, globular star clusters, planetary nebulae, galaxies, and quasars.

★ **Webb Society Deep-Sky Observer's Handbook,** edited by Kenneth Glyn Jones. Available from Sky Publishing. Prices range from $11.95 to $17.95 per volume. A series of independent volumes for the serious amateur astronomer. Volume 1: **Double Stars;** Volume 2: **Planetary and Gaseous Nebulae;** Volume 3: **Open and Globular Clusters;** Volume 4: **Galaxies;** Volume 5: **Clusters of Galaxies;** Volume 6: **Anonymous Galaxies;** Volume 7: **The Southern Sky.**

ON THE TRAIL OF COMETS

In the quiet of the night David Levy hunts a quarry that lies hidden among the stars, disguised by wispy nebula, and cloaked in the aura of distant galaxies. His target is the once mysterious comets that in times past were omens, portents of dire straits for rulers and their subjects. Today, scientists know they more closely resemble "dirty snowballs" that either visit our Solar System briefly, or take up a regular orbit around the Sun. But their romantic image lingers, enticing dedicated followers who labor long into the night in search of new comets.

Levy is one of those searchers; he speaks of his effort with a quiet reverence for the comets that follow their lonely paths through the Solar System. As he describes his quest to amateur astronomy clubs, he sprinkles in references to other comet hunters, music, literature, and science. He displays a modest acceptance of his accomplishments (he has discovered sixteen comets) as he encourages others to share in his passion for the night skies.

It's appropriate that he enjoys music and quietness, for those penchants, along with a seemingly endless reservoir of patience, help him on his quest to discover yet another comet that will bear his name.

His inspiration to search for comets came after reading Leslie C. Peltier's **Starlight Nights,** when he was seventeen. The search for comets, Levy says, is a "way of communing with the sky." He has been hunting comets since 1968, starting in Montreal, Canada. Since

1979 he has lived in Tucson, Arizona, where he regularly scans the skies with 6-inch and 16-inch reflectors and an 8-inch Schmidt camera which allows him to peer deeper into space with photographs.

His search is methodical, with slow sweeps back and forth within 90 degrees of the Sun's setting point; 45 degrees on each side of that path, and from the horizon up to about 45 degrees. Each sweep takes several minutes, and requires a thorough knowledge of the sky. In fact, Levy says hunting comets is an excellent method to learn the night sky. As he searches, Levy listens to music by Joan Baez, or to classical recordings.

When he finds a comet, he verifies it with one of his charts, and often turns to friends at Kitt Peak for further confirmation.

Although he speaks softly, Levy "loves the intensity of the competition" among comet searchers. "It's a very competitive field," he notes, with observers all over the world vying for the honor of being the first to spot a new comet. He estimates he has spent at least 800 hours over the past 18 years in his comet searches. His first find, discovered Nov. 15, 1984, came while his father was terminally ill in the hospital.

Levy writes extensively about astronomy, with books such as **The Sky: A User's Guide, Observing Variable Stars: A Guide for the Beginner,** and, most recently, a biography of Clyde Tombaugh to his credit. He also has a monthly column in **Sky & Telescope.** His formal training, however, was in English. He brings that lyrical mindset to his calling. Astronomy, he says can be understood and enjoyed without the formulas and mathematics. In a sense, he says, if there are "no equations, no physics, it's magic" and the sights he views through his telescope are awe inspiring.

Furthermore, he believes that amateurs, who usually lack the expensive equipment and complex measuring devices of professionals, often are better observers. This enables them to spot subtle changes in the atmosphere of Mars or one of the other planets, for example, and alert professional astronomers.

But the most lasting impact an amateur can have, Levy suggests, is to teach others about astronomy. "There are kids that have not seen the sky," he says, and encourages amateurs to draw children into the field. "The most important thing we as amateurs can do," he insists, "is to inspire the next generation to get into astronomy" and the sciences.

5

ASTRO-PHOTOGRAPHY

THE NUTS AND BOLTS OF ASTROPHOTOGRAPHY

Taking beautiful photos of the night sky is not an easy task. Although an amateur astrophotographer can begin by using a simple camera with a shutter that can be kept open for long exposures, getting the truly great shots takes a telescope, hypered film, a drive that can follow the stars, and a great deal of patience. Many astrophotographers also swear by cooled cameras and cold film, but you shouldn't purchase the equipment needed to gas-cool film without at least trying your hand at conventional film.

Many astrophotographers prefer to develop their own film. This enables them to experiment with contrasts, with filters, and with stacking negatives together to make a composite shot taken with different-colored filters. But do-it-yourself developing is not necessary if you make contact with a local studio and explain what you're shooting. Explaining that you have taken deep space shots is essential; some developers, especially overnight services, don't have the facilities or experience to deal with this kind of photography, and may think you made an error by not exposing the film sufficiently. By patiently explaining that yes, you are taking pictures of the night sky, and yes, you do intend for only a few little "bright dots" to show, you can obtain some excellent developments of your work.

Catadioptrics have proven to be excellent for astrophotography. Pictured here, the Celestron C8 series of catadioptrics. (Courtesy of Celestron)

A common problem for astrophotographers, especially those living in light-polluted areas, is that the brightness of the sky gradually overpowers the light coming from the stars and casts a "fog" across the image. Filters can ease some of these problems and even reduce the interference from certain kinds of street lights. But your best bet is still to get away from it all and do your work under dark skies.

Learning to take high-quality shots is very much a matter of "learning by doing." But there are a number of books, as well as excellent articles in magazines such as **Astronomy** and **Sky and Telescope,** that can help you along the way. Some of the more useful publications are listed below. This section also includes companies that provide developing services, supply equipment, or sell guides and books on the subject. Many of the telescope suppliers listed in Chapter 3 also cater to amateur astrophotographers.

Books
and Brochures

★ **Astrofilters for Observation and Astrophotography,** by Barbera, Capen, Carvalho, Steeg. Available from Optica b/c Company, at address below. $6.95. Discuses the uses of filters to enhance photos and observations.

★ **Astrophotography,** by Barry Gordon. Available from Willmann-Bell, P.O. Box 25025, Richmond, VA 12125. Tel 1–800–825–STAR. 208 pages, $18.95.

★ **Astrophotography: A Step-by-Step Approach,** by R. T. Little. Macmillan, 866 Third Ave., New York, NY 10022. 79 pages, $19.95.

★ **Astrophotography Basics.** Eastman Kodak Co., Customer Service Pamphlet P–150. 22–page pamphlet. $2.

★ **Astrophotography for the Amateur,** by Michael Covington. Cambridge University Press, 40 W. 20th St., New York, NY 10011. 168 pages, $24.95.

★ **Astrophotography II,** by Patrick Martinez. Available from Willmann-Bell, P.O. Box

The Lagoon Nebula (M8, NGC 6523) photographed with the JMI NGT-18 and an off-axis guider/camera.

25025, Richmond, VA 12125. Tel. 1–800–825–STAR. 174 pages, $18.85.

★ **Handbook for Star Trackers,** by Jim Ballard. Available from Sky Publishing Corporation, 49 Bay State Rd., Cambridge, MA 02138. Tel. (617) 864–7360. $9.95. A guide that explains how to use common hardware-store items to build an accurate camera tracking platform.

★ **Introduction to Observing and Photographing the Solar System,** by Tom Dobbins, Don Parker & Charles Capen. Available from Sky Publishing Corporation, 49 Bay State Rd., Cambridge, MA 02138. Tel. (617) 864–7360. $19.95.

★ **A Manual of Celestial Photography,** by E.S. King. Available from Sky Publishing Corporation, 49 Bay State Rd., Cambridge, MA 02138. Tel. (617) 864–7360. $9.95. A classic reissued by Sky Publishing Corporation, this book explains the fundamentals of taking shots of the night sky.

★ **Sky Shooting—Photography for Amateur Astronomers,** by R. Mayall & M. Mayall. Available from Sky Publishing Corporation, 49 Bay State Rd., Cambridge, MA 02138. Tel. (617) 864–7360. $5.95. A starter book for sky photography.

Equipment, Film, and Developing Services

★ **AstroEnhance,** 719 S. Harbor Blvd., Drawer 222, Fullerton, CA 92632. Offers high-tech computer-enhancing to transform astrophotographs, color or black and white, into false-colored images.

★ **Grindstone Lab,** 18 Grindstone Lane, Sudbury, MA 01776. Tel. (508) 443–3500. Specializes in color enlargements of astrophotographs.

★ **Lumicon,** 2111 Research Dr. #5, Livermore, CA 94550. Tel. (415) 447–9570. Fax (415) 447–9589. Sells astrophotography supplies, including film hypersensitization kits, hypered film, guides, filters, and other accessories.

★ **Optica b/c Company,** 4100 MacArthur Blvd., Oakland, CA 94619. Astrophotography systems and supplies. Also sells how-to books on astrophotography. Catalog $1.

★ **Roger W. Tuthill, Inc.,** Box 1086, Mountainside, NJ 07092. Tel. 1–800–223–1063; in New Jersey, call (908) 232–1786. Fax (908) 232–3804. Sells astrophotography equipment, books, and guides.

★ **University Optics, Inc.,** P.O. Box 1205, Ann Arbor, MI 48106. Tel. 1–800–521–

2828. Books and supplies for astrophotography.

★ **Willmann-Bell Inc.,** P.O. Box 25025, Richmond, VA 12125. Orders, call 1–800– 825–STAR. For information, call (804) 320–7016. Astronomy and astrophotography equipment and books.

CHARGE-COUPLED DEVICES

To many amateur astronomers, buying new equipment seems to be nearly as enjoyable as the act of observing. With each new piece of equipment, they expect to uncover new vistas, catch small, obscure objects that previously were visible only to those with professional equipment, or seek out new detail in familiar objects.

Over the past decade, the charge-coupled device (CCD) has entered the domain of the amateur astronomer. It previously was a tool only professionals could afford; today, although CCDs are still not cheap, prices have declined and the equipment has improved to the point where more amateurs can afford them.

A CCD basically consists of a light-sensitive semiconductor that, like the silver halide in traditional photographic film, reacts to the incoming photons. In the case of the CCD, the incoming light builds up an electrical charge of picture elements or pixels. The pixels collect the electrons triggered by the light, and eventually, via computer and a screen, display the "picture." At this point the images are "raw" and can be manipulated via computer software programs. The manipulation includes highlighting regions or special areas of the target, subtracting "dark" images caused by the heat of the equipment, or with some software, enhancing the pixels to draw up more detail. Most CCD cameras are cooled to decrease the dark current caused by the electrical noise of the CCD circuits.

In many ways, a CCD camera is used like the cameras traditionally used by astrophotographers. It must be guided to stay with the target, and, like a camera, has a "shutter" that determines the length of the exposure. One major advantage of a CCD camera is the short exposure time needed to capture even faint objects. An exposure of a few seconds can equal several minutes at the camera. Additionally, the problem of film "fog" is substantially reduced.

Once the incoming light strikes the CCD, it is transferred to an image controller, which translates the data into a format that can be used for a video display. The controllers are connected to a computer, (not part of the standard equipment sold by most CCD companies). Although some models have self-contained units that can process images, if you want to save the images permanently you will need a computer.

After you have saved the image, you can retrieve it just as you would any other computer file. In this respect, the file is similar to printing a finished picture from a traditional photographic negative. You can adjust the brightness and contrast, just as in film negatives, but with some advantages. If you don't like the image, simply start over with no loss of paper or chemicals. Also, you can stretch the image or eliminate unwanted areas much more easily than in film work.

Film, however, still holds an advantage in resolution of an image.

Just what can you expect from a CCD? It depends, in part, on what you want. Keith and Susan Gardner, editors of **CCD News,** recommend you ask yourself a few questions before you buy. For example, do you want your equipment for tracking, imaging, or both? If you just want it to track, many CCD cameras will do that without a computer; tracking and imaging, however, require a computer.

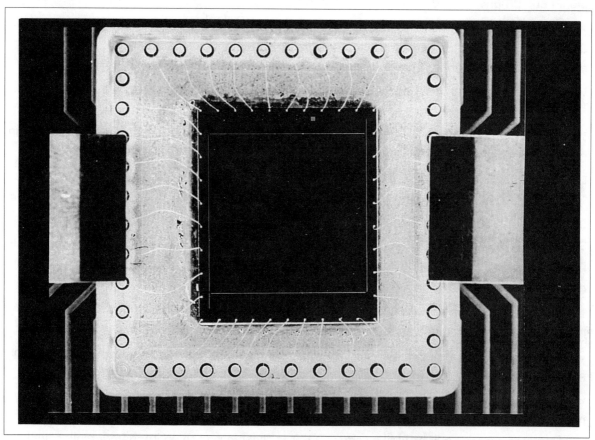

Close-up of a charge-coupled device showing the array of sensitive picture elements, or pixels, that can be read off by a computer as a digital image. (National Optical Astronomy Observatories)

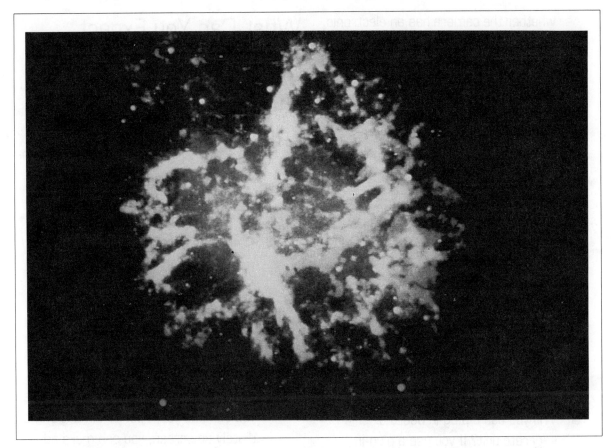

This image of the Crab Nebula (M1) was reconstructed from exposures made through three separate filters and recombined in the Image Reduction Analysis Facility at Kitt Peak National Observatory. All images were taken at the observatory's 0.9–meter telescope with a CCD.
(National Optical Astronomy Observatories)

If you're considering a CCD for tracking, Keith and Susan recommend checking with suppliers to determine if the CCD camera is compatible with your drive's electronics. "Connecting them together is not a trivial matter," they say, and recommend you have at least a minimum of electronics knowledge before attempting to do it yourself.

Selecting a CCD

The editors of **CCD News** suggest you keep some of the following points in mind when shopping for a CCD.

■ Cameras without coolers cannot do long integrations on deep sky objects, while cooled cameras give you the ability to take longer exposures and get less background or thermal noise. Although some lower-cost cameras don't have coolers, they can be suitable for planetary and lunar work. Choose a camera to fit your viewing preferences. For example, determine whether the camera has an electronic shutter so you can image bright objects. If there is no shutter, you must use filters or a mask to stop the scope down.

- Remember that chip size severely limits the amount of sky you look at. Ideally, the Gardners recommend you choose the largest chip you can afford. A side note, however: the larger the chip, the more memory it will use to store an image, which can affect the performance of your computer and the time it takes to view an image.

- Determine what image size the CCD camera will deliver with the telescope you use. Some cameras give very small fields.

- Will you use a plug-in board or separate unit? If you use a plug-in board, you'll need an expansion slot in your computer. A laptop computer, although great in terms of portability, does not always have an expansion slot.

- For photometric work, an 8–bit camera can only give you limited applications (8 bit can only give 256 levels of intensity). The Gardners recommend you have at least a 12–bit camera, which is capable of more than 3,000 levels of intensity.

- For best results, use a VGA display on your computer. If necessary, take a demonstration disk from the supplier to a computer store and try it out with different displays.

What Can You Expect from a CCD?

Among the recommendations from the Gardners are:

- An ability to capture any object with instant results, and to capture and save those images on disk and manipulate them later.

- The speed of a CCD camera allows you to take short exposures, which minimizes the periodic errors in your drive. Also, CCDs can work even in light-polluted skies.

- With a CCD camera, you can retake an image if it isn't what you want, without wasting film. In addition, since you can see your results almost immediately on screen, you can make adjustments that night instead of waiting for another night.

Unfortunately, there is a lack of CCD standards, and each supplier uses different file formats, so be aware of this when buying image-processing software.

The Gardners also find that many newcomers to the field are disappointed with their first results. Often, Keith says, the newcomer doesn't realize that the clean, clear images shown in magazines are processed. A "raw image" usually has dark areas that are the result of thermal noise from the camera itself.

Finding reading materials for CCD work also can be a problem. The Gardners say they launched their magazine in part

A lunar close-up taken with a SpectraSource CCD imaging system. (Courtesy of SpectraSource Instruments)

because of their difficulty in finding technical information about their hobby. The magazine provides in-depth technical tips on using CCDs, with articles from experts at the amateur and professional level. See below for subscription information.

CCD Manufacturers

★ **Astro-Link,** P.O. Box 1978, Spring Valley, CA 92077. Tel. (619) 449–4722.

★ **Catenary Systems,** 470 Belleview, St. Louis, MO 63119. Tel. (314) 962–7833. Image-processing software for the personal computer.

★ **ELECTRIM Corporation,** P.O. Box 2074, Princeton, NJ 08543. Tel. (609) 799–7248.

★ **First Magnitude Corporation,** 519 South Fifth St., Laramie, WY 82070. Tel. (307) 766–6267. Free literature. Manufactures slow-scan, cooled, digital cameras for scientific, educational, and industrial use. Also has linear CCDs for spectroscopy. Software included with equipment. Prices start at $9,500 for StarScape CCD cameras. Payment by C.O.D., cashiers check, personal check (which is cleared before shipment), or institutional purchase order. Provides documentation and telephone support for products.

★ **Mico Luminetics, Inc.,** 3447 Greenfield Ave., Los Angeles, CA 90034. Tel. (213) 839–0690. Fax (213) 836–4733.

★ **Patterson Electronics,** 360 East First St., Tustin, CA 92680. Tel. (714) 544–4127.

★ **Photometrics Ltd.,** 3440 Britannia Dr., Tucson, AZ 85706. Tel. (602) 889–9933. Fax (602) 573–1944. The Star I System with a liquid circulation camera head, or with a passive air dissipation camera head, starts at $12,100; the CCD is another $2,750 to $4,725. This price does not include other options, such as the controller software and tape drive. Write for catalog.

★ **Prime Focus Imaging,** 128 Elpis Rd., Camden, NY 13316. Tel. (315) 245–3596.

★ **Santa Barbara Instrument Group,** 1482 East Valley Rd., Suite 601, Santa Barbara, CA 93108. Tel. (805) 969–1851. Fax (805) 969– 0299. Brochures available at no charge. Also furnishes a demonstration diskette for a personal computer, at a cost of $5. Orders must be accompanied by a $200 deposit, with the remainder due 10 days prior to shipment. Most sales handled through the main office, or offices overseas. Prices start at $890, plus options.

★ **SpectraSource,** P.O. Box 1045, Agoura Hills, CA 91376–1045. Tel. (818) 707–2655. Fax (818) 707–9035. Provides free data pack and demonstration disk. The company suggests that the optimum equipment for astronomical applications with the Lynxx series of cameras is a short focal length, fast optical system. The company uses a 10–inch f/3 Newtonian most often. The suggested computer component is an IBM PC/XT or AT compatible with 640K RAM, and EGA or VGA graphics. Also has a Macintosh-based system. Prices for CCD imaging systems start at $9,875 for a complete system.

★ **TRIFID Corporation,** 744 Office Parkway, Suite 224, St. Louis, MO 63141–7128. Tel. (314) 991–3095. Provides image-processing software.

★ **Western Research Company Inc.,** 2127 E. Speedway, Suite 209, Tucson, AZ 85719. Tel. (602) 325–4505.

Magazine

★ **CCD News,** 31651 Avon Rd., Avon, OH 44011. One-year subscription (four issues) costs $5.

Brochure

★ **Photometrics Ltd.,** 3440 Britannia Dr., Tucson, AZ 85706. Tel. (602) 889–9933. Photometrics provides a background brochure that explains many of the concepts of Charge-Coupled Devices.

Books

★ **CCDS in Astronomy,** edited by A.G. Davis Philip, Donald S. Hayes, and Saul J. Adelman. Available from L. Davis Press., Inc., 1125 Oxford Place, Schenectady, NY 12308. $27 plus $4 postage and handling. A collection of papers on using CCD observations in astronomy.

★ **CCD Astronomy,** by Christian Bull. Available from Willmann-Bell Inc., P.O. Box 35025, Richmond, VA 23235. $24.95. A hands-on approach by the French amateur astronomer. The book details the design and construction of a CCD camera, and covers operating the CCD once you have it.

★ **Introduction to Astronomical Image Processing with Imagepro Software,** by Richard Berry. Available from Willmann-Bell Inc., P.O. Box 35025, Richmond, VA 23235. $29.95. A manual for the amateur astronomer. Covers image processing without heavy emphasis on mathematics.

The Orange Country Astronomers are another good source of information for CCD enthusiasts. Members of this club have compiled publications from seminars they hold on Electronics Oriented Astronomy. Write to: OCA Publications, P.O. Box 1762, Costa Mesa, CA 92628. For more information about the club, see the **Local Astronomy Clubs** section in Chapter 2.

6

OBSERVATORIES

OBSERVATORIES OF NORTH AMERICA

An observatory, no matter what the size, easily conjures up images of exploring the unknown, of seeing distant places, of learning. It is, in part, a symbol of humanity's attempts to look up, to push back the boundaries of ignorance, to expand what is known, to dispel that which is false.

The great observatories of North America—Mount Wilson, McDonald, Yerkes, Lick, Palomar, Kitt Peak, Mauna Kea—have gained worldwide recognition and have attracted some of the worlds' best scientists. But their telescopes are not the only instruments being trained on the skies. Universities, private researchers, and even amateur clubs across the country have built and are building instruments capable of seeing far back in time.

Reserving time on one of the major instruments is a competitive process; worthy projects far outnumber available time. Financing new observatories continues to be a problem, as the requirements for new technology carry a tremendous price tag. In recent years, the U.S. has lagged behind Europe when it comes to building new instruments. What this will mean for the future is uncertain. For today's professionals, it almost certainly means less time testing theories through observation.

Further complicating matters for many of the older observatories is the continuing problem of light pollution. Early observatories, constructed in days when transportation was more difficult, often were built to be easily accessible by the astronomers who would use them. Even those built "in the country" in the last century are today surrounded by development. Some universities have coped by moving the entire instrument, others by simply using the older observatory as a teaching tool while using more distant facilities for actual research.

Despite the problems facing today's observatories, there **are** some new and exciting projects, including the new telescopes at Mauna Kea on Hawaii, and plans for instruments on Mount Graham in Arizona. Even amateurs are building ever larger instruments as they adapt the new technologies to their needs.

In all, it means that—although there are some troubled times for science—there are also some bright spots.

The following listing includes data on many of the research, university, municipal and public, private, and club observatories in the U.S. and Canada. A vast majority offer public tours, and some even permit public viewing in special instances. For information about tours or to find out how to obtain observing time, write or call the facility directly.

Arizona

★ **Grasslands Observatory,** 5100 N. Sabino Foothills Dr., Tucson, AZ 85715.

★ **Kitt Peak National Observatory.** See **National Optical Astronomy Observatories,** below.

★ **Lowell Observatory,** 1400 W. Mars Hill Road, Flagstaff, AZ 86001. Tel. (602) 621–1558.

★ **Michigan Dartmouth MIT Observatory,** HC 04, P.O. Box 7520, Tucson, AZ 85735. Tel. (602) 620–5360.

★ **Mount Graham International Observatory.** This site, located in the Pinaleno Mountains, will house several telescopes when completed during this decade. They are:

■ **Submillimeter Telescope.** This will feature a 10–meter dish antenna that will be the most precise radio reflector ever built. Partners are: University of Arizona, Max Planck Institute for Radio astronomy in Bonn, Germany.

■ **Vatican Advanced Technology Telescope.** This 1.8–meter telescope will be used for optical and infrared astronomy. The Vatican Observatory and the University of Arizona are partners.

■ **Columbus Project.** This instrument will be the world's largest and most powerful telescope for optical and infrared astronomy. Two mirrors, each 8 meters in diameter, will be cast and polished at the Steward Observatory Mirror Laboratory. They will work in binocular fashion to equal the power of a single 12–meter telescope.

Partners are the University of Arizona, Ohio State University, and the Arcetri Observatory, Italy. This project has been plagued by delays, including objections by environmentalists over the danger to the red squirrels atop the mountain, and Ohio State University trustees recently rejected participation in the project.

★ **Multiple Mirror Telescope**. See **Fred Whipple Observatory.**

★ **National Optical Astronomy Observatories,** P.O. Box 26732, Tucson, AZ 85726–

6732. Tel. (602) 325–9204 for public information office. The NOAO is operated by the Association of Universities for Research in Astronomy, under contract to the National Science Foundation. The Observatories consist of three major astronomical centers, including Kitt Peak National Observatory near Tucson, Cerro Tololo Inter-American Observatory in Chile, and the National Solar Observatory with facilities at Kitt Peak, Arizona, and Sacramento Peak, New Mexico. The facilities are operated for U.S. astronomers. Observing time is allocated

View of the National Optical Astronomy Observatories facilities on Kitt Peak, showing the 2.1–meter telescope (large dome in foreground) and the McMath Solar Telescope (triangular building), the largest solar telescope in the world. (National Optical Astronomy Observatories)

on the basis of the relative merit of research proposals.

Kitt Peak National Observatory contains the world's largest single collection of optical telescopes. The Cerro Tololo facility in northern Chile also is the site for a large number of U.S. and European observatories.

Research at the sites covers virtually all aspects of astronomy, including studies about asteroids, red shift of galaxies, binary stars, hydrogen emissions, evolution of galaxies, low metal stars, star formation, star clusters, quasars, and many other subjects of interest.

The NOAO also has an active Advanced Optical Telescope Technology Program, and is constantly improving imaging techniques, computer services, and optical improvements.

A planned project, the 8–meter Telescope Project, has received support from the National Science Foundation. The 8–meter telescopes would be placed atop Mauna Kea in Hawaii, and in Chile.

★ **Northern Arizona University Campus Observatory,** Department of Physics and Astronomy, Box 6010, Flagstaff, AZ 86011. Tel. (602) 523–2661.

★ **Steward Observatory,** directed by the University of Arizona, Tucson, AZ 85721. Tel. (602) 621–6524. Fax (602) 621–1532. Telex: 46175. The Steward Observatory staff operates the University's research telescopes, located at various sites throughout southern Arizona. The telescopes are open to astronomers from all of the state's universities. About 10 percent of the time on the research telescopes is available to professional astronomers outside the state's university system. The Steward Observatory's research activities include studies of extragalactic astronomy, galactic and stellar astronomy, Solar System studies, and theoretical astrophysics. Scientists are trying to answer questions about the early Universe and the formation of galaxies. They also are searching for planets around other stars. The research telescopes are not open to the general public or amateurs, although the campus telescope, which is used for undergraduate instruction, is occasionally open for public viewing.

■ **Steward Observatory Mirror Laboratory** makes and polishes lightweight mirrors that are a radical departure from conventional solid-glass mirrors. They are honeycombed on the inside, and can be made larger and lighter than traditional solid glass. A series of mirrors that are 8 meters (26 feet) or more in diameter will be cast in 1992. The technological breakthroughs at this laboratory may mean previously unthinkable sizes for Earth-bound telescopes might be possible.

★ **United States Naval Observatory,** Flagstaff Station, P.O. Box 1149, Flagstaff, AZ

86002. Tel. (602) 779–5132. Site of the 1978 discovery of Pluto's moon, Charon.

★ **University of Arizona Telescopes,** directed by the University of Arizona, Tucson, AZ 85721. Tel. (602) 621–6524. On Kitt Peak, the university operates a 90–inch reflector and 36–inch reflector; plus a 72–inch computer-controlled telescope that makes a nightly survey of a selected swath of the sky. This Charge-Coupled Device/Transit Instrument records data that might be missed without continuous observations. In the Santa Catalina Mountains, the university has a 60–inch reflector and 40–inch reflector on Mount Lemmon; and a 61–inch reflector on Mount Bigelow. See also **Steward Observatory; Fred Whipple Observatory (Multiple Mirror Telescope); Mount Graham International Observatory.**

★ **Fred Lawrence Whipple Observatory,** P.O. Box 97, Amado, AZ 85645. Tel. (602) 398–2432. The Observatory, located on Mount Hopkins, is the largest field installation of the Smithsonian Astrophysical Observatory outside Cambridge, Massachusetts. Research at the Whipple Observatory includes spectroscopic observations of extragalactic, stellar, and planetary bodies; gamma-ray and cosmic-ray astronomy; solar energy research; and environmental studies. The instruments include 1.5–m and 61–cm reflecting telescopes, a 10–m optical array, a Baker-Nunn satellite tracking camera, plus other telescopes.

Tours are available by reservation. There is a maximum of 22 visitors each tour day. Children under 6 are not permitted. Tickets cost $5 for adults; $2.50 for children 6 to 12; and $4.50 for Smithsonian Associates.

The Mount Hopkins site also is home to the **Multiple Mirror Telescope,** a telescope which combines six individual 1.8–m reflecting telescopes in an array to produce the light-gathering capacity of a single 4.5–m telescope. The instrument, the third largest in the world, is used for infrared and optical astronomy. It is used by Smithsonian, University of Arizona, and guest astronomers.

See also **Harvard-Smithsonian Center for Astrophysics,** Massachusetts.

Arkansas

★ **River Ridge Observatory,** P.O. Box 5142 Little Rock, AK 72225. Tel. (501) 569–3021.

California

★ **Big Bear Solar Observatory,** 40386 North Shore Drive, Big Bear City, CA 92314. Tel. (714) 866–5791 or (818) 356–3857. Contact William Marquette or Dr. Harold Zirin. Professional astronomers may write to CIT, 1201 E. California Blvd., Pasadena, CA 91125, Mail Code 264–33, to arrange observing time. There is no cost for professional research

Got a Project for the Hubble?

If so, the Space Telescope Science Institute (StSci) wants to hear from you. StSci operates the Hubble Space Telescope under contract with the Association of Universities for Research in Astronomy, Inc. StSci allocates time on the 2.4–meter (94.5–inch) telescope, which was placed into orbit in 1990. Although flaws were detected in the primary mirror, the telescope remains a useful observational tool. The Hubble was launched by the U.S., but observing time is allocated to the international astronomy community. Also, in an unusual move, the agency has set aside small amounts of observing time for amateurs who have programs that meet strict guidelines and show some useful research goals. For further information:

PROFESSIONALS SHOULD CONTACT:

User Support Branch, Space Telescope Science Institute, 3700 San Martin Dr., Baltimore, MD 21218.

AMATEURS SHOULD CONTACT:

AAVSP (American Association of Variable Star Observers), 25 Birch St., Cambridge, MA 02138. Tel. (617) 354–0484.

time. The Observatory, built in 1969, is owned and operated by the California Institute of Technology. The dome is located in the lake, which ensures steady air, free of rising heat currents.

Among the observatory's major findings are:

- Determined most accurate solar p-mode frequencies to date. (These are used to infer sound speed vs. depth inside the Sun, and accurate determination of depth of convection zone.)

- Best measurements of p-mode amplitudes and linewidths.

- Best measurement of Sun's internal rotation profile.

- First good measurement of solar cycle variations in p-mode frequencies.

- High resolution magnetogram in the Quiet Sun.

- High resolution white light observations.

- Discovery of canceling magnetic fields on the quiet sun and in active regions.

- Identifying canceling magnetic fields in active regions.

- Development of a new model for the formation of filaments.

★ **Brackett Observatory,** department of Physics and Astronomy, Pomona College, Claremont, CA 91711. Tel. (714) 621–8000.

★ **Chabot Observatory,** 4917 Mountain Blvd., Oakland, CA 94619. Tel. (415) 531–4560.

★ **Fremont Peak Observatory Association,** P.O. Box 1110, San Juan Bautista, CA 95045. Tel. (408) 623–4255. Founded in 1984, the facility is devoted to providing public education and interpretation of astronomy to Fremont Peaks State Park visitors. The 30–inch, f/4.8 Newtonian was installed in 1986. Members in the Association receive a quarterly publication, **The Fremont Peak Observer,** and use of the instruments after training. Membership is $10 annually plus a $10 one-time initiation fee for general members; $30 annually plus one-time $10 initiation fee for contributing members; $50 annually for sustaining member, plus $10 one-time initiation fee; and $300 one-time fee for life member.

★ **Griffith Observatory,** 2800 East Observatory Road, Los Angeles, CA 90027. Tel. (213) 664–1181. Operated by the Department of Recreation and Parks of Los Angeles, the Observatory is open to the public from 7 to 9:45 p.m. Tuesday through Sunday during the winter, and from dark until 9:45 p.m. during the summer. No admission charge. Publishes the **Griffith Observer,** a magazine covering observing tips.

★ **Hat Creek Radio Observatory,** Radio Astronomy Laboratory, University of California, Route 2, Box 500, Cassel, CA 96016. Tel. (916) 335–2364.

★ **Leuschner Observatory,** Astronomy Department, University of California, Berkeley, CA 94720. Tel. (415) 642–5275.

★ **University of California Observatories/Lick Observatory,** University of Santa Cruz, CA 95064. Tel. (408) 459–5939. One of the premier observatories in the world, the site on Mount Hamilton features the famous Lick 36–inch refractor; the 40–inch Nickel Telescope; the Crossley 36–inch reflector; the 20–inch Carnegie Astrograph; and the Shane 120–inch reflector. The 120–inch reflector began operation in 1959, and remains one of the world's most productive telescopes. The universities also are participating in construction of the Ten Meter Telescope at Mauna Kea in Hawaii, which, when completed, will make it the largest in the world.

The Lick Observatory staff, over the years, produced some of the best ground-based photographs of the outer planets, as well as of comets. Members continue their study of the Universe and astrometric programs, such as the measurement of absolute stellar proper motions with respect to galaxies. Studies of variable stars and supernovas also are continuing, as are studies of galactic star clusters.

★ **Mount Laguna,** Astronomy Department, San Diego State University, San Diego, CA 92182. Tel. (619) 595–6182.

★ **Mount Wilson Observatory,** Mount Wilson Institute, 740 Holladay Road, Pasadena, CA 91116. Tel. (818) 793–3100. Mount Wilson was once known for innovative research, but light pollution unfortunately has curtailed much of the possible work that can be done from the site built by George Ellery Hale. Mount Wilson saw first light in 1917, and, with a 2.5–m (100–inch) telescope, was the largest telescope in the world for 30 years. For years it was the primary instrument used by Edwin P. Hubble in his study of galaxies. The 100–inch is no longer operational, but the Mount Wilson Institute, which operates the facility, is raising money to reopen the telescope. Other instruments at Mount Wilson include a 60–inch reflecting telescope; a 60–foot Solar Tower Telescope; and a 150–foot Solar Tower Telescope. Some fundamental research continues, as well as educational programs for undergraduates. Among the discoveries made at Mount Wilson are: magnetic nature of sunspots, by Hale, 1908; the Earth's position in the Milky Way galaxy, by Harlow Shapley, 1917; the speed of light measured by reflecting a beam of light between Mount Wilson and Mount San Antonio, Albert Michelson, 1920; three moons of Jupiter found by Seth Nicholson; discovery of two distinct classes of stars, young blue stars and cold red stars, by Walter Baade,

1940s; mapping of the lunar surface in preparation for the Apollo Moon landings.

★ **Palmer Observatory—Gladwin Planetarium, Santa Barbara Museum of Natural History,** 2559 Puesta del Sol Road, Santa Barbara, CA 93105. Tel. (805) 682–4711. The observatory is part of the museum, and is open Saturday nights after the planetarium show and for special events. It features 5–inch, 8–inch, 16–inch, and 29–inch telescopes. All facilities are operated jointly by the museum and Santa Barbara City College. See listing in Chapter 7.

★ **Palomar Mount Observatory,** California Institute of Technology, San Diego, CA 92060. The observatory houses the Hale Telescope, a 5.08–meter (200–inch) reflecting telescope that for many years was the largest in the world. It saw first light in 1949, and has been instrumental in deep-sky observations and research. In addition to Caltech, other partners in the observatory are Cornell University and Carnegie Institution of Washington.

★ **N.A. Richardson Astronomical Observatory,** San Bernardino Valley College, 701 S. Mount Vernon Ave., San Bernardino, CA 92410. Tel. (714) 888–6511.

★ **San Fernando Observatory,** 14031 San Fernando Rd., Sylmar, CA 91342. Tel. (818) 367–9333.

★ **San Francisco State University Observatory,** Department of Physics and

Astronomy, San Francisco, CA 94132. Tel. (415) 338–1852.

★ **Sonoma State University Observatory,** Department of Physics and Astronomy, Rohnert Park, CA 94928. Tel. (707) 664–2267.

★ **Stony Ridge Observatory,** P.O. Box 874, Big Bear City, CA 92314.

★ **Table Mount Observatory,** Jet Propulsion Laboratory, California Institute of Technology, P.O. Box 367, Wrightwood, CA 92397. Tel. (619) 249–6610. Fax (619) 249–5392. Originally a station of the Smithsonian Institution that was established to study the variability of the solar constant, the facility became part of the Jet Propulsion Laboratory in the 1960s when the JPL mission expanded. The primary objective of the observatory is the study of Solar System objects. There are five telescopes: a 1.2–m reflector; a 1.04–m reflector; a 0.6–m reflector; a 0.4–m reflector; and a 0.27–m Schmidt

camera. A 1.2–m reflector was completed in 1991. Professional astronomers may request observing time by contacting: Director, Division of Earth and Space Sciences, Jet Propulsion Laboratory, 4800 Oak Grove Dr., Pasadena, CA 91109. The facility is not open for public viewing.

Accomplishments of TMO include: asteroid studies to determine rotation rate, albedo, and orbit parameters of asteroids; and discovery of the sodium cloud around Io. Studies of Mars, Venus, and comets are ongoing projects.

The Observatory is being upgraded with modern instruments, infrared and optical, and computer controls.

Colorado

★ **Black Forest Observatory,** 12815 Porcupine Lane, Colorado Springs, CO 80908. Tel. (719) 495–3828. The observatory bills itself as a non-profit independent educational corporation. The

Left, the main building of the U.S. Naval Observatory; right, the dome housing the observatory's 26–inch refractor.

telescopes are: 32–inch f/9 Cassegrain on a German equatorial mount; a 17.5–inch f/4.5 Newtonian on an alt-azimuth mount; a 10–inch f/16 Cassegrain on a German equatorial mount; an 8–inch f/10 Schmidt-Cassegrain on a fork mount; a 6–inch f/16 Maksutov-Cassegrain on a fork mount; a 3–inch f/15 refractor on a German equatorial mount.

The Observatory holds public viewings and will be offering observatory time on a prepaid reservation basis to amateur and professional astronomers. There are currently no formal research projects underway.

★ **Chamberlin Observatory,** Physics Department, University of Denver, Denver, CO 80208. Tel. (303) 871–2238.

★ **Sommers-Bausch Observatory,** University of Colorado, Boulder, CO 80309. Tel. (303) 492–6732.

★ **Tiara Observatory,** P.O. Box 1059, Colorado Springs, CO 80901. Tel. (719) 597–3603. Prof. Terry E. Schmidt, director. The observatory was founded in 1969, with the pier for the first telescope poured on July 20, as Neil Armstrong walked on the Moon. The observatory has seven buildings, and is the largest professional observatory in Colorado. The instruments are: 16–inch, f/11 Cassegrain; 16–inch f/4.5 Newton; four astrographs mounted together for red, blue, yellow, and no filter photography; 6–inch horizontal refractor fed by an 8–inch flat mirror

for planetary and lunar work; an 8–inch Schmidt camera for comet work; a meteor research building with three-prism spectrographs, two color index cameras, a radiant camera, three meteor train spectrographs, a color train camera, and an image intensifier. There are also solar eclipse telescopes.

Since the institution is devoted to research it does not hold public viewing sessions often. However, special group sessions occasionally can be arranged by contacting the director.

Professional astronomers may reserve time, also by contacting the director. Costs are kept at a "minimum."

The observatory concentrates on inner Solar System research concerning comets, meteors, meteorites, meteorite craters, solar eclipses, Mars, zodiacal light, gegenschein, lunar libration clouds, and inner Solar System debris. The research files contain more than 200 meteor spectra. The meteorite collection has more than 518 different falls and finds, and the observatory runs a worldwide meteorite recovery program. It also offers color slides of solar eclipses.

Other findings include: first to discover the 1973 dust storm on Mars that engulfed the planet; first observatory to successfully do photoelectric photometry on Halley's Comet to determine the rotation of the nucleus. Also, determined the rotation periods of many asteroids. Currently the observatory is tying together observations to explain the phenomena associated with inner Solar System debris, with the major emphasis on meteors and meteorites.

The observatory is owned and operated by Tersch Enterprises, Colorado Springs, which supplies astronomical slides to buyers worldwide. Five percent of the observatory time is devoted to taking new photos, with the remaining 95 percent to research.

Connecticut

★ **The Stamford Observatory,** 39 Scofieldtown Rd., Stamford, CT 06903. Tel. (203) 322-1648. The observatory is part of the Stamford Museum & Nature Center, and is open to the public Friday from 8 p.m. to 10 p.m. The observatory's 22-inch research telescope is the second largest in Connecticut. Admission is: adults, $3; children under 12, $2. The Fairfield County Astronomical Society holds its regular meeting at the observatory the first Friday of each month. Amateur telescope facilities are available. The research facility's principal program is the study of variable stars.

★ **Western Connecticut State University Observatory,** 181 White S. Danbury, CT 06810. (203) 797-2774.

★ **Van Vleck Observatory,** Wesleyan University, Middletown, CT 06457. Tel. (203) 347-9411.

Delaware

★ **Mount Cuba Astronomical Observatory,** Box 3915, Greenville, DE 19807. Tel. (302) 654-6407.

District of Columbia

★ **U.S. Naval Observatory,** 34th St. and Massachusetts Ave., NW, Washington, D.C. 20392. Tel. (202) 653-1507. When founded in 1830, the purpose of the observatory was to create and store navigational charts for the U.S. Navy. Since then, it has become the official timekeeper for the United States, and also the site of several important discoveries, including Asaph Hall's discovery of the two moons of Mars. The observatory maintains an astronomical library which includes many rare books, including treatises by Galileo and Copernicus. Public tours are given every Monday night except federal holidays on a space available basis. Call or write the observatory for more information.

Florida

★ **Fox Observatory,** Operated by the South Florida Amateur Astronomers Association, Robert Markham Park, 16000 W. State Road 84, Fort Lauderdale, FL 33326. The observatory houses a 14-inch reflector and a 6.5-inch refractor.

Members built the Fox Observatory and donated it to Broward County in 1976.

★ **Gibson Observatory,** 4801 Dreher Trail North, West Palm Beach, FL 33405–3099. Tel. (407) 832–1988. The observatory is part of the planetarium of the South Florida Science Museum. The observatory houses a 15.5–inch Newtonian, three C–8s, two C–5s, and two 4–inch refractors, plus several 6–inch Newtonians. Public viewing sessions held. See Gibson Observatory Astronomer's Group in the **Local Astronomy Clubs** section of Chapter 2.

Georgia

★ **Bradley Observatory and Hard Labor Creek Observatory,** Agnes Scott College, Decatur, GA 30030. Recently moved a 30–inch telescope to the Hard Labor Creek Observatory. It previously was on the Agnes Scott College Campus. The telescope was built in 1930 and owned by a Pennsylvania amateur. It was sold to the college in 1949, but forced to move in 1990 because of light pollution. Public observing is available at the Agnes Scott campus on the first Friday of each month, October through May. The program consists of a lecture and slide show, planetarium show, and a look through a 14–inch telescope. At the Hard Labor Creek Observatory, public viewing is scheduled about ten times per year with the 30–inch and 16–inch telescopes.

Professional astronomers may reserve time at either observatory by contacting the Agnes Scott College or Georgia State University. Decisions are made on a case-by-case basis and generally there is no charge for research purposes. In the future, Dr. Alberto C. Sadun, director of the observatory, says the telescope primarily will be devoted to the investigation of Active Galactic Nuclei (AGN) such as quasars and BL Lac objects. Other phenomena related to active galaxies to be studied include jets, multiple nuclei, and other unusual morphology. The observatory plans to add instrumentation, photoelectric photometry, photography, and CCD electronic photography.

★ **Fernbank Science Center Observatory,** 156 Heaton Park, Atlanta, GA 30307. Tel. (404) 378–4311. Houses a 36–inch reflecting telescope used for photography of compact galaxies, photometry of double stars and asteroids, and spectroscopy of stars. Is part of the Fernbank Science Center.

★ **Valdosta State College Observatory,** Department of Physics, Astronomy, and Geology, Valdosta, GA 31698. Tel. (912) 333–5752.

Hawaii

★ **Canada-France-Hawaii Telescope,** P.O. Box 1597, Kamulea, HI 96743. Tel. (808) 885–7944. Fax (808) 885–7288.

Telex 633147. Summit (808) 935–4511. This major observatory was founded jointly by the National Research Council of Canada, the French National Center for Scientific Research, and the University of Hawaii. The 3.6–meter telescope is atop Mauna Kea on the island of Hawaii. It saw first light on Aug. 6, 1979, and has been involved in serious astronomy work since.

Astronomers seeking access to the telescope must submit their observation program to a committee in charge of assigning observing time. Approximately 6 percent of observations are of Solar System objects; 12 percent of interstellar space; 36 percent of the stars of our galaxy; and 46 percent of objects outside our galaxy.

Some accomplishments include: determining the ratio of the relative abundance of deuterium and hydrogen in the atmosphere of Mars; observing the occultation of two satellites of Jupiter (the passage of Callisto in front of Io); analyzing interstellar space to show the presence of molecular clouds, three of which are less than 16 light-years away from the Solar System; discovering indications of carbon stars in several galaxies very close to our own; measuring the abundance of lithium in dwarf stars of solar type. Also, the Observatory has concluded that globular clusters, made up of several hundreds of thousands of stars in a roughly spherical configuration, date back to the origin of our galaxy. And the observatory's study of galaxies shows the presence of central cores that are much denser than surrounding regions, which may be super-massive black holes. The Observatory also is studying the diffuse environments of quasars.

★ **Mauna Kea Observatory,** P.O. Box 4729, Hilo, HI 96721. Tel. (808) 935–3373. One of the newer observatory sites in the world, the Mauna Kea site includes a number of facilities, including: a 3.0–meter (120–inch) Infrared Telescope Facility built by NASA and operated by the University of Hawaii; a 3.8–meter United Kingdom Infrared Telescope; and the 10–meter Keck Telescope. Several countries and universities operate telescopes atop the mountain, which, at 13,800–feet, is clear and dry.

Illinois

★ **Walter H. Blacke Observatory,** Illinois College, Jacksonville, IL 62650. A part of the college, the observatory has 14–inch and 10–inch Celestron telescopes. See the **Local Astronomy Clubs** section in Chapter 2 for more information.

★ **Dearborn Observatory/Lindheimer Astronomical Research Center, Northwestern University,** Department of Physics and Astronomy, 2145 Sheridan Road, Evanston, IL 60208–3112. Dr. Melville Ulmer, director. Since 1967 the Astronomy Department has performed photometry and spectroscopy of distant galaxies and quasars; provided catalogues of physical characteristics of stars; undertaken X-ray and radio astronomy; studied the evolution of dense white dwarfs and neutron stars. Other areas of study in recent years include: mass transfer in binary stars; comparison of the X-ray center of clusters of galaxies and optical centers; common envelope evolution of interacting binary systems; flux-limited diffusion theory; studies of the galactic center; gamma-ray astrophysics; Herbig Haro objects; the hydrodynamics of accretion; infrared observations of 20 interacting galaxies; interstellar matter: a network of string-like ionized features in the Orion Nebula; X-ray bursts; and X-ray mirrors.

Northwestern also uses the Corralitos Observatory, the school's remote satellite observatory. Since 1926, the Dearborn Observatory in Evanston has offered free tours as a community service.

★ **Illinois Wesleyan University Observatory,** Bloomington, IL 61702. Tel. (309) 556–3176.

★ **Northern Illinois University Observatory,** Physics Department, De Kalb, IL 60115. Tel. (815) 753–1772.

★ **University of Illinois Observatory,** Astronomy Department, 103 Astronomy Building, 1002 W. Green St., Urbana, IL 61801. Tel. (217) 333–3090.

Indiana

★ **Goethe Link Observatory,** Indiana University Astronomy Department, Swain Hall W. 319, Bloomington, IN 47405. Tel. (812) 855–6911.

★ **J.I. Holcomb Observatory,** 4600 Sunset Ave., Butler University, Indianapolis, IN 46208. Tel. (317) 283–9282. Ronald G. Samec, director. Houses a 38–inch Cassegrain reflector. A three-phase funding program is underway to re-gear and add motors to the telescope; add a microcomputer to drive the telescope; and to add a CCD camera for research.

★ **McKim Observatory,** Department of Physics & Astronomy, DePauw University, Greencastle, IN 46135. Tel. (317) 658–4654. Built in 1884, the observatory contains the original equipment acquired when the facility was built. A meridian circle transit telescope manufactured by Fauth and Company is used to observe the transit of the Sun across the local meridian. The main telescope is the 9.5–inch clear aperture refractor built by Warner and Swasey. The objective lens was produced by Alvan Clark and Sons. Regular public tours are arranged.

★ **Wahnsiedler Observatory,** Lynnville City Park, operated by the Evansville Astronomical Society. Tel. (812) 922–5681. Open to the public the third Friday of each month, except August. No admission. The entrance to the Lynnville City park is one mile west of the Lynnville exit of Interstate 64 on Indiana State Route 68.

Iowa

★ **Drake University Municipal Observatory,** Des Moines, IA 50311. Tel. (515) 271–3033.

★ **Erwin W. Fick Observatory,** Physics Department, Iowa State University, Ames, IA 50011. Tel. (515) 294–3668.

★ **Witte Observatory,** 610 Walnut, Burlington, IA 52601–5902. The observatory equipment includes a 12–inch f/15 Alvan Clark refracting telescope; an 8–inch f/7 Fecker refracting telescope; CCD camera with Amiga computer and related software; slide projector; VCR. Meeting place for Southeastern Astronomy Club. See **Local Astronomy Clubs** section in Chapter 2.

Kansas

★ **Lake Afton Public Observatory,** MacArthur Road at 247th St. W., Wichita, KS 67213. Tel. (316) 794–8995.

★ **Powell Observatory,** Louisburg, KS. The Observatory is owned and operated by Astronomical Society of Kansas City, P.O. Box 400, Blue Springs, KS 64013. The observatory has a 30–inch Newtonian

which is computer controlled and a 4–inch refractor. See **Local Astronomy Clubs** section in Chapter 2 for more information.

★ **Clyde W. Tombaugh Observatory,** Department of Physics and Astronomy, University of Kansas, Lawrence, KS 66045. Tel. (913) 864–4626.

Kentucky

★ **Golden Pond Observatory,** Paducah, Kentucky. The Observatory has an Ash Dome, 12.5–inch reflector, and a 4.5–inch refractor.

★ **Roberts Observatory,** Berea College, Berea, KY 40404. Tel. (606) 986–9342, ext. 6240. Contact Smith Powell or Hamdy Kemp. Founded in 1929, on the campus, the observatory began with a 4–inch refractor. In 1972, a 16–inch Boller & Chivens reflector was installed. Open to the public one night per week. Not involved in research, and generally not open to astronomers outside the school, but special proposals would be considered.

Maryland

★ **Harford County Astronomical Society Observatory,** P.O. Box 906, Bel Air, MD 21014. The observatory is on the campus of the Harford Community College. The observatory has a 16–inch Cassegrain, a meeting room, a library, and a computing room nearby. A public observatory open house is held each month.

★ **University of Maryland Observatory,** Astronomy Program, College Park, MD 20742. Tel. (301) 454-3001.

Massachusetts

★ **Amherst College Observatory,** Dept. of Astronomy, Amherst College, Amherst, MA 01002. Tel. (413) 542-2138. The observatory has an 18-inch Clark refractor, and frequently holds public sessions in cooperation with the Amherst Area Amateur Astronomers Association.

★ **Harvard-Smithsonian Center for Astrophysics,** 60 Garden St., Cambridge, MA 02138. Tel. (617) 495-7461. The Center for Astrophysics (CFA) combines the Harvard College Observatory and the Smithsonian Astrophysical Observatory under a single director. The joint center was formed in 1973 following several years of cooperation. There are approximately 140 Smithsonian and Harvard scientists working at the center. Among the topics under study are:

■ **High Energy Astrophysics**—X-ray astronomy using instruments aboard satellites, rockets, and the Space Shuttle; development of new instrumentation for future space missions; research into the amount of matter in the Universe, and the origin, evolution, and ultimate fate of the Universe.

■ **Optical and Infrared Astronomy**—Extragalactic and galactic astronomy, studying the large-scale structure of the Universe, clusters of stars and of galaxies, and the formation and evolution of stars by using data from ground-based observations; and spectroscopy and imaging techniques.

■ **Planetary Sciences**—Studies of the planets and their satellites, and small bodies of the solar system.

■ **Solar and Stellar Physics**—Theoretical investigations of solar and stellar processes; studies of the Sun and stars via spaceflight instruments; construction of model stellar atmospheres.

■ **Theoretical Astrophysics**—Analyses and mathematical models of astronomical systems to study interiors of stars, the properties of atoms and molecules in interstellar space, spiral structure in galaxies, high temperature plasmas, formation of planets, and theories of the early Universe.

The Center was a pioneer in development of instrumentation for orbiting observatories, and participated in the "CFA Redshift Survey," a precise determination of distances to approximately 2,000 galaxies.

Observing facilities include: The Whipple Observatory, in Arizona; Oak Ridge Observatory, at Harvard University, which has a 61–inch reflector; sky patrol cameras; an 84–foot radio antenna, now being used in a search for extraterrestrial intelligence; and the George R. Agassiz Station at Fort Davis, Texas, which features 28–foot and 85–foot radio antennas involved in solar research and Very Long Baseline Interferometry.

The Harvard College Observatory has a collection of approximately 400,000 astronomical photographic plates, the largest of its kind in the world. The earliest plates were taken in the mid–1880s, and the collection continues to grow. The **Henry Draper Catalog** of the spectra of more than 200,000 stars was classified using such plates.

The facilities are open only to astronomers affiliated or associated with the CFA.Public tours are scheduled the third Thursday of every month.

★ **Hopkins Observatory,** Williams College, Williamstown, MA 01267. Tel. (413) 597–2188.

★ **Maria Mitchell Observatory,** 3 Vestal St., Nantucket, MA 02554. Tel. (508) 228–9273.

★ **Wheaton College Observatory,** Wheaton College, Norton, MA 02766. Tel. (508) 285–7722, ext. 422. The observatory is located on the roof of the college Science Center. There are seven telescopes; two computerized 14–inch scopes and four Celestron 8 telescopes. A CCD television camera is mounted on one 14–inch telescope. The observatory is designed for use by students taking astronomy courses, but small research projects are possible. The department is searching for supernovas in other galaxies by using CCD images. The observatory is open to the public each clear Thursday even while college is in session. There are, on average, 50 visitors per night. In the future, the observatory staff plans to do photometry as well as direct imaging, and later to produce color pictures.

Michigan

★ **Michigan State University Observatory,** Department of Physics and Astronomy, Physics-Astronomy Building, East Lansing, MI 48824–1116. Tel. (517) 353–6784. The observatory was built in 1970, and the main instrument is a 0.6–m reflector by Boller and Chivens. A solar telescope also is in use. The 0.6–m telescope is mainly used for photometric studies using a CCD detector.

Current programs involve photometry of RR Lyrae variable stars in both the galactic field and in globular star clusters. Solar work involves imaging of the solar disk related to studies of solar oscillations. The 0.6–m also has been used in the development of a new infrared array camera.

Public viewing is available one weekend each month from spring through fall. Astronomers interested in observing with the 0.6–m should contact Professor Jeff Kuhn in the Dept. of Physics and Astronomy.

★ **Peach Mountain Observatory,** 9287 Chestnut Circle, Dexter, MI 48130. The University Lowbrow Astronomers operate a 24–inch McMath telescope at Peach Mountain. Club members may reserve the telescope for exclusive use during the week. The club maintains a library of books and astronomical software.

★ **Stargate Observatory,** P.O. Box 1505, Warren, MI 48090–1505. Owned by the Warren Astronomical Society and Rotary International, in conjunction with the Rotary International. The observatory features a 12.5–inch Cassegrain telescope. It is open to all club members. Areas of interest of members of the society include solar, lunar/planetary, cosmology, deep sky, and computer studies.

★ **James C. Veen Observatory,** 3308 Kissing Rock Road, Lowell, MI 49331. Tel. (616) 897–7065. The observatory has four fully equipped optical telescopes, a meeting room, library and darkroom. The observatory is open to the public twice a month from April through October.

Minnesota

★ **Macalester College Observatory,** 1600 Grand Ave., St. Paul, MN 55105. Tel. (612) 696–6383.

Mississippi

★ **The Rainwater Observatory & Planetarium,** at the French Camp Academy, French Camp, MS 39745. Tel. (601) 547–6970 or 6865 or 6113. The observatory has 17 telescopes and is open to individuals and groups by appointment. Ten of the telescopes are equatorial driven, and housed in four movable-roof buildings. The largest is a 20.5–inch reflector. Also has a Meade DS–16 with refigured optics; a 12.5–inch Ritchey-Cretien Cassegrain; a 10–inch Schmidt-Cassegrain; three 6–inch Newtonians; a 4–inch Unitron refractor; a 5.7–inch rich field refractor; a 4–inch SCT; 95mm binocular telescope; 80mm refractor; and two 9.5–inch Maksutov Cassegrains. Also has five telescopes for solar viewing. Has a library, a complete array of nebular and color filters, and access to the school's darkroom.

Missouri

★ **Laws Observatory,** 223 Physics Building, University of Missouri- Columbia, Columbia, MO 65211. Tel. (314) 882–3335.

Was one of the first observatories built west of the Allegheny Mountains. In 1880, a 7.5–inch Merz refractor was added and used for photometric and astrometric work by Professors Milton Updegraff, Frederick H. Seares, and Robert H. Baker. Harlow Shapley received his first experience in observational astronomy at the Laws Observatory. By 1920, the observatory had ceased active observational research. The Central Missouri Amateur Astronomers plan to relocate the telescope to their Wildhaven Observatory north of Columbia. Currently, the observatory has a 16–inch Celestron telescope used for undergraduate and graduate training and for a weekly public viewing program in conjunction with the Central Missouri Amateur Astronomers. The University Department of Physics and Astronomy, in collaboration with the Southwest Missouri State University, jointly operate the Baker Observatory, which houses a research-grade 16–inch telescope on permanent loan from Cerro Tololo Inter-American Observatory. A Photometris Ltd. CCD photometric system is being used for observational programs on variable stars, star clusters, and photometry of nearby bright galaxies.

Nebraska

★ **Behlen Observatory,** Department of Physics and Astronomy, University of Nebraska, Lincoln, NE 68588. Tel. (402) 472–2770.

New Hampshire

★ **Shattuck Observatory,** Wilder Hall, Dartmouth College, Hanover, NH 03755. Tel. (603) 646–2034.

★ **University of New Hampshire Observatory,** Physics Department, DeMeritt Hall, Durham, NH 03824. Tel. (603) 862–1950.

New Jersey

★ **Princeton University Observatory,** Peyton Hall, Princeton, NJ 08544. Tel. (609) 452–3800.

★ **William Miller Sperry Observatory,** Union County College, 1033 Springfield Ave., Cranford, NJ, 07016. Tel. (908) 709–7520. Dedicated in 1967, the observatory is the home of the Amateur Astronomers Inc. The observatory houses a 10–inch f/15 refractor built by members of the AAI and a 24–inch Cassegrain reflecting telescope. Darkroom facilities, a computer room, and a machine shop also are available.

New Mexico

★ **Apache Point Observatory,** P.O. Box 59, 2001 Apache Point Rd., Sunspot, NM

88349. Tel. (505) 437–6822. A cooperative effort of the University of Chicago, Washington State University, the University of Washington, New Mexico State, and Princeton University. This is one of the newest observatories in the Southwest.

★ **National Radio Astronomy Observatory,** P.O. Box O, Socorro, NM 87801–0387. Tel. (505) 835–7000. TWX (910) 9881710. Fax (505) 835–7027. National Radio Astronomy Observatory Very Large Array is operated by the Associated Universities Research Association under a cooperative agreement with the National Science Foundation. The observatory consists of an array of 27 dish-shaped antennas on the Plains of San Augstin. Each antenna has a 25–meter (82–foot) diameter, an accuracy of better than 0.05 inch, and focuses radio waves as short as 0.4 inch. Observations generally go on 24 hours a day, seven days a week. More than 400 programs are scheduled annually, involving more than 700 astronomers from around the world. In 1990, more than 230 scientific papers based on new VLA data were published.

Only professional astronomers may use the facilities. Observing time is allocated on the basis of proposals, which should be sent to NRAO, Edgemont Road, Charlottesville, VA 22903–2475. Deadlines are the 15 of February, June, and October for the next configuration, following review. The facility averages about 50 experiments each month.

The NRAO plans to build a Very Long Baseline Array with a series of additions, including placing four VLBA data recorders at the VLA site in New Mexico (to be done as soon as money is available). On the long-term wish list, the NRAO hopes to construct four additional antennas in New Mexico and Arizona, and link the VLA via optic fibers to the new antennas and to nearby VLBA antennas. Plans also call for replacing the receivers operating on the 21, 6, 2, and 1.3 cm wavelength with new VLBA-style receivers as soon as the dollars are available, and to expand the bandwidth of the VLA observations from 100 MHz to 2000 MHz by transmitting the received signals via optic fibers to the correlator and replacing the correlator with high-speed design.

★ **National Solar Observatory,** P.O. Box 62, Sunspot, NM 88349–0062. Tel. (505) 434–7000. Fax (505) 434–7029 or 7009. Telex: 1561030. The National Solar Observatory has facilities at Sacramento Peak, New Mexico, Kitt Peak, and Tucson, Arizona. It is a division of the National Optical Astronomy Observatories, and is operated by the Association of Universities for Research in Astronomy, Inc. (AURA).

At the Sacramento Peak facility, the primary instrument is the Vacuum Tower Telescope, which has 0.2 arc seconds resolution and has proven excellent for work on the intricacies of the surface features on the Sun.

The Kitt Peak and Tucson facilities feature a 1.5–meter McMath Telescope on Kitt Peak. It is the largest solar telescope in the world. This telescope can be used in solar, stellar, and planetary observations, and is one of the few telescopes in the world that is regularly used 24 hours per day. The other major NSO telescope on Kitt Peak is the Vacuum Telescope, which is used to observe the solar magnetic field.

The equipment and facilities of the National Solar Observatory are available for research and educational programs in solar physics, solar-stellar physics, and related fields. Data obtained with NSO telescopes are in the public domain.

The Director of the NSO allocates use of the facilities on the basis of scientific proposals that are reviewed by each site's Telescope Allocation Committee. Proposals are considered quarterly. Submission deadlines are: Winter Quarter, October 15; Spring Quarter, January 15; Summer Quarter, April 15; and Fall Quarter, July 15.

New York

★ **Dudley Observatory**, 69 Union Ave., Schenectady, NY 12308. Tel. (518) 382–7583. No longer an active observatory.

★ **Kopernik Observatory,** Underwood Road, Vestal, NY 13850. Tel. (607) 748–3685. Observatory is part of the Roberson Center for the Arts and Sciences. Houses a 12–inch Tinsley and a 14–inch Celestron. An active amateur astronomy society opens the scopes to the public on Friday and sometimes Wednesdays. Holds star parties and an annual Astro-Fest in May.

★ **Martz Observatory,** 176 Robin Hill Road, Frewsburg, NY 14738. Tel. (716) 483–0343. The observatory has 30–inch, 17.5–inch, and 8–inch Newtonians; a library; 50–seat meeting room; and a planetarium projector. It was opened in 1965 and is operated by the Marshal Martz Memorial Astronomical Association. It is used primarily for public education; tours are available by reservation. The club plans to add a 30–inch Dobson telescope and convert the original instrument to a CCD imaging device.

North Carolina

★ **Three College Observatory,** Department of Physics and Astronomy, University of North Carolina at Greensboro, Greensboro, NC 27412. Tel. (919) 334–5669.

North Dakota

★ **Minot State University Observatory,** Minot State University, Minot, ND 58701. Tel. (701) 256–3620.

Ohio

★ **Apollo Observatory,** 2629 Ridge Ave., Dayton, OH 45414. Tel. (513) 275–7433 or 275–7431. The Apollo Observatory site has a 50–cm Cassegrain plus eight other telescopes, and a library with more than 500 books. Nearby is the John Bryan State Park Observatory, which has a dome and a 12–inch and 16–inch reflector, plus a darkroom and telescope-building room. Both facilities are used by the Miami Valley Astronomical Society.

★ **Perkins Observatory,** P.O. Box 449, Delaware, Ohio 43015. Tel. (614) 363–1257. Founded in 1923, the observatory originally was operated by Ohio Wesleyan University. In 1931, The Ohio State University signed a joint agreement with OWU. The first telescope used a 60–inch mirror from the Harvard College Observatory. A 69–inch mirror was completed in 1928, and used until 1961, when the mirror was relocated to a site near Flagstaff, Arizona. Today, the observatory serves as a meeting site for the Columbus Astronomical Society and holds monthly viewing nights for the public. The telescope is a 32–inch reflecting telescope.

Also on the grounds is the "Big Ear" radio telescope. This radio telescope today is used primarily for the Search for Extraterrestrial Intelligence. This search is the longest, continually operating search in the world.

The observatory public viewing sessions are held one Thursday of each month. Additionally, the Columbus Astronomical Society holds several public viewing sessions each year.

★ **Warren Rupp Observatory,** P.O. Box 1118, Mansfield, OH 44901. Tel. (419) 524–7814. Operated by the Richland Astronomical Society, the 31–inch telescope is used primarily by club members and for the club's public education programs.

Oregon

★ **Pine Mountain Observatory,** P.M.O Bend-Burns State Route, Bend OR 97701. Tel. (503) 382–8331.

★ **Vernonia Peak Observatory,** 55371 McDonald Road, Vernonia, OR 97064. Tel. (503) 429–2430.

Pennsylvania

★ **Allegheny Observatory,** Observatory Station, University of Pittsburgh, Pittsburgh, PA 15214. Tel. (412) 321–2400.

★ **Edinboro University Observatory,** Edinboro University, Edinboro, PA 16444. Tel. (814) 732–2469. The observatory houses a 16–inch Schmidt-Cassegrain telescope, with camera adapters and a photometer. The system also is used during the day via an aperture diaphragm energy reduction filter, making the solar beam f/30, and a solar H-alpha filter. In addition, four portable telescopes are available for students.

In 1982, under the direction of faculty astronomer Dr. James C. LoPresto, the University added a Solar Observational Laboratory, which houses an eight-inch flat Heliostat. The priority is education about the Sun.

★ **Keystone Junior College Observatory,** P.O. Box 50, LaPlume, PA 18440–0200. Tel. (717) 945–5141, ext. 3110 or 2004. Thomas G. Cupillari, observatory director. The observatory boasts a 9.5–inch glass from Alvan Clark & Sons. The instrument was built in 1882 for Beloit College, WI. Keystone shares its observatory with the public and permits students in the public schools and colleges to use it free of charge. Evening viewing hours are scheduled and lecture programs conducted on Wednesdays in early September through mid-November and March through May, and on Mondays and Wednesdays in July. The Lackawanna Astronomical Society and Keystone work closely together. The Society has its own telescope at the site and shares the use of the service building with its darkroom and reference library.

★ **Nicholas E. Wagman Observatory,** Deer Lakes Park, Pittsburgh, PA 15116. Contact the Amateur Astronomers Association of Pittsburgh, Inc., P.O. Box 314, Glenshaw, PA 15116. Tel. (412) 224–2510. The Association owns and operates the Nicholas E. Wagman Observatory, which houses a 12.5–inch Newtonian. Plans are to add a classroom, a permanently mounted 10–inch Schiefspiegler, and an 11–inch Brashear refractor.

Rhode Island

★ **Ladd Observatory,** Brown University, 210 Doyle Ave., Providence, RI 02912. David Targan, director. The observatory was founded in 1891, at the insistence of Prof. Winslow Upton. The observatory has a 12–inch refractor with a 15–foot focal length, a meeting room, a "library" of transparent photographs, and other astronomical instruments. Although located in a residential area where light pollution limits the research work, the telescope still is used as a teaching aid and for public shows. Open every Wednesday with volunteers guiding the telescope.

South Carolina

★ **Charles E. Daniel Observatory,** 504 Roper Mountain Rd., Greenville, SC 29615. Tel. (803) 297–0232. The observatory has a 23–inch refractor designed by Alvan Clark which originally served at Princeton's Halstead Observatory. Today the instrument is used by local amateur astronomers and Greenville county schools. It is open for tours each Friday.

Tennessee

★ **A.J. Dyer Observatory,** Vanderbilt University, Box 1803 Station B., Nashville, TN 37235. Tel. (615) 373–4897. The observatory was dedicated in 1953. Its principal instruments are a 24–inch reflecting telescope and a 12–inch reflecting telescope. The 24–inch telescope has a camera and photoelectric photometry. A 16–inch automatic photoelectric telescope is located on Mount Hopkins in Arizona. The observatory is open to the general public approximately eight nights per year. Professional astronomers may request observing time by contacting the director. The cost is "negotiable."

Among the research programs are: a study of starburst in early-type galaxies; observations of atmospheric eclipses of zeta Aurigae binaries; spectroscopic observations of eclipsing binaries.

Texas

★ **McDonald Observatory,** P.O. Box 1337, Fort Davis, TX 79734. Tel. (915) 426–3640. One of the larger sites in the U.S., the McDonald Observatory has a 2.7–meter (107–inch) telescope; a 2.1–meter (80–inch); a 0.8–meter (30–inch); a 0.9–meter (36–inch); and a 0.8–meter (30–inch) laser telescope. Also, ground

will be broken soon for an 8–meter (320–inch) Multiple Mirror Telescope for Spectroscope Surveys. The new telescope will consist of 85 1–meter telescopes that will work as one. It will be funded by the University of Texas, the University of Munich, Rutgers University, and Penn State University.

McDonald conducts a public education program every day of operations, starting at 9:30 a.m. There is no cost. Public viewing times are scheduled regularly, and the 107–inch telescope is open periodically. Only 60 people can attend viewing sessions on the 107–inch, and reservations must be made in advance.

Professionals may reserve time on the instruments by contacting: Dr. Tom Barnes, University of Texas at Austin, RLM 15.208, Austin, TX 78701. Tel. (512) 471–1301.

Utah

★ **Physics Department Observatory,** 201 James Fletcher Bldg., Univ. of Utah, Salt Lake City, UT 84112. Tel. (801) 581–7140.

Vermont

★ **Green Mountain Observatory,** P.O. Box 782, Williston, VT 05495. Tel. (802) 878–3459.

Virginia

★ **Leander McCormick Observatory,** Department of Astronomy, University of Virginia, P.O. Box 3818, Charlottesville, VA 22903–0818. Tel. (804) 924–7494. The Observatory was built around 1883 with a donation from the developer of the McCormick reaper. Operated by the University of Virginia, the observatory features a 66–cm refractor; a 76–cm reflector; and a 100–cm astrometric reflector. The observatory plate file has 140,000 plates, taken since 1914, to study stellar positions and motions.

The observatory is used for student research and training, and for astrometric programs.Among the major research programs are: stars and stellar evolution, including interpretation of globular cluster photometry; ultraviolet spectral properties of normal stars; interstellar medium studies; and galaxies and active galactic nuclei studies.

Public viewing is scheduled the first and third Friday evenings.

Washington

★ **Goldendale Observatory,** 1602 Observatory Drive, Goldendale, WA 98620. Tel. (509) 773–3141. Contact Stephen R. Stout. A public telescope operated by The Washington State Parks and Recreation Commission. It was operated by The Goldendale Observatory Corporation, a non–profit, volunteer organization, from 1973 until 1980. The observatory has a 24.5–inch reflecting telescope. Other instruments include 10 portable telescopes, special camera accessories, a science library, and an 8–inch mounted telescope. The observatory serves the public and amateur astronomers in the area, but is not used in professional work. Tours are available. Amateurs may reserve the facility after 11 p.m.

West Virginia

★ **National Radio Astronomy Observatory,** P.O. Box 2, Green Bank, WV 24944. Tel. (304) 456–2011. The site of the first NRAO telescopes, the 140–foot, the 300–foot, and the Interferometer. The site also contains an array of three radio telescopes, each with a diameter of 85 feet. This array detected steady radio emission from stars and confirmed Einstein's theory of relativity by measuring the bending of radio waves near the Sun. The 300–foot telescope at the site collapsed recently, and has not been rebuilt. Applications for observing time at the Green Bank site are approved by the director of NRAO. Send proposals to: NRAO, Edgemont Rd., Charlottesville, VA 22903–2475.

Wisconsin

★ **Modine-Benstead Observatory,** the Racine Astronomical Society, Inc., P.O. Box 085694, Racine, WI 53403. The observatory houses a 16–inch Cassegrain/Newtonian; a 14–inch Schmidt-Cassegrain; a 12.5–inch Newtonian; an 8–inch Schmidt Camera; a 6–inch refractor; and a 4–inch Schmidt-Cassegrain; plus a meeting room, a small library, a rudimentary workshop, and a darkroom. The observatory is open to the public every clear Thursday from May through September.

★ **Yerkes Observatory,** 373 W. Geneva St., P.O. Box 258, Williams Bay, WI 53191. Tel. (414) 245–5555. One of the great observatories of the U.S., Yerkes began operation in the late 1890s. The instruments at this facility include the world's largest refractor, a 40–inch instrument which still is in use; a 41–inch reflector; and a 24–inch reflector. The observatory takes part in studies of the proper motion of stars, distances to the stars, and astronomical studies from the Antarctic. Staff astronomers also are associated with the new observatory at Apache Point, New Mexico.

The Observatory conducts public tours and viewing throughout the year, primarily on Saturdays. It also has a sales shop, and has a large number of prints of famous astronomers who have visited or worked at the site.

Private viewing can be scheduled for the 24–inch telescope, and professional astronomers can apply for time on the Yerkes instrument or the Apache Point instrument.

Wyoming

★ **Wyoming Infrared Observatory,** Department of Physics and Astronomy, University of Wyoming, Laramie, WY 892071. Tel. (307) 766–6150.

Canada

★ **Burke-Gaffney Observatory,** Department of Astronomy, Saint Mary's University, Halifax, Nova Scotia, Canada B3H 3C3. Tel. (902) 420–5633. The main instrument of the observatory is a 40–cm Cassegrain reflecting telescope. It is used primarily for teaching, and students may use the spectrographs, photoelectric photometer, and electrostatic image intensifier tube. Students at the university also use the Canada-France-Hawaii telescope, plus other telescopes in Canada, Arizona, and Chile. Current research includes studies of star clusters, the structure of the Milky Way, pulsating Cepheid variable stars, the creation of molecules in comets, and interstellar gas clouds.

Special tours can be arranged by contacting the department of astronomy. Free public tours are held on Saturdays, beginning at 7 p.m. November through April; or 9 p.m. May through October.

★ **Climenhaga Observatory,** Department of Physics and Astronomy, P.O. Box 3055, Victoria, B.C., Canada V8W 3P6. Tel. (604) 721–7698. The 0.5–meter telescope has been used for studies of period changes in eclipsing binaries. The facilities also include control programs that allow automatic centering, spiral searches, and multiple star sequences.

★ **Devon Astronomical Observatory,** Department of Physics, 412 Avadh Bhatia Physics Laboratory, University of Alberta, Edmonton, Canada T6G 2J1. Tel. (403) 432–5286 or (403) 432–4127. Established in 1967, the observatory has a 20–inch folded Cassegrain/Cassegrain telescope equipped with a two-star pulse counting photometer. The principal research is in high precision photometry of eclipsing binaries and intrinsically variable early-type stars. The observatory is not open to the general public, except under special circumstances. Although the telescope is, in principle, open to outside professional astronomers, in practice, there is too little available time for them. The telescope is used by graduate and advanced undergraduate students under the supervision of Dr. B.E. Martin, and Dr. Douglas P. Hube. Proposed developments include the addition of a Charge-Coupled Device photometric and imaging system.

The University also operates a Campus Observatory, which includes a 12–inch Cassegrain and a 14–inch Cassegrain, plus smaller instruments. The Campus Observatory is on the roof of the physics building, and is open to the public on Friday evenings, and by arrangement. It is used primarily by undergraduate students.

★ **Dominion Astrophysical Observatory,** Herzberg Institute of Astrophysics, National Research Council Canada, 5071 W. Saanich Road, Victoria, B.C., Canada V8X 4M6. Tel. (604) 363–0001. Fax (604) 363–0045. Telex 049–7295. The DAO uses two major reflecting telescopes: a 1.2–meter and a 1.8–meter. Astronomers in Canada also have access to the 3.6 meter Canada-France-Hawaii Telescope in Hawaii. (See listing under Hawaii). The DAO serves as a major tool in research and for graduate students. In the past few years, about 60 percent of the nights at the observatory have been assigned to visiting scientists. The average is about 50 scientists per year. The DAO also is open to the public. Some research projects include a study of the luminous spiral galaxies, a review of cosmic stance scales, a study of the systematic differences between globular clusters in the Milky Way and those associated with the Magellanic Clouds, and studies of binary and variable stars, star clusters, and interstellar matter.

★ **David Dunlap Observatory,** Box 360, Richmond Hill, Ont., Canada L4C 4Y6. Tel. (416) 884–2112. The observatory, founded in 1935, is part of the University of Toronto. It boasts a 74–inch reflecting telescope and is used by professional astronomers and astronomy students. The primary research emphasis is on the spectrographic study of the stars. Public tours available.

★ **Science North Solar Observatory,** 100 Ramsey Lake Road, Sudbury, Ontario, Canada P3E 5S9. Tel. (705) 522–3701. This public education observatory is part of the Science North complex. It is a public hands-on Science Activity Centre opened in 1980. The 17.5–inch solar telescope allows a seated audience of 30 to look down on a giant rotating screen and see the solar disc. The Observatory also includes a Hydrogen-Alpha telescope and a "spectrum heliostat" that creates a 20–foot solar spectrum display.

Amateurs may use the Solar Imaging project. Contact Steve Dodson at the center. There is no charge for time on the instruments, but a reservation is required so the session does not interfere with the public viewing schedule.

★ **Gordon MacMillian Southam Observatory,** 1100 Chestnut Street, Vancouver, B.C., Canada V6J 3J9. Tel. (604) 738–2855. The observatory is part of the H.R. Mac-Millian Planetarium operated by the British Columbia Space Sciences Society, an educational group. A 20–inch telescope and smaller instruments are used to introduce the public to the night sky.

Puerto Rico

★ **Arecibo Observatory,** National Astronomy and Ionosphere Center, Arecibo, Puerto Rico 00613. The largest radio telescope in the world, the 1,000–foot dish is dug out of the earth.

7 | Planetariums and Museums

Whether you're planning a month-long vacation, or simply a day trip, there are a vast number of museums and planetariums across the country that can offer you a pleasant afternoon exploring the history of science, astronomy, or the space program, or an evening "under the stars."

Many hold special events for amateurs (check ahead before your trip) and will arrange group tours and programs for your civic or school group.

If you're traveling, and want a break from the rigors of the road, a planetarium/museum can give you a relaxing and educational respite from traffic.

Alabama

Birmingham

Robert R. Meyer Planetarium, Birmingham-Southern College, Arkadelphia Road, Box A–36, Birmingham, AL 35254. Tel. (205) 226–4700. Seats 87.

Florence

University of North Alabama Planetarium, Box 5150, Florence, AL 35632. Tel. (205) 760–4334. Seats 70.

Huntsville

U.S. Space and Rocket Center, Huntsville, AL 35807. Tel. 1–800–633–7280.

Montgomery

W.A. Gayle Planetarium, 1010 Forest Ave., Montgomery, AL 36106. Tel. (205) 832–2625. Seats 237.

Von Braun Planetarium, P.O. Box 1142, Huntsville, AL 35807. Tel. (205) 837–9359. Seats 100.

Arizona

Tucson

Flandrau Planetarium/Science Center, University of Arizona, North Cherry Ave., Tucson, AZ 85721. Tel. (602) 621–4515. Jack Johnson, Director. Open 10 a.m. to 5 p.m. weekdays; 7 to 9 p.m. Wednesday through Saturday; 1 to 5 p.m. Saturday and Sunday. There is no charge for viewing exhibits. Call for group tours. Holds special attractions, depending on astronomical events. Supported by the state and University of Arizona.

Arkansas

Little Rock

University of Arkansas at Little Rock Planetarium, 2801 S. University, Little Rock, AR 72204. Tel. (501) 569–3259. Open Tuesday through Friday by reservation. Public shows at 7:30 p.m. Friday and 2:30 p.m. Sunday. Public shows admission: adults, $3; children, $2. Group instructional programs are offered by reservation only. Hosts Star Parties during the summer, plus a telescope workshop during the winter.

California

Berkeley

Lawrence Hall of Science, University of California, Berkeley, CA 94720. Tel. (415) 642–2858. Open daily, 10 a.m. to 4:30 p.m.. Admission is $4 for adults; $3 for ages 7–18; $2 for senior citizens and students. Group discounts available. Call in advance, at (415) 642–5134. Special astronomy attractions include planetarium programs, Wizard's Lab, "Saturday Night Stargazing," after-school classes, workshops in astronomy, physics, and telescope making and astrophotography. Supported by University of California at Berkeley, and self-supporting.

Cupertino

Minolta Planetarium, 21250 Stevens Creek Blvd., Cupertino, CA 95014. Tel. (408) 864–8814. Open 9 a.m. to 5 p.m. Monday through Friday. Admission: adults, $4; seniors, $3; under 18, $3; group discounts, $2. Holds family Astronomy Nights the last Friday of the month; also special shows for Astronomy Day and eclipse information. Operated by the De Anza College/Community Services.

Redding

Schreder Planetarium, 1644 Magnolia Ave., Redding, CA 96001. Offers school programs from 9 a.m. to 2 p.m. Tuesday through Friday; public programs at 7 and

8:30 p.m. Fridays. Admission: adults, $2.50; students, $2; children 6 to 12, $1.50. Group tours can be scheduled. Occasionally holds special classes for amateurs. Operated by the Shasta County Office of Education.

Sacramento

Sacramento Science Center, 3615 Auburn Blvd., Sacramento, CA 95821. Tel. (916) 449–8256. Contact Denise Benavides. Open noon to 5 p.m. Wednesday through Friday; 10 a.m. to 5 p.m. Saturday and Sunday. Admission: adults, $2.50; children, 6 to 15, $1. Classes for amateur astronomers scheduled during the summer, school year, and holidays.

San Francisco

Exploratorium, The Museum of Science, Art and Human Perception, 3601 Lyon St., San Francisco, CA 94123. Tel. (415) 561–0317. Admission: adults, $6; seniors, $3; youth, ages 6 to 17, $2; under 6, free. Special events scheduled throughout the year. Call for reservations and discounts.

Planetarium Institute, Department of Physics and Astronomy, San Francisco State University, San Francisco, CA 94132. Tel. (415) 338–1852. Open Wednesdays during the noon hour during the fall and spring school terms. Closed June, July, and August. No admission fee. Seats 50. Call for reservations. Funded by the school of science of SFSU.

San Jose

The Rosicrucian Museums, Planetarium and Science Center, 1342 Naglee Ave., San Jose, CA 95191–0001. Tel. (408) 287–9172. Sponsored by the Rosicrucian Order. The Planetarium and Science Center is open from 9 a.m. to 4:15 p.m. Tuesdays through Sunday. Admission to the Science Center is free, show tickets are: adults, $3; seniors and students, $2.50; children ages 7 to 15, $1.50; children 5 and 6, free. Children under 5 normally are not admitted to the planetarium shows. The star projector displays approximately 2,200 stars plus the Sun, the Moon, and the five visible planets.

Santa Ana

Tessmann Planetarium, Rancho Santiago College, Santa Ana, CA 92706. Tel. (213) 927–2942 or (714) 623–8902. Shows each Sunday at 2 p.m., hosted by the Orange County Astronomers.

Santa Barbara

Gladwin Planetarium, Santa Barbara Museum of Natural History, 2559 Puesta del Sol Road, Santa Barbara, CA 93105. Tel. (805) 682–3224 for show and event information. The Planetarium has a Spitz projector and 8–meter dome. Shows every Saturday and Sunday, free with museum admission. Saturday show, at 7 p.m. during Standard Time, 8 p.m. during Daylight Savings Time, has a fee of $3 for adults,

$1.50 for children. An observation follows. The Palmer Observatory is open Saturday nights after the planetarium show and for special events. It features 5–inch, 8–inch, 16–inch, and 29–inch telescopes. All facilities are operated jointly by the museum and Santa Barbara City College. For school programs, call (805) 682–4711, ext. 317. Group tours, extension 326.

Colorado

Boulder

Fiske Planetarium, University of Colorado, Boulder, CO 80309–0408. Tel. (303) 492–5002. Open 8 a.m. to 5 p.m. Monday through Friday. Evening shows are $3 and $1.75; laser shows, $3.50; and after-hours shows, $1.50 to $2.25. Groups, minimum of 20, pay $2 each, and must make reservations. Holds planetarium shows, star talks and occasional scientific lectures. Operated by the University of Colorado, Astrophysical, Planetary and Atmospheric Sciences department.

Colorado Springs

United States Air Force Academy Planetarium, 50 ATS/DOP, Colorado Springs, CO 80840. Tel. (719) 472–2779. Open noon to 3:30 p.m. daily, June through August, except Monday. September to May, open Sundays only. No admission fee. Operated by the USAF Academy.

Denver

Gates Planetarium, Denver Museum of Natural History, 2001 Colorado Blvd., Denver, CO 80205–5798. Tel. (Office) (303) 370–6317. For reservations, (303) 370–7009. Fax (303) 331–6492. Open 12:30 to 2:30 p.m. Monday through Friday, 11:30 a.m. to 3:30 p.m. Saturday and Sunday. Admission to the museum / planetarium: adults, $6; seniors and children, $3.50. Planetarium only: adults, $3; seniors and children, $2. Minimum group, 30. Offers a wide variety of astronomical classes and events, including programs on astrophotography, telescopes, and general astronomy; live star talks about the Colorado skies; star parties. Also offers classes on interpreting the stars through the eyes of other cultures. Telephone hotline for astronomy events: (303) 370–6316.

Connecticut

New Haven

Southern Connecticut State University Planetarium, 501 Crescent St., New Haven, CT 06515. Tel. (203) 397–4347. Open by appointment only; free to elementary schools. Observing sessions available on 12–inch Newtonian.

Stamford

Stamford Museum & Nature Center, 39 Schofieldtown Rd., Stamford, CT 06903. Tel. (203) 322-1646. Monday through Saturday and holidays, 9 a.m. to 5 p.m.; Sundays 1 to 5 p.m. Closed Thanksgiving, Christmas, and New Year's Day. Planetarium open Sundays at 3:30 p.m. Museum entrance fee: adults, $4; under 14 and seniors, $3. Stamford residents half price and free on Wednesdays. Planetarium show: adults, $2; children age 5 and up, $1, plus museum entrance fee. Groups, for 10 or more, must have appointments. The planetarium is part of the Center that includes early New England farm life displays. The non-profit organization is funded through membership, entrance fees, class fees, and other projects. School talks featuring astronomy are available by appointment.

District of Columbia

Einstein Planetarium, National Air & Space Museum, 7th St. and Independence Ave. SW, Washington, DC 20560. The Einstein Planetarium is just one of the many attractions at the National Air & Space Museum. The first show starts at 11:30 a.m. on weekdays; 10:50 a.m. on weekends. The last show begins at 4:50 p.m. weekdays and weekends. Admission is $2.75 for adults; $1.75 for children, students, and senior citizens. Admission to the museum itself is free. Although the museum's main focus is on air and space memorabilia, there are also displays of astronomical significance, including a bona fide Moon rock that visitors can touch.

Rock Creek Nature Center, 5200 Glover Rd. NW, Washington, DC 20007. Operates 9 a.m. to 5 p.m. Wednesday through Sunday. Shows are scheduled frequently, and last 45 minutes. Admission is free, with group tours arranged for groups of 10, age 7 and over. Has a hallway and wall astronomy display featuring the Moon, Solar System, meteor crater, Saturn, etc. Once a month holds a special "Exploring the Sky" in association with the National Capitol Astronomers. The Center is supported by the federal government.

Florida

Bradenton

Bishop Planetarium/South Florida Museum, 201 10th St., Bradenton, FL 34205. (813) 746-4132. Open 10 a.m. to 5 p.m. Tuesday through Saturday; Sunday, noon to 5 p.m. Admission to star show and museum: adults, $5; children 5 to 12, $2.50; under 5, free; admission to evening star shows: adults, $3.25; children 5 to 12, $2; under 5, free. Includes observatory admission. The observatory is open 9 to 10 p.m. Friday and Saturday, weather permitting. Observatory has a 6-inch f/12 refractor. Solar observing 11:30 a.m. to 1 p.m.

Saturday. Observatory open for special events. The Planetarium/Museum is a private, non-profit organization. Offers a general astronomy class for adults once a year.

Cocoa

Astronaut Memorial Space Science Center, Brevard Community College, 1519 Clearlake Rd., Cocoa, FL 32922. Tel. (407) 631–7889. Open Wednesdays, Fridays, and Saturdays at 4 p.m.; and Saturdays from 7 to 10 p.m. The cost is $1 per person per show. Features movies and lectures on astronomy subjects. Funded by Florida. Also has an observatory, which is open Friday and Saturday nights from dark until 10 p.m. Admission free.

Davie

Buehler Planetarium, Broward Community College, 3501 Southeast Davie Road, Davie, FL 33314. Tel. (305) 475–6681. Open 8 a.m. to 5 p.m. Seats 101. The planetarium features a Zeiss System 1015, plus a mid-sized GOTO auxiliary planetarium. Broward Community College operates the planetarium. Admission: adults, $3; children under 12 and seniors, $3. School programs are offered weekday mornings during the school year. Also offers a mobile astronomy program that travels to local schools. An observatory is open each clear Wednesday, Friday, and Saturday. Admission is $2 per person, free with a stub from the planetarium show. Of-

fers a monthly publication, **Florida Skies,** for $5 per year.

Jacksonville

Alexander Brest Planetarium/Museum of Science and History, 1025 Gulf Life Drive, Jacksonville, FL 32207. Tel. (904) 396–7062. Mike D. Reynolds, Director. Museum hours, 10 a.m. to 5 p.m. Monday through Saturday, and 1 to 5 p.m. Sunday. Daily Public Planetarium shows, except Monday, which is reserved for school groups. Admission: adults, $5; children, $3; under 4 free. Planetarium shows included in museum admission. Spacial attractions include "Sky over Jacksonville," Astronomy Day, National Spaceweek, and viewing of special NASA events such as Shuttle launches or Voyager fly-bys. The planetarium is a 60–foot dome with Jena Spacemaster Project. Seats 215. Special programs for amateurs include instruction in mirror grinding, how to buy a telescope, and construction of a simple telescope, and special lectures with the cooperation of the Northeast Florida Astronomical Society.

Kennedy Space Center

NASA Kennedy Space Center's Spaceport USA, Kennedy Space Center, 32899. Tel. (407) 452–2121. Fax (407) 452–3043. Managed and operated by TW Recreational Services Inc., for NASA. Admission is free; bus tours are $6 for adults, $3 for children. Also has IMAX movie; adults, $2.75; children, $1.75.

Recreation area designed to show past, present, and future of space exploration. For visitor information, call 1–800–USA–1969.

Melbourne

Space Coast Science Center, Box 36–1816, Melbourne, FL 32936. Tel. (407) 259–5572. Open 10 a.m. to 5 p.m. Tuesday through Saturday; noon to 5 p.m. Sunday; closed Monday. Admission: adults, $3; children 2 to 17, $2. Offers discount for groups of 10 or more.

Miami

Miami Space Transit Planetarium, 3280 S. Miami Ave., Miami, FL 33129. Tel. (305) 854–4244. Fax (305) 285–5801. Open 10 a.m. to 6 p.m. daily; weekends until 7 p.m. Laser shows Friday, Saturday, and Sunday nights. Admission to the Planetarium: adults, $5; children 3–12 and senior citizens, $2.50; laser shows: adults, $6; children and senior citizens, $3. Groups of 20 or more must have advance reservations. Special projects include "Star Hustler," with Jack Horkehimer, on the PBS Astronomy series.

Orlando

Orlando Science Center, John Young Planetarium, 810 E. Rollins St., Orlando, FL 32803. Tel. (407) 896–7151. Open 9 a.m. to 5 p.m., Monday through Thursday; 9 a.m. to 9 p.m. Friday; 9 a.m. to 5 p.m.

Saturday; and noon to 5 p.m. Sunday. General admission: adults, $4; children, seniors, $3; combination pass, including planetarium: adults, $5.50; children/seniors, $4.50. Center includes all types of science exhibits. Offers camps on a variety of subjects, including astronomy, for youngsters.

St. Petersburgh

St. Petersburgh Junior College Planetarium, P.O. Box 13489, St. Petersburgh, FL 33733–3489. Tel. (813) 341–4320. Fax (813) 341–4770. Kenneth E. Perkins, Director. The Planetarium has a 7.3–meter domed ceiling, a Goto projector, and an automated planetarium operating system. Offers group shows Tuesday through Friday by appointment, no charge. Public shows on Fridays are $1 per person. Also has viewing after the Friday night shows, with an 11–inch Celestron. The Planetarium is operated by the College.

Georgia

Atlanta

Fernbank Science Center, Jim Cherry Memorial Planetarium, 156 Heaton Park, Atlanta, GA 30307. Tel. (404) 378–4311. Planetarium seats 500 and has a 70–foot diameter projection dome. Open 8 p.m. Tuesday through Friday; 11 a.m. Saturday; and 3 p.m. Wednesday, Friday, Saturday, and Sunday. Admission: adults, $2; students, $1. Holds seasonal and holiday shows. Operated by the DeKalb County School system.

Columbus

Patterson Planetarium, 2900 Woodruff Farm Rd., Columbus, GA 31907. Tel. (404) 568–1730. Open 8 a.m. to 5 p.m., with public shows held through the year on pre-scheduled basis. Admission is free. Holds special lectures, workshops, telescope observations every Tuesday during the summer. Operated by the Muscogee County School District. Holds special programs for amateur astronomers once or twice yearly.

Rock Spring

Walker County Science Center, P.O. Box 10, Hwy. 95, Rock Spring, GA 30739. Tel. (404) 764–1111. Regular planetarium shows from 9 a.m. to 4 p.m. Monday through Friday. Admission, $1.50 per person. Planetarium has 32 seats and a 24–foot dome and schedules programs for all grade levels. It is operated and financed by the Walker County School System. Holds programs offering tips on observing, how to use your telescope, etc., during the school year.

Hawaii

Honolulu

Bishop Museum, State Museum of Natural and Cultural History, 1525 Bernice St., Honolulu, HI 96817–0916. Tel. (808) 847–3511. Main galleries open 9 a.m. to 5 p.m. daily. General admission: adults, $5.95, includes planetarium; children under 6 free. Planetarium opens 11 a.m. Monday through Saturday. Planetarium admission only: adults, $2.50; children 6 to 17, $1.25. For school group tours and education programs, call (808) 848–4108. Seats 77. Recently added a portable Star-Lab planetarium for schools on all islands.

Illinois

Chicago

Adler Planetarium, 1300 South Lake Shore Drive, Chicago, IL 60605. Tel. (312) 322–0300 for a recording on the Planetarium services. Open 9:30 a.m. to 4:30 p.m. daily; Fridays until 9 p.m. Features a history of astronomy collection, telescope exhibits, sky theater, planet wall, and Hall of Space Exploration. The history collection contains instruments for time finding, and surveying and modeling the Universe, and date from the 1100s. The Planetarium arranges free group Sky Shows for school students. Regular admission is: adults, $3; children 6 to 17, $1.50. Seats 430, and has a 68–foot sky dome. Uses a Zeiss Mark VI planetarium projector, plus special effects.

Students can make telescopes in the workshop, and various community programs are offered through the year. Subjects range from beginning stargazing to particle physics. Also has a gift shop, cafeteria, and library, and a research center for scholars to study artifacts from the History of Astronomy collection. The Planetarium opened in 1930, and was operated by the Chicago Park District until 1976, when it became a private, not-for-profit corporation managed by a board of trustees.

Museum of Science and Industry, 57th Street and Lake Shore Drive, Chicago, IL 60637. Tel. (312) 684–1414. Museum features the Omnimax Theater in the Henry Crown Space Center. Tickets to the theater are: adults, $5; seniors, $4; and children, 5 through 11, $2. Combined museum/theater tickets are: adults, $8; seniors, $6; children, $4.

Lakeview

Lakeview Museum of Arts & Sciences, 1125 W. Lake Ave., Lakeview, IL 61614–5985. Tel. (309) 686–7000. Planetarium open weekends and Wednesday evenings. Admission to the planetarium: adults, $2.25; students, $1.25. Museum free. Holds classes for children about space science and astronomy.

Normal

Illinois State University Planetarium, Physics Dept., Illinois State University, Normal, IL 61761–6901. Tel. (309) 438–8756, or (309) 438–2496 for a recorded message. Carl J. Wenning, Director. The Planetarium offers programs for preschool, elementary and secondary school, and college level astronomy and space-related classes. Admission is $1 per person with a minimum group fee of $20.

River Grove

Cernan Earth & Space Center, Triton College, 2000 Fifth Ave., River Grove, IL 60171. Tel. (708) 456–0300 ext. 372 or (708) 456–5886. Bart Benjamin, Director. Open 9 a.m. to 5 p.m. Mondays; 9 a.m. to 9 p.m. Tuesdays through Thursdays; 9 a.m. to 10 p.m. Fridays; 1 to 10 p.m. Saturdays; and 1 to 4 p.m. Sundays. Admission: adults, $4; children 12 and under and senior citizens, $2. The Center is named for astronaut Eugene A. Cernan, who flew aboard the Gemini 9, Apollo 10, and Apollo 17 missions. The 44–foot dome planetarium seats 100. Features Earth and space-related shows. Open to the public, and sponsors special events, workshops, and other programs plus a series of monthly Skywatch programs on the lawn outside the Center. A membership program offers free admission to each new planetarium program and laser light show, discounts in the Star Store gift shop, discounts for astronomical magazines, a monthly sky map, and a member's newsletter. Museum exhibits include Apollo artifacts.

Rockford

Discovery Center, 711 N. Main St., Rockford, IL 61103. Tel. (815) 963–6769.

The Center is open Tuesday through Saturday from 11 a.m. to 5 p.m.; Sunday from 1 to 5 p.m. Admission is: adults $2; children and seniors, $1.50; children under 2 and members free. Planetarium tickets are $.50. Reservations can be made by calling the Center. The Center sponsors four Young Astronaut Clubs that meet monthly, and also offers science classes and workshops on a regular basis.

Time Museum, 7801 E. State St., P.O. Box 5285, Rockford, IL 61125. Open 10 a.m. to 5 p.m. Tuesday through Sunday. Admission: adults, $3; seniors, $2; students, $2; children 6 to 18, $1; under 6, free. Groups of 15 or more by appointment, at a group rate of $2 per person.

Indiana

Evansville

Evansville Museum of Arts and Science, 411 S.E. Riverside Drive, Evansville, IN 47713. Tel. (812) 425–2406. Mitch Luman, director of planetarium. Open 10 a.m. to 5 p.m. Tuesday through Saturday; noon to 5 p.m. Sunday. Museum visitors asked to consider a $1 donation per person. Planetarium admission is: adults, $2; ages 3–12, $1. Showtimes in the Koch Planetarium are 1 p.m. Tuesday through Friday during June, July, and August; 1 and 3 p.m. Saturday and Sunday. Group tours are available.

Fort Wayne

E.C. Schouweiler Planetarium, St. Francis College, 2701 Sprint St., Fort Wayne, IN 46808. Tel. (219) 434–3278. Andrew L. Henning, Director. Open by appointment only. Admission: adults, $2; children, $1. Special shows include "Star of Bethlehem," and "Special Star Show." Holds an "Astronomy for casual observers" class for five Tuesdays evenings after Easter.

Indianapolis

The Children's Museum, P.O. Box 3000, Indianapolis, IN 46206. Tel. (317) 924–4014 or (317) 924–5431. Fax (317) 921–4019. The SpaceQuest Planetarium seats 130 people, and is the largest public planetarium in Indiana. Features group tours (call in advance), and special shows in recognition of Astronomy Day and Space Day.

J.I. Holcomb Planetarium, Butler University, 4600 Sunset Ave., Indianapolis, IN 46208. Ronald G. Samec, director. Tel. (317) 283–9282, office; (317) 283–9749, scheduling. Open 8 and 9:15 p.m. Fridays and Saturdays. Admission: adults, $2; students and children, $1. Features a seasonal star show, plus private tours. Large groups, maximum of 50, $20 per tour. Small groups, maximum of 12, $12 per tour.

Iowa

Des Moines

Science Center of Iowa, 4500 Grand Ave., Greenwood-Ashworth Park, Des Moines, IA 50312. Tel. (515) 274–6868. Open 10 a.m. to 5 p.m. Monday through Saturday; 1 to 5 p.m. Sunday. Admission: 13 and over, $4; ages 5–12, $2. Reservations must be made at least two weeks early for groups of 20 or more. Financed by admissions and public donations. The Des Moines Astronomical Society meets at the center and provides information on astronomy.

Kansas

Wichita

Omnisphere & Science Center, 220 S. Main, Wichita, KS 67202. Tel. (316) 264–3174. Open 8 a.m. to 5 p.m. Tuesday through Friday; 1 to 5 p.m. Saturday and Sunday. Admission to shows: adults, $3; ages 3–12, $2; museum only, $1. Group reservations available. Holds Planetarium shows, science demonstrations, and exhibits dealing with the Space Shuttle and space. Operated and financed by the City of Wichita.

Kentucky

Berea

Weatherford Planetarium, Berea College, Berea, KY 40404. Tel. (606) 986–9342, ext. 6240. Open for public shows at 4 p.m. Saturdays and Sundays. Admission is $1. School groups pay $10 per group.

Georgetown

Georgetown College Planetarium, 400 E. College St., Georgetown, KY 40324–1696. Tel. (502) 863–8436. Contact Sharon Smith. Open by appointment only. Admission fees range from 25 cents to $3. Sometimes offers special Christmas program.

Louisville

Museum of History and Science, 727 W. Main St., Louisville, KY 40202. Tel. (502) 561–6111. Open 9 a.m. to 9 p.m. Friday and Saturday; 9 a.m to 5 p.m. Monday through Thursday; noon to 5 p.m. Sunday. Admission to museum and shows: adults, $6; children and senior citizens, $5; museum only: adults, $4; children and senior citizens, $3. Has IMAX, plus temporary exhibits. Also offers a STARLAB portable planetarium. Call (502) 561–6103.

Rauch Memorial Planetarium, University of Louisville, Louisville, KY 40292. Tel. (502) 588–6665. The planetarium holds school shows daily, at 9:30 a.m., 11 a.m., and 12:30 p.m., with a feature show at 1 p.m.

Saturday. General shows are scheduled for 10 a.m. Tuesdays and Thursdays during June, July, and August. Admission is: Adults, $3.50; children 12 and under, $2.50; senior citizens, $2.50; and University of Louisville students, $2.50. Reservations must be made at least 48 hours prior to the tour. The Planetarium holds special activities linked with astronomical events, such as eclipses, and an annual Christmas show. Also works closely with the Louisville Astronomical Society.

Louisiana

Lafayette

Lafayette Natural History Museum, Planetarium and Nature Station, 637 Girard Park Drive, Lafayette, LA 70503–2896. Tel. (318) 268–5544. Fax (318) 261–8041. David E. Hostetter, curator of the planetarium. Open 9 a.m. to 5 p.m. Monday, Wednesday, Thursday, and Friday; 9 a.m. to 9 p.m. Tuesdays; and 1 p.m. to 5 p.m. Saturdays and Sundays. Tuesday programs are followed by Telescope Night, when visitors may use the Museum's Celestron 8 telescope. Admission is free. Groups wishing to schedule tours should call at least two weeks in advance. Seats 58; uses a Spitz A4 star projector under a 30–foot dome. Also sponsors star parties, classes on buying and using telescopes, and events in honor of Spaceweek.

Maine

Easton

Francis M. Malcolm Science Center, P.O. Box 186, Easton, ME 04740. Contact Lawrence Berz, Planetarium Coordinator. Operates 9 a.m. to 4 p.m. Monday-Friday. Admission is: adults, $1.50; students/senior citizens, free. Public programs; adults, $3. Group reservations fees are: adults, $25; students, $15. Offers planetarium sky theatre, regular public programs. Hosts astronomy club meetings.

Portland

Southworth Planetarium, University of Southern Maine, 96 Falmount St., Portland, ME 04103. Tel. (207) 780–4249. Roy A. Gallant, Director. Open at 6:30 p.m. Fridays and Saturdays. Admission: school groups, $2.50 per person; $25 per group minimum. Reservations must be made at least one week in advance. Public shows: adults, $3; children and senior citizens, $2.50. Offers various shows, plus laser light shows featuring music from popular bands. Also has observing sessions on some Sundays, and offers courses in celestial navigation.

Maryland

Baltimore

Davis Planetarium, Maryland Science Center, 601 Light St., Baltimore, MD 21230. Tel. (301) 685–2370. Seats 50. Open 10 a.m. to 5 p.m. Monday through Friday; 10 a.m. to 6 p.m. Saturday and Sunday. Planetarium is part of the Science Center.

K. Price Bryan Planetarium, College of Notre Dame of Maryland, 4701 N. Charles St., Baltimore, MD 21210. Contact J.D. Rieuzi, Tel. (301) 532–5702. Open irregular hours. Free admission. School groups are given special seasonal programs.

Greenbelt

Goddard Space Flight Center, Greenbelt, MD 20771. Tel. (301) 286–8981. Open 10 a.m. to 4 p.m. Wednesday through Sunday. No admission charge. Groups of 20 or more should call for advance reservations. On Sunday, holds special events such as talks by NASA scientists, engineers, or officials on topics such as the Hubble Space Telescope, supernovas, or the Space Station. These events begin at 1 p.m. There also is a Teacher Resource Laboratory. Holds a Star Watch the second Saturday evening of each month to view the Moon, the planets, and the stars. Members of the Goddard Astronomy club provide telescopes.

Hagerstown

Washington County Planetarium and Space Science Center, 823 Commonwealth Avenue, Hagerstown, MD 21740. Tel. (301) 791–4172. Rodney L. Martin, Director. Open Tuesdays at 7 p.m. during the school year, and during school days for education groups, Sept. through June only. There is no charge, but groups must make advance reservations. Holds special events for Astronomy Day, and star parties sponsored by the Tristate Astronomers Club, which also offers mirror-making classes, observing tips, etc. The Planetarium is operated by the Washington County Board of Education.

Massachusetts

Amherst

Bassett Planetarium, Dept. of Astronomy, Amherst College, Amherst, MA 01002. Tel. (413) 542–2138. Ronald B. Woodland, Director. Open Monday through Friday during the school year, for school and other groups by special arrangement. From Sept. through June, open at 3 p.m. Sundays. Call for group tours. The Amherst Area Amateur Astronomers Association conducts classes and observing sessions at the planetarium and at the Amherst College Observatory (which has an 18–inch Clark refractor). The Association and Amherst work closely together to sponsor special projects.

Boston

The Children's Museum, 300 Congress St., Boston, MA 02210. Tel. (617) 426–6500. Science, nature, and cultural museum dedicated to education for children. Admission: adults, $6; children 2 to 15 and seniors, $5; 1–year–old, $1; under 1, free.

Museum of Science, Charles Hayden Planetarium, Science Park, Boston, MA 02114–1099. Tel. (617) 589–0270. Open 9 a.m. to 5 p.m. Monday through Sunday; until 9 p.m. Fridays. Admission to exhibit halls: adults, $6; ages 4 to 14 and seniors, $4.50; children under 3, free. Planetarium shows: adults, $6; ages 4 to 14 and seniors, $4.50; Omni Theater: adults, $6; ages 4 to 14 and seniors, $4.50; laser show: adults, $6; ages 4 to 14 and seniors, $4.50. Combination tickets are available. Planetarium has a Zeiss projector. Daily program includes shows on the skies over Boston as well as celestial phenomena such as black holes and supernovas.

Michigan

Alpena

Jesse Besser Museum, 491 Johnson St., Alpena, MI 49707. Tel. (517) 356–2202. Dennis Bodem, Museum Director. Operates from 10 a.m. to 5 p.m. Monday, Tuesday, Wednesday, and Friday; 10 a.m. to 9 p.m. Thursday; and noon to 5 p.m. Saturday and Sunday. Planetarium public shows are 12:30 p.m. Wednesdays; and 2 and 4 p.m. Sunday. Admission to the planetarium is $1.50 for adults; $1 for those under 18 or over 65; children under five free. Admission to the museum is free. For group tours, contact Jim Bruton; 14 days advance notice required. The museum has a 30–foot diameter planetarium and Foucault pendulum. The Huron Amateur Astronomers meet each month at the museum, and sponsor star parties. Celebrates Astronomy Day each year.

Ann Arbor

Exhibit Museum, The University of Michigan, 1109 Geddes Ave., Ann Arbor, MI 48109–1079. Tel. (313) 764–0478. Open 9 a.m. to 5 p.m. Tuesday through Saturday; 1 to 5 p.m. Sunday. Planetarium shows Tuesday through Friday only. Seats 41.

Detroit

Children's Museum, Detroit Public Schools, 67 East Kirby, Detroit, MI 48202. Tel. (517) 494–1210. Open 8:15 a.m. to 4:45 p.m. Monday through Friday; 9 a.m. to 4 p.m. Saturdays, from October to May. Admission free. Group tours by reservation only. Holds special programs on Saturdays and during school vacations. Workshops and programs, such as Young Astronauts Clubs, are designed for children.

East Lansing

Abrams Planetarium, Michigan State University, East Lansing, MI 48824. Tel. (517) 355–4672. David Batch, director. Admission: adults, $2.50; students and senior citizens, $2; children 12 and under, $1.50. Features shows Fridays and Saturdays at 8 p.m.; Sundays at 4 p.m. Schedules special events, occasional observing nights at the Michigan State University observatory. The Planetarium also produces the popular **Sky Calendar,** and maintains a sky information hotline.

Flint

Robert T. Longway Planetarium, 1310 East Kearsley St., Flint, MI 48503. Tel. (313) 760–1181. Fax (313) 760–6774. Operating hours Monday through Friday, 8 a.m. to 5 p.m. Programs scheduled on a reservation basis. Admission is: adults, $3; children, $2; group rates are $2.50 adults; $1.50 for children. Advance reservations necessary. Offers a variety of astronomy-related programs, laser shows, and special Christmas programs. Also offers free viewing of all launches, missions, and landings of the Space Shuttle. Seats 292, and has an inner dome of 60–feet. Uses a Spitz Model B and is capable of reproducing 3083 stars. The Planetarium is owned and operated by the Flint Community Schools. The Genesee Astronomical Society holds monthly meetings and offers classes in mirror-making, observing tips, and telescope tips.

Grand Rapids

Chaffee Planetarium, 54 Jefferson, SE, Grand Rapids, MI 49503. Tel. (616) 456–3977. Contact Gary Tomlinson. The planetarium is Astronomy Day Head-quarters. Open Friday and Saturday at 8 p.m. Admission is $3 for adults; $1.50 for children and senior citizens. Group tours available (min. of 20). Sometimes offers classes for amateur astronomers. The Chaffee Planetarium director also arranges tours to the James C. Veen Observatory, operated by the Grand Rapids Amateur Astronomical Association. The observatory is open to the public from 8:30 p.m. to 11 p.m. the second Saturday and last Friday each month, April through October. Admission is $1 for adults, 50 cents for children under 12. The maximum group size is 40.

Kalamazoo

Kalamazoo Public Museum & Planetarium, 315 S. Rose St., Kalamazoo, MI 49007. Tel. (616) 345–7092. Open 9 a.m. to 5 p.m. Tuesday through Saturday during school year; Wednesday until 9 p.m.; and 1 to 5 p.m. Sundays. Summer hours, 9 a.m. to 5 p.m. Tuesday through Saturday. Admission fee varies. Operated by the Kalamazoo Valley Community College.

Lansing

Impression 5 Science Museum, 200 Museum Drive, Lansing, MI 48933–1905. Tel. (517) 485–8116. Fax (517) 485–

8125. Plans an astronomy exhibit in cooperation with the Lansing Community College.

Minnesota

Hibbing

Paulucci Space Theatre, Arrowhead Community College Region, U.S. Hwy 169 & 23rd St., Hibbing, MN 55746. Tel. (218) 262-6720. Open Friday, Saturday, and Sunday during school year; seven days a week during the summer. Admission: adults, $3; seniors, $2.50; 17 and under, $1.50. Must have reservations for group tours. Has a gift shop. Operated by State of Minnesota.

Marshall

Southwest State University Planetarium, Marshall, MN 56258. Tel. (507) 537-6196. Open 8 a.m. to 5 p.m. during academic year, by reservation only. No summer programs. Group rates start at $15 for school groups to "much higher fees" for weekends. Public shows, $2 per person. Funded by Southwest State University.

Minneapolis

Minneapolis Planetarium, 300 Nicollet Mall, Minneapolis, MN 55401. (612) 372-6644. Open year round. Showtimes change during the winter and summer. Admission: adults, $3.50; children 12 or under, $2; laser light shows, $5 per person. Group shows by reservation only (call (612) 372-6543. The planetarium is in the Minneapolis Public Library and is operated by Friends of the Minneapolis Public Library.

Mississippi

Jackson

Russell C. Davis Planetarium, 201 E. Pascagoula St., Jackson, MS 39201. Tel. (601) 960-1550. Seats 237. School shows at 9 a.m., 10:30 a.m., and noon, by appointment, Tuesday through Friday. Public shows at 8 p.m. Tuesday through Saturday, with Saturday and Sunday matinees. Summer shows start at noon. Admission: adults, $4; children 12 and under $2.50. Group shows available. Programs at special times cost at least $150. Each year the Davis Planetarium invites speakers from NASA, other planetariums, or observatories to speak on astronomical subjects. Also offers a quarterly popular-level astronomy class with an emphasis on observational astronomy and using a telescope. Sponsors a Space Station program for seventh and eighth graders.

Missouri

Kansas City

Kansas City Museum/Planetarium, 3218 Gladstone Blvd., Kansas City, MO 64123. Tel. (816) 483-7827. Seats 50.

St. Louis

St. Louis Science Center and McDonnel Star Theater, 5100 Clayton Road, Forest Park, St. Louis, MO 63110. Tel. (314) 289–4444. Seats 228.

Montana

Bozeman

Taylor Planetarium, Montana State University, Bozeman, MT 59717. Tel. (406) 994–2251. Michael L. Murray, Program Assistant. The planetarium is part of the Museum of the Rockies, which is a department of Montana State University. The planetarium has a 40–foot domed facility, seats 104, and features a Digistar and modern automation and multi-media hardware. Also offers a 13–inch Odyssey and an 8–inch Schmidt-Cassegrain for classes and public star parties from late spring through mid-autumn. Astronomy classes offered.

Nebraska

Fremont

Lueinghoener Planetarium, Midland Lutheran College, 900 N. Clarkson, Fremont, NE 68025. Tel. (402) 721–5480, ext. 6328. Programs by arrangement, $50 admission. Programs based on current astronomical events. Offers adult non-credit astronomy classes and holds open observatories.

Lincoln

Jenson Planetarium, 5000 Saint Paul Ave., Lincoln, NE 68504–2796. Tel. (402) 465–2246. Open by appointment. Programs mostly for local public schools. Funded by Nebraska Wesleyan University, physics department.

Ralph Mueller Planetarium, University of Nebraska at Lincoln, 212 Morrill Hall, Lincoln, NE 68588–0338. Tel. (402) 472–6302. During school year shows at 2 p.m. Saturday and Sunday; summer hours Tuesday through Saturday 1:30 and 2:30 p.m.; and 2 p.m. Sundays. Admission: adults, $2.50; students and children, $1.50; laser shows: $4; children 12 and under, $2. Holds private shows by reservation through museum reservations office. Special events for Astronomy Day, Spaceweek, and events connected with astronomical events. Prairie Astronomy Club holds events there as well.

Nevada

Reno

Fleischmann Planetarium, University of Nevada-Reno, Reno, NV 89557–0010. Tel. (702) 784–4812. Fax (702) 784–4822. Hours vary with the season. Admission: Adults, $5; children 12 and under and seniors 60 and over, $3.50. Does not offer group tours. Has a small museum and gift

Vacationing under the Stars

Scheduling a trip to view an astronomical event generally is a personal matter. As often as not, you simply want to find a dark spot where the seeing is good, where light pollution is nonexistent, where you can observe to your heart's content. You don't want lots of strangers around; other astronomy buffs are fine, but not unwelcome guests.

Occasionally, there are special events when tour guides can be of help in planning transportation and lodging. During the solar eclipse of 1991, for example, cruise lines and tour agencies stepped forward to get eclipse-watchers to the prime viewing sites. For the most part, these businesses do not plan astronomical tours on a regular basis; determining your destination for the best site to view an occultation or a lunar eclipse will depend on your own initiative. The following firms, however, have demonstrated a willingness to work with astronomers eager to travel to odd corners of the Earth for "just the right view." As always, call or write to the firms for more information.

TOUR COMPANIES

All-Earth Travel, Inc., 10592 Champagne Rd., Alta Loma, CA 91701. Tel. (714) 941–2451.

Arctic Odysseys, Box 37T, Medina, WA 98039. Tel. (206) 455–1960.

Explorers Tours, 5 Queen Anne's Court, Windsor, SL4 1DG, England. Tel. 011 44 753 842184. Fax 011 44 753 861512.

Horizon Travel & Tours, 6760 University Ave., Suite 100, San Diego, CA 92115. Tel. (619) 287–8880. Fax (619) 287–8883.

Jack Peak Travel, 1221 Lincoln Ave., San Jose, CA 95125. Tel. (408) 286–2222. Toll-free, in California only, 1–800–632–7900. Nationwide, 1–800–331–8620.

Roughrider Expeditions, 1117 Lincoln, Grand Forks, ND 58201. Tel. 1–800–437–5301.

Scientific Expeditions Inc., 227 West Miami Ave., Suite 3, Venice, FL 34285. Tel. 1–800–344–6867.

Travelbug International, 8369 Vickers St., Suite F., San Diego, CA 92111. Tel. 1–800–247–1900. Fax (619) 279–8687.

Tropical Adventures, 2516 Sea Palm, El Paso, TX 79936. Tel. (915) 595–1003.

LODGING

Star Hill Inn, Box IA, Sapello, NM 87745. Tel. (505) 425–5605. This inn, near Santa Fe, is one of the few in the country to actively court astronomers who want to vacation in the mountains where they can use their telescopes, plus enjoy skiing, golf, tennis, fishing, and hiking. Call or write for reservations or more information.

shop, and publishes a monthly newsletter, the **Fleischmann Flyer.** Offers free public telescope viewing, holds model rocketry classes and special shows. The Planetarium is a non-profit organization, primarily self-funded, but is connected to the University of Nevada system. Works with local amateur astronomers, but does not hold special classes for amateurs.

New Hampshire

Concord

The Christa McAuliffe Planetarium, 3 Institute Drive, Concord, NH 03301. Tel. (603) 271-2842. Open 9 a.m. to 4 p.m. Tuesday through Thursday; 9 a.m. to 7 p.m. Friday; noon to 7 p.m. Saturday; noon to 4 p.m. Sunday. Admission: adults, $4; seniors, college students, and children, $2.50. Group rates available. Seats 91. Named in honor of Christa McAuliffe, a Concord teacher who perished in the space shuttle Challenger disaster in 1986.

New Jersey

Mountainside

Trailside Nature and Science Center, Coles Avenue & New Providence Road, Mountainside, NJ 07092. Tel. (201) 789-3670. Open Sunday through Thursday. Sunday public shows at 2 and 3:30 p.m.; Monday through Thursday by registration,

shows between 9 a.m. and 5 p.m. Admission: $2 per person; $1.70, senior citizens. Minimum group fee $25. Groups of 26 or more $1.50 per person. Groups must register. Summer workshops offered to elementary grades 1 through 5.

Newark

The Newark Museum, 49 Washington St., Box 540, Newark, NJ 07101-0540. Tel. (201) 596-6615. Open noon to 5 p.m. Tuesday through Sunday. Admission: school groups $2 per person; other groups, $2 per person with minimum charge of $25; adults, $4; children under 12, $2. Special events not regularly scheduled.

Toms River

Robert J. Novians Planetarium, at Ocean County College, CN 2001, Toms River, NJ 08754-2001. Tel. (908) 255-0343. Admission: adults, $3; all others, $2. Group rates available. Features a variety of shows for adults, and special programs for schools. Offers credit and non-credit courses in astronomy and related subjects.

Trenton

New Jersey State Museum, 205 W. State St., CN-530, Trenton, NJ 08625-0530. Tel. (609) 292-6347. Richard D. Peery, Assistant Curator. Open 9 a.m. to 4:45 p.m. Tuesday through Saturday. Admission to the museum is free. Admission to the planetarium is $1 per person. Holds free weekday programs October through June, for school and community groups. Marks Space Day and holds public star parties in the spring and fall.

New Mexico

Alamogordo

Space Center, P.O. Box 533, Alamogordo, NM 88311–0553. Tel. (505) 437–2840. The Space Center includes the International Space Hall of Fame (a museum dedicated to the pioneers of Space Science); the Clyde Tombaugh Space Theater; the Joseph P. Stapp Air and Space Park; the Astronaut Memorial Garden; and Shuttle Camp (a summer space science camp for children grades three through nine). The museum is open daily from 9 a.m. to 6 p.m. Admission for adults is $2.25. The theater is open daily, and admission is $3.75 for day programs; $4 for evening programs. Groups of 10 or more may make reservations. School groups, Scouts, and other youth groups can visit the museum and planetarium for a combined price of $2.50 per student. Each night during June through August the theater presents laser light shows; the first Saturday of each month the planetarium presents a free "Skywatch" program. The Space Center is a Division of the Office of Cultural Affairs, New Mexico.

New York

Binghamton

Link Planetarium, 30 Front St., 13905. Tel. (607) 772–0660. Open 10 a.m. to 5 p.m. Tuesday, Wednesday, Thursday and Saturday; 10 a.m. to 9 p.m. Friday and noon to 5 p.m. Sunday. Admission is: adults, $4; students, seniors, $2.50. Planetarium is associated with the Robertson Center for the Arts and Sciences. Seats 60, and permits reservations for groups of 15 or more.

Centerport, Long Island

Vanderbilt Museum, 180 Little Neck Road, P.O. Box F, Centerport, NY 11721–0605. Planetarium Tel. (516) 262–7800. Located with Vanderbilt Museum. Offers special "Young People's Shows" Saturday mornings for children under 8. Also has regular Sky Shows, and special shows for selected celestial events, such as the appearance of a comet, or the celebration of a solstice or an equinox. Adult education courses are provided in astronomy, meteorology, and celestial navigation. Displays include meteorites and space photographs. The Planetarium is open year round. Museum hours are Tuesday through Saturday, 10 a.m. to 4 p.m.; Sundays and holidays, noon to 5 p.m. From November through March, hours are Tuesday through Sunday, noon to 4 p.m. Admission fees are:

adults, $5 (group $4.50); Senior citizens/students $4; children under 12, $2.

Corona

New York Hall of Science, 47–01 111th St., Corona, NY 11368. Tel. (718) 699–0005. Open 10 a.m. to 5 p.m. Wednesday through Sunday. Group tours Monday and Tuesday, 10 a.m. to 2 p.m. Admission: adults, $3.50; children and senior citizens, $2.50. Special programs include "Seeing the Light," "Feedback," "Realm of the Atom," and "Structures." Offers portable planetarium rentals for teachers.

New York City

American Museum-Hayden Planetarium, Central Park West at 79th St., New York City, NY 10024–5192. Tel. (212) 769–5000. Operating hours October through June: Monday through Friday, 12:30 to 4:45 p.m., Saturday 10 a.m. to 5:45 p.m., Sunday, noon through 5:45 p.m. July through September: Monday through Friday, 12:30 to 4:45 p.m.; Saturday and Sunday, noon to 4:45 p.m. Admission fees are $4 adults; $3 students with I.D., senior citizens, and members of the American Museum of Natural History, $2, children 2–12. Prices subject to change. Special attractions and events include daily Sky Shows, two floors of astronomical exhibits, special children's shows, weekend laser shows, lectures, and live concerts. Offers astronomy classes for beginner through advanced intermediate. Mixes popular non-astronomy concepts, such as jazz festivals and Sesame Street characters, with astronomy.

Northeast Bronx Planetarium, 750 Baychester Ave., Bronx, NY 10475. Tel. (212) 379–1616. Terry Buchalter, Planetarium Director. Open 8 a.m. to 4 p.m., Monday through Friday, for schools and groups in the North Bronx. All school groups must make appointments in advance, via a "Planetarium Visit Request Form." Seats 180, and offers programs designed for elementary through high school groups. Admission is $30 per class. The Planetarium is operated by the New York City Board of Education, District 11, and is part of the Northeast Bronx Science Center.

Newburgh

Newburgh Free Academy Planetarium, 201 Fullerton Ave., Newburgh, NY 12550. Tel. (914) 563–7500. No open schedule. Admission for adults, $1.75; for students and senior citizens, $1.25. Offers a special Christmas show and occasional observing night. Operated by the Newburgh City School District.

Oneonta

State University of New York, College at Oneonta, Oneonta, NY 13820. Open 9 a.m. to 4 p.m. Arranges group tours; holds programs for public schools, Christmas programs, and special event shows such as eclipses. Also holds sessions at the college observatory.

Schenectady

Schenectady Museum & Planetarium, Nott Terrace Heights, Schenectady, NY 12308. Tel. (518) 382–7890. Richard Monda, Director. Open 10 a.m. to 4:30 p.m. weekdays; noon to 5 p.m. weekends. Public planetarium shows are presented on weekends during the school year. Combined museum/planetarium admission is: adults, $4; children, $2. This includes one planetarium show. Admission to additional planetarium shows is: adults, $2; children, $1. Group admission rates are: $55 minimum for first 25 people; additional charge of $2 for each person after first 25. Special events include International Astronomy Day, with the Albany Area Amateur Astronomers, a laser light show and a "Concert Under the Stars." The local astronomy club holds monthly club meetings at the planetarium.

Syracuse

The Discovery Center, 321 S. Clinton St., Syracuse, NY 13202. Tel. (315) 425–9068. Open 10 a.m. to 5 p.m. Tuesday through Saturday; noon to 5 p.m. Sunday. Admission: adults, $2.50; children 2 to 11, $1.50; members free; planetarium admission, 50 cents additional. Group discounts available for 15 or more. Reservations must be made seven days in advance. The Rotary Planetarium offers three shows daily, as well as special programs. Has a continuous monitor of the NASA-Select satellite broadcasts providing launch coverage, briefings, and science projects. Exhibits include a gravity well, lunar landing game, and landsat photo-mosaics. Holds workshops on designing your own telescope, as well as observing sessions. Provides observational information to local television stations.

North Carolina

Chapel Hill

Morehead Planetarium, CB #3480, Morehead Planetarium Bldg., The University of North Carolina at Chapel Hill, Chapel Hill, NC 27599–3480. Tel. (919) 962–1236. Open 12:30 to 5 p.m. and 6:30 to 9:30 p.m. Sunday through Friday; 6:30 to 9:30 p.m. Saturday. Admission is: adults, $3; children, students, and senior citizens, $2.50. Call for group tours. Holds Star Shows and shows films. Operated and financed by the State of North Carolina. Offers courses for amateur astronomers, teacher renewal credit courses, and astronomy day camps for children.

Greensboro

Edward R. Zane Planetarium, Natural Science Center, Greensboro, NC 27408. Tel. (919) 288–3769. Roger D. Joyner, planetarium curator. Open 8 a.m. to 5 p.m. Monday through Saturday and 1 to 5 p.m. Sunday. Closed Thanksgiving Day, Christmas Day, and New Year's Day. Museum admission fees are: adults,

$2.50; children $1.50; Non-Greensboro residents, adults, $3.50; children, $2.50. Admission to the planetarium is an additional $1. Group reservations available. Museum associated with the Greensboro Astronomy Club, which meets at the center the third Friday in each month. Club holds monthly observing sessions.

Lumberton

Robeson County Planetarium, Robeson County Educational Resource Center, Hwys. 72 and 71, Box 1328, Lumberton, NC 28358. Tel. (919) 739–3302. Seats 80. Available to school groups and community church and civic organizations. Visits must be confirmed by reservations at least two weeks in advance. Schools outside Robeson County are charged $1 per student. Offers astronomy seminars and workshops, plus public programs.

Salisbury

Horizons Unlimited, 1636 Parkview Circle, Salisbury, NC 28144. Tel. (704) 639–3004. A natural science, local history, space science, and health education center. Open 8 a.m. to 5 p.m. Monday through Friday. No admission charge for students in the Rowan-Salisbury Schools. Teachers request programs. Operates the Margaret C. Woodson Planetarium/rooftop observatory. Holds various special programs for school children, including one called Moon Madness; has scale models of the Solar System and viewing programs.

Winston-Salem

Nature Science Center, Museum Drive, Winston-Salem, NC 27105. Tel. (919) 767–6730. David D. Bonney II, Executive Director. Open 10 a.m. to 5 p.m. Admission to the museum is $3.50 for adults, $2.50 for children; admission to the planetarium is $1.00 extra for adults, 50 cents for children. Groups get a reduced admission fee into the museum, but pay $1.50 per person for planetarium shows. Planetarium shows are at 3 p.m. Monday through Friday; 10:30 a.m., 12:30 p.m., 2 p.m., and 3:30 p.m. Saturday; and 1:30 and 3:30 p.m. Sunday. Schedules shows to coincide with museum displays. Plans to build a 150–seat planetarium by 1993.

North Dakota

Valley City

Valley City State University Planetarium, Valley City, ND 58072. Tel. (701) 845–7452. Joseph C. Stickler, Planetarium Director. No admission charges, and all shows are scheduled by groups. Operated by volunteers. Each year schedules special shows such as Native American Astronomy. Also schedules a few telescope sessions for the public and for college astronomy classes.

Ohio

Bay Village

Lake Erie Nature and Science Center, Schuele Planetarium, 28728 Wolf Rd., Bay Village, OH 44140. Tel. (216) 835–9912. Open Saturday afternoons, 3 to 4 p.m.; Friday evenings, 7:30 to 8:30. Admission: adults, $2; children under 12 and seniors, $1. Special group planetarium programs cost $60 for up to 75 people.

Bowling Green

Bowling Green State University Planetarium, Dept. of Physics & Astronomy, Bowling Green, OH 43403. Dale Smith, Director. Tel. (419) 372–8666. Open September to May. Public shows: 8 p.m. Tuesday and Friday; 7:30 p.m. Sunday. School shows, Tuesday and Thursday, daytime, by reservation. Public shows: $1 donation suggested; school shows, $1. Major shows held each year. Occasional special shows. Stargazing held after Friday and Sunday shows.

Canton

Hoover-Price Planetarium, McKinley Museum, Box 20070, Canton, OH 44701. Tel. (216) 455–7043. Jane W. Mahoney, Director. The museum is open 9 a.m. to 5 p.m. during the winter; 9 a.m. to 7 p.m during the summer. The planetarium is open 9:30 a.m. to 2:30 p.m. Monday through Friday; 2 to 4 p.m. Saturday and Sunday. Museum admission includes planetarium: adults, $5; seniors, $4; youth, $3. Call or write for group tour information. Seats 65. Features a Spitz A–3P projector capable of projecting 6,000 stars in color, and of simulating motions of the Earth, stars, and planets. Holds special programs, such as galaxies, Babylonian-Assyrian skies, Star of Bethlehem, and special education programs.

Cincinnati

Cincinnati Museum of Natural History, 1301 Wester Ave., Cincinnati, OH 45203. Tel. (513) 287–7020. The museum features various programs for adults and students, including classes on how to build a simple telescope and classes on NASA materials. Admission to the Planetarium is: $2.50 for adults; $2 for children under 12. Tickets go on sale 45 minutes before each show. No reserve tickets.

Cleveland

NASA Lewis Research Center, 21000 Brookpark Road, Cleveland, OH 44135. Tel. (216) 433–2001. Open 9 a.m. to 4 p.m. weekdays; 10 a.m. to 3 p.m. Saturdays; and 1 to 5 p.m. Sundays. Admission is free. You need at least 20 people to schedule a program. Presents educational programs for different grades. Also schedules adult programs covering topics such as living and working in space, space spinoffs, and history of spaceflight. Center specializes in aircraft propulsion, space propulsion, spacecraft technology, and energy and technology use.

Columbus

Columbus Center of Science and Industry, 280 E. Broad St., Columbus, OH 43215-3773. Tel. (614) 228-2674. Fax (614) 228-6363. Open 10 a.m. to 5 p.m. Monday through Saturday; 1 to 5:30 p.m. Sundays. Admission to the center includes the planetarium: Adults, $5; students/seniors/children, $3.

Ohio State University Planetarium, 174 W. 18th Ave., Columbus, OH 43210. Occasionally used for beginning college classes. Public shows first Wednesday of each month. No admission charge. No group tours. Operated by the OSU Astronomy Department.

Sylvania

Copernicus Planetarium, Lourdes College, Sylvania, OH 43560-2898. Tel. (419) 885-3211. Delores Kurek, Director. Open 9:30 a.m. to 2:30 p.m. Mondays, Wednesdays, and Thursdays. Public shows at 7:30 p.m. Friday. Closed in summer. Admission: adults, $2; children and senior citizens, $1. School and scout groups, 50 cents. Seats 60, and does not schedule tours. Holds special programs and observing night, plus occasional teachers' workshops.

Youngstown

Ward Beecher Planetarium, Youngstown State University, Youngstown, OH 44555-

3616. Tel. (216) 742-3616. Fax (216) 742-1998. Open Fridays at 8 p.m. and Saturdays at 2 p.m. and 8 p.m. Admission, by reservation, is free. Sometimes opens the roof-top observatory shows. Holds laser light shows in May and October. The Mahoning Valley Astronomical Society meets in the Planetarium during the winter. The club meets the last Saturday of each month. Offers some classes for amateurs.

Oklahoma

Oklahoma City

Omniplex Science Museum and Kirkpatrick Planetarium, 2100 NE. 52nd St., Oklahoma City, OK 73111. Tel. (405) 424-5545. Seats 120.

Oregon

Gresham

Mount Hood Community College, 26000 S.E. Stark St., Gresham, OR 97030. Tel. (503) 667-7292. Contact Douglas McCarty, Planetarium Director. Planetarium consists of a 30-foot hemispherical dome, with seating for 70. Offers programs on stars and constellations, the Solar System, general astronomy, and special shows. A special discounted facility-use fee of $30 is charged to schools and youth groups. College also has a solar observatory that is used for public viewing and for supplementing college astronomy classes. The college finances both facilities. Special observing sessions are held, usually on Saturday evenings, and the Rose City Astronomers sometimes meet in the planetarium.

Pennsylvania

Edinboro

Edinboro University Planetarium, Edinboro, PA 16444. Open during school year by appointment only. No admission charge. Also has a 14-inch telescope.

Harrisburg

Spectrum, The Museum of Scientific Discovery, Strawberry Square, Box 934, Harrisburg, PA 17108. Tel. (717) 233-7969. Open 10 a.m. to 6 p.m. Tuesday through Sunday; noon to 5 p.m. Sunday. Admission: adults, $3; ages 3 to 17, $2.50; under 3, free. Offers various scientific exhibits, including some astronomy displays.

Indiana

Indiana University of Pennsylvania Planetarium, Geoscience Dept., 114 Walsh Hall, Indiana, PA 15705. Open by appointment only. Fees: $25 for school groups; $10 for scouts, civic groups, and churches. Holds special programs for school groups and events such as viewing Halley's Comet. Holds special classes for amateurs "when requested."

Lock Haven

Ulmer Planetarium, Lock Haven University, Lock Haven, PA 17745. No special hours; shows arranged for public schools and other organizations. Admission is free. Usually holds a Christmas program and a program in the spring, plus shows for university students. Operated by the Departments of Chemistry, Physics, and Geoscience, and the University.

Meadville

Allegheny College Planetarium, Physics Department, Meadville, PA 16355. Planetarium primarily used as a meeting place for astronomy classes. Has a 9.5-inch refractor, and can arrange night tours.

Philadelphia

The Franklin Institute Science Museum, Fels Planetarium, Benjamin Franklin Parkway at 20th St., Philadelphia, PA 19103-1194. Tel. (215) 448-1208. Museum open 9:30 a.m. to 5 p.m. daily, with Omniverse Theater open most evenings until 9 p.m. Separate tickets available for exhibits, Omniverse Theater, and Fels Planetarium. For planetarium only: adults, $5; children and seniors, $4. Combination ticket to exhibits, theater, and planetarium: adults, $12.50; children and seniors, $10.50.

Reading

Reading School District Planetarium, 1211 Parkside Drive South, Redding, PA 19611–1441. Tel. (215) 371–5854. Admission: adults, $3; students, $2. Special shows for groups available for $200 in advance. Open to classes or groups. Call first. Programs include views of the Solar System, films, talks on Native American sky legends, and current astronomical events.

Williamsport

Detwiler Planetarium, Lycoming College, Williamsport, PA 17701–5192. Tel. (717) 321–4284. Public shows announced in local papers and on local radio stations. Programs presented to school groups by arrangement. Admission free. Group tours call ahead. The Planetarium is owned by Lycoming College, and operated by the faculty and students of the Department of Astronomy and Physics.

Rhode Island

Providence

Cormack Planetarium, Museum of Natural History, Friends of the Park Museum, Roger Williams Park, Providence, RI 02905. Tel. (401) 785–9450. Fax (401) 941–5920. Michael Umbricht, Coordinator. Programs offered at 1 and 3 p.m. Saturdays and Sundays. During school vacations extra programs are added. Admission is: adults, $1; children 50 cents; children under 4 not admitted. Admission to the Museum is free. Group reservations available. The charge is $1.50 per student, with chaperons free. Holds special lectures and movies during Astronomy Week, plus educational courses and workshops such as "How to Choose a Telescope" and "Learning the Night Sky."

South Carolina

Columbia

Gibbes Planetarium, 1112 Bull St., Columbia, SC 29201. Tel. (803) 799–2810. Seats 55.

Greenville

Howell Memorial Planetarium, Bob Jones University, Greenville, SC 29614. Tel. (803) 242–5100. Seats 90.

Roper Mountain Science Center, 504 Roper Mountain Road, Greenville, SC 29615. (803) 297–0232. Seats 175.

Orangeburg

Stanback Museum and Planetarium, South Carolina State College, Orangeburg, SC 29117. Tel. (803) 536–7174. Seats 82.

Rock Hill

Museum of York County and Settlemyre Planetarium, 4621 Mount Gallant Road,

Rock Hill, SC 29730. Tel. (803) 297–2121. Seats 64.

Tennessee

Johnson City

East Tennessee State University Planetarium, Department of Physics, Box 22060A, East Tennessee State University, Johnson City, TN 37614–0002. Tel. (615) 929–6906. Planetarium mainly used for astronomy courses at the university, although public programs are offered on occasion. No admission fee. Seats 50. Three shows offered per year, typically near the Fall Equinox, the Winter Solstice, and Spring Equinox. Also holds some Star Parties.

Texas

Abilene

Morgan Jones Planetarium, Box 981, Abilene, TX 79604. Open 8 a.m. to 5 p.m. Monday through Thursday; 8 a.m. to 4:30 p.m. Friday. Group tours scheduled twice a year. Operated by the Abilene School District.

Dallas

Science Place Planetarium, Southwest Museum of Science and Technology, P.O. Box 151469, Dallas, TX 75315–1469. Tel. (214) 428–8351. Open 9:30 a.m. to 5:30 p.m. Monday through Saturday; noon to 5:30 p.m. Sunday. Admission is $2 per person. Visitors also can buy combination tickets that include the museum: adults, $5.50; children and senior citizens, $2.50. Group tours are scheduled through the scheduling coordinator at (214) 428–5555. Planetarium seats 65. Offers special shows for school groups and children, as well as adults. Marks astronomical events, such as eclipses and comets, with special programs. In the summer, the planetarium conducts general astronomy classes for children, and a star party/safari to a local wildlife ranch. Also plans some special observing trips to view comets or other astronomical events.

El Paso

El Paso ISD Planetarium, 6531 Boeing Drive, P.O. Box 20100, El Paso, TS 79925. Tel. (915) 779–4316. John Peterson, Consultant. The planetarium is operated by the El Paso Independent School District. Its main star projector can display 1,354 stars, the planets, Sun, and Moon. The public programs cost $2 per person. Programs include a tour of the night sky and simulated space flight. Seats 120. For information about what's in the sky each month, call "Star Line" at (915) 779–4317, after work hours.

Fort Worth

Noble Planetarium, Fort Worth Museum of Science and History, 1501 Montgomery

St., Fort Worth, TX 76107. Tel. (817) 732–1631. Fax (817) 732–7635. Open seven days a week, with programs scheduled daily. Holds school programs during the school year. Holds public observing sessions with help of local astronomy clubs.

Houston

NASA Johnson Space Center, 2101 NASA Rd. 1, Houston, TX 77058. Tel. (713) 483–4273 for tours of 25 or more; for 24–hour recording on visitor information, call (713) 483–4321. Admission is free; gates open from 9 a.m. to 4 p.m.; buildings close at 4:30 p.m. Tours are self-guided, but Mission Control briefings can be scheduled in advance. Closed only on Christmas Day. Operated by the U.S. Government.

Midland

Marian Blakemore Planetarium, Museum of the Southwest, 1705 W. Missouri, Midland, TX 79701. Tel. (915) 683–2882. Mark Hartman, Planetarium Director. Planetarium open 9 a.m. to 5 p.m. Tuesday through Friday; public programs at 2 and 3:30 p.m. Sunday and at 7:30 p.m. Tuesdays. Admission is free. Group tours available. Special programs at the planetarium are based on important astronomical events. Also serves as the meeting place for the West Texas Astronomers club.

San Angelo

Angelo State University Planetarium, Dept. of Physics, Angelo State University, San Angelo, TX 76909. Planetarium shows at 8 p.m. Thursdays and 2 p.m Saturdays. Admission: adults, $2; students and senior citizens, $1.

Tyler

Hudnall Planetarium, Tyler Junior College, Box 9020, Tyler, TX 75711. Tel. (214) 510–2312. Public shows at 1 p.m. Wednesday and 2 p.m. Sunday, during school year. Admission: adults, $1.50; children and senior citizens, $1. Seats 110. Holds monthly Star Parties, and summer children's classes. Operated by Tyler Junior College. Holds observing sessions and monthly meetings for amateurs.

Utah

Provo

Sarah Summerhays Planetarium, Brigham Young University, 297 Eyring Science Center, Provo, UT 84602. Tel. (801) 378–3436. Open by appointment, and at 7:30 and 8:30 p.m. Fridays. Admission is $1. Holds an open observatory on Friday evening. Operated by Brigham Young University.

Salt Lake City

Hansen Planetarium, 15 S. State St., Salt Lake City, UT 84111. Tel. (801) 531-8038. Open 9 a.m. to 9 p.m. Monday through Thursday; 9 a.m. to 1 a.m. Friday and Saturday; 1 to 4 p.m. Sunday. No admission fee. For group tours call in advance. Holds star shows, special events, and Christmas specials. Hosts classes on telescope making, astronomy classes for students and groups.

Vermont

Johnsbury

Fairbanks Museum, Main St., Johnsbury, VT 05819. Tel. (802) 748-2372.

Virginia

Arlington

Arlington Public Schools Planetarium, 1426 N. Quincy St., Arlington, VA 22207. Tel. (703) 358-6070. The planetarium is open from 8 a.m. to 4:30 p.m. weekdays for school groups and weekends for the public. For public programs, admission is: adults, $2; children 12 and under and senior citizens, $1. Groups requesting a private program can call the Planetarium Office to reserve a time. Fee is $50. Sponsors activities for Astronomy Day and Young Astronaut Day and hosts professional astronomer seminars one Wednesday a month. The Northern Virginia Astronomy Club meets at the Planetarium on the third Wednesday of each month.

Chatham

Pittsylvania County Planetarium, Educational and Cultural Center, 37 Pruden St., Box 232, Chatham, VA 24531. Tel. (804) 432-2761. Open 8:30 a.m. to 4:30 p.m. Monday through Friday. Groups by appointment. Seats 87. Public programs on some Sundays, at 3 p.m. No admission fee. Operated by Pittsylvania County Public Schools. Special attractions: planetarium with analog projection, auxiliary digital simulation; mini-museum of local science. Hosts binocular and telescope use sessions about one night per month.

Chesapeake

Chesapeake Planetarium, P.O. Box 15204, Chesapeake, VA 23320. Tel. (804) 547-0153, ext. 281. Robert J. Hitt Jr., Director. Open 8 a.m. to 4 p.m. Monday through Friday. Public programs held at 8 p.m. Thursday. Admission is free. Reservations must be made due to limited seating. Planetarium used during school hours to present programs to Chesapeake school classes.

Harrisonburg

Eastern Mennonite College Museum & Planetarium, Harrisonburg, VA 22801. Tel.

(703) 432–4400. Joseph W. Mast, Planetarium Director. The Planetarium is associated with the D. Ralph Hostetter Museum of Natural History. Built in 1967, the Planetarium features a Spitz A–4 Projector that shows the Sun, major planets, and more than 1,200 stars on the 30–foot dome. The shows are at 2:30 p.m. Admission is $1.50 per person. Groups larger than 20 must make reservations, and there is a minimum fee of $30. Special Sunday afternoon programs are offered from October to March on the first and third Sundays, no admission fee. The facility is supported by the Eastern Mennonite College.

Newport News

Virginia Living Museum, 524 J. Clyde Morris Blvd., Newport News, VA 23601. Tel. (804) 595–1900. Admission, Museum/Observatory: adults, $4.50; children, 3 to 12, $3. Planetarium: adults, $2; children, 3 to 12, $1.50. Combination: adults, $5; children, 3 to 12, $3.50. Offers classes on astronomy for students and adults.

Richmond

Science Museum of Virginia, 2500 West. Broad St., Richmond, VA 23220. Tel. (804) 367–1083. The museum features exhibits on aerospace, astronomy, crystals, computers, electricity, and visual perception, and a Foucault pendulum. The Ethyl UNIVERSE Planetarium Space Theater

features OMNIMAX films and planetarium shows in a five-story, domed theater. Hours are: Sept.-May, 9:30 a.m. to 5 p.m., Thursday until 9 p.m.; Memorial Day to Labor Day, open 9:30 a.m. to 5 p.m., Thursday, Friday, and Saturday until 9 p.m. Admission to exhibits only is $3.50 for adults, $3 for others; exhibits and film or show: $5.50 for adults, $5 others; exhibits, film, and show: $6.50 adults, $6 others. Group rates are available. Holds special classes throughout the year, some involving astronomy.

Wallops Island

NASA GSFC/Wallops Flight Facility, Box 98, Wallops Island, VA 23337. Tel. (804) 824–2297. Open 10 a.m. to 4 p.m. Thursday through Monday from September through June; and 10 a.m. to 4 p.m. in July and August. Admission is free. Tours of the facility available; reservations are required at least three weeks prior to tour date. Visitor Center has space and aeronautics exhibits such as a Moon rock, space suit, models of space vehicles. No programs for amateur astronomers.

Washington

Pullman

Washington State University Planetarium, Washington State University, Pullman, WA 99164. Tel. (509) 335–8518. No regular operating hours; open for special events. No admission fee. Tours for schools and groups during school year only. Supported by Washington State University.

Seattle

Pacific Science Center, 200 Second Ave. N., Seattle, WA 98109. Tel. (206) 443–3611. Open 10 a.m. to 5 p.m. Monday through Friday; 10 a.m. to 6 p.m. Saturday, Sunday, and holidays. Summer hours, 10 a.m. to 6 p.m. Admission: adults, 14 to 64, $6; juniors, 6 to 13, $5; seniors, $5; children, $4. Rotates major exhibits, hosts traveling exhibits and about 12 special events per year. Offers hands-on astronomy classes for children and adults, plus a Starlab Planetarium with regular shows.

West Virginia

Parkersburg

Dwight O. Conner Planetarium, 2101 Dudley Ave., Parkersburg, WV 26101. Tel. (304) 420–9595, ext. 57. Maximum seating, 70 adults. Holds special Christmas season programs. Open 8 a.m. to 4 p.m. with arranged programs. Admission for citizens of Wood County free.

Wisconsin

LaCrosse

University of Wisconsin-LaCrosse Planetarium, University of Wisconsin-La-Crosse, LaCrosse, WI 54601. Tel. (608) 785–8669. All public planetarium lectures are at 7 p.m. Mondays, except for the Saturday Dec. 15 program, which begins at 1 p.m. School groups and private programs may be scheduled by calling the planetarium. The charge per program, for groups up to 60 children or 50 adults, is $10 for groups of 20 or less; 50 cents per person for groups of more than 20 but less than 40; and $20 for groups of 40 or more. Holds programs on the Moon, the sky, black holes, cosmology, ancient observatories, and the space telescope.

Milwaukee

Milwaukee Public Museum, 800 W. Wells St., Milwaukee, WI 53233–1478. Tel. (414) 278–2713. Open 9 a.m. to 5 p.m. daily. Holidays, 11 a.m. to 4 p.m. Admission: adults, $4.50; children ages 4 to 17, $2.50; college students and Milwaukee County Senior Citizens, $3.

Wyoming

Casper

Casper Planetarium, 904 N. Poplar St., Casper, WY 82601. Operates from 7:30

a.m. to 3:30 p.m. during the school year; 7:30 a.m. to 9:30 p.m. June through Labor Day. Admission is $2 per person and $5 per family, with public shows nightly at 8 p.m. For group shows, call and arrange tours. Offers Thanksgiving through Christmas shows, plus laser shows when possible. Operated by the Natrona County School District. The Central Wyoming Astronomy Society is based at the planetarium and regularly sponsors classes for amateur astronomers.

Canada

Calgary

Alberta Science Centre/Centennial Planetarium, 701 11 Street SW, P.O. Box 2100, Station "M," Location 73, Calgary, Alberta, T2P 2M5. Tel. (403) 221-3711. Fax (403) 237-0186. Winter hours, 1 to 9 p.m. Wednesday through Saturday, 1 to 5 p.m. Sunday; Summer hours, 11 a.m. to 9 p.m. Admission to star show: adults, $5.75; seniors/youth, $3; admission to laser show: adults, $6.75; seniors/youth, $5.75. Admission to exhibits: adults, $4; seniors/youth, $3. Exhibits/star show: adults, $6.75; seniors/youth, $4.50. Group tours conducted for a minimum of 10 people. Call for reservations. Holds telescope-building courses for amateur astronomers throughout the year. Marks Astronomy Day with astronomy displays, slide shows, films, and planetarium shows.

Also opens the observatory. The facility has a gift shop which sells science novelties, books, shirts, and astronomical items.

Montreal

Planetarium Dow of the Ville de Montreal, 1000 rue Saint-Jacques Ouest, Montreal, H3C 1G7. Tel. (514) 872-3611. Fax (514) 872-8102. Shows in English and French daily. Times vary. Admission: adults, $2; youths 5 to 17, $2.50; senior citizens, $2.50; children 4 and under, free. Groups of 25 or more are eligible for a discount on Tuesday through Friday. Seats 385 viewers.

Ottawa

National Museum of Science and Technology, Box 9724, Ottawa Terminal, Ottawa, Ontario, K1G 5A3. Tel. (613) 991-9219. Has an observatory, plus planetarium. Has programs in French and English. Starting times vary with the season. Organized groups need a minimum of 20 people. Admission: adults, $4; students/seniors, $2.75; children 5 to 15, $1.75; families, $9. Offers a number of programs designed for astronomers, including astrophotography and viewing programs. The Museum also publishes **Sky News** four times a year, in both French and English. Subscription is free. Call (613) 991-0607. The publication includes sky maps, observing tips, and calendar tips.

Toronto

McLaughlin Planetarium, Royal Ontario Museum, 100 Queen's Park, Toronto, Ontario, Canada M5S 2C6. Tel. (416) 586–5736 for group registration. For advance tickets, call Ticketmaster at (416) 872–1111. Open 10 a.m. to 6 p.m. Mondays; 10 a.m. to 9 p.m. Tuesdays, Wednesdays, Thursdays, and Sundays; 10 a.m. to 8 p.m. Fridays and Saturdays. Admission: adults, $5; seniors, students, children, $3. The 50–seat mini-theater presents multi-panel slide shows about current astronomical events and about the McLaughlin Planetarium. Has a gift shop with astronomical items and games.

Ontario Science Centre, 770 Don Mills Road, Don Mills, Ontario, Canada M3C 1T3. Tel. (416) 429–4100. Open 10 a.m. to 6 p.m. daily; until 9 p.m. Fridays. Admission: adults, $5.50; youths 13 to 17, $4.50; under 12, $2; family, $14. Tour operators receive 20 percent discount for groups, and private groups of more than 25 receive a 10 percent discount. Special events held during the holidays and throughout the year. The Science Centre is funded by the Ontario Ministry of Culture and Communications. The Centre has a STARLAB demonstration every day, and holds special stargazing trips and lectures during the summer.

Vancouver

H.R. MacMillan Planetarium, 1100 Chestnut St., Vancouver, BC V6J 3J9. Tel. (604) 736–4431. Admission, $1.50. Operated by the British Columbia Space Sciences Society. Offers courses in astronomy, lectures and tips on observing, and special observing sessions at the Southam Observatory.

8

U.S. SPACE-BASED ASTRONOMY PROJECTS

NASA PROJECTS AND PUBLICATIONS

Over the past few decades, the U.S. space program has sent a number of scientific instruments into orbit, and, on occasion, out of the Solar System, in an attempt to expand our knowledge of the planets, the Sun, and the Universe. The National Aeronautics and Space Administration has deployed and maintained equipment that sent back remarkable pictures of Mars and the outer planets, as well as spacecraft that examined solar winds or X-ray sources. NASA has maintained an open policy of sharing its findings with the world and with astronomers not directly involved in the programs.

NASA's giant publishing departments churn out material on everything from model rockets to the Space Shuttle to the composition of Saturn's moons. The Jet Propulsion Laboratory and Goddard Space Center, for example, have volumes of pamphlets, brochures, books, and papers on each of NASA's missions. Other NASA offices can provide information on the more technical aspects of space technology and aeronautics. Chances are, one of the agencies below can answer your questions about space exploration and research or can refer you to an agency that can. You may also be able to obtain some helpful information or materials at a nearby NASA Teacher Resource Center. (See **Teaching Resources** in Chapter 10.) In addition, you can get up-to-the-minute information on NASA missions by calling one of the NASA hotlines or bulletin boards listed in Chapter 1.

NASA Public Affairs Points of Contact

★ **NASA Headquarters,** CODE S., Washington, D.C., 20546. Tel. (202) 453–4164 or (202) 453–8455. Fax (202) 426–6111. This office oversees the work of the facilities listed below. Can provide information on past and upcoming NASA projects.

★ **Ames Research Center,** Mail Stop 204–12, Ames Research Center, Moffett Field, CA 94035. Tel. (415) 694–5091, ext. 464. Fax (415) 694–3953. Concentrates on computer science and applications; experimental aerodynamics; flight simulation; life sciences; space sciences; interplanetary missions; infrared astronomy; airborne science and applications.

★ **Goddard Space Flight Center,** Code 130, Goddard Space Flight Center, Greenbelt, MD 20771. Tel. (301) 286–5565, ext. 888. Fax (301) 286–8142. The Space Flight Center has supported all the country's major space programs.

★ **Jet Propulsion Laboratory,** MS 180–200, Jet Propulsion Laboratory, 4800 Oak Grove Dr., Pasadena, CA 91109. Tel. (818) 354–5011, ext. 792. Fax (818) 354–4537. JPL has been the lead agency in exploration of the Solar System via satellites.

★ **Johnson Space Center,** Mail Code AP3, Johnson Space Center, Houston, TX 77058. Tel. (713) 483–8646, ext. 525. Fax (713) 483–2000. The Center has been involved in planning, tracking, and mission control of many U.S. space launches. Details about the missions and accomplishments of the missions are available.

★ **Kennedy Space Center,** PA-PIB, Kennedy Space Center, FL 32899. Tel. (407) 867–2468, ext. 823. Fax (407) 867–2692. Primarily the take-off site for U.S. space vehicles. Serves as ground support.

★ **Langley Research Center,** MS 115, Langley Research Center, Hampton, VA 23665. Tel. (804) 865–3006, ext. 928. Fax (804) 865–4000. Works mainly in basic research in aeronautics and space technology.

★ **Lewis Research Center,** Mail Code 3–11, Lewis Research Center, 21000 Brookpark Rd., Cleveland, OH 44135. Tel. (216) 433–2902, ext. 297. Lewis Center works on propulsion systems, flight research, and biomedical engineering, among other areas.

★ **Lunar and Planetary Programs Office,** c/o Deputy Director, Code SL, NASA Headquarters, Washington, DC 20546. Tel. (202) 755–3730. Can answer inquiries about participation in NASA-supported programs of research on lunar samples and other aspects of lunar science.

★ **Lunar Science Institute,** Data Center, Code L, 3303 NASA Road #1, Houston, TX 77058. Tel. (713) 488–5200. Can provide information about lunar science and about data resources available for scientific and educational purposes.

★ **Marshall Space Flight Center,** Mail Stop CA10, Marshall Space Flight Center, Huntsville, AL 35812. Tel. (205) 544–0034, ext. 824. Fax (205) 544–5852. The Marshall Center has managed several space projects, including the Redstone rocket that put astronaut Alan Shepard into space in 1961. The center also oversaw the launch in 1965 of three Pegasus micrometeoroid detection satellites; and the High Energy Astronomy Observatories launched in 1977, 1978, and 1979 to study stars and star-like objects.

★ **Stennis Space Center,** Mail Code AB–10, John C. Stennis Space Center, Bay St. Louis, MS 39529. Tel. (601) 688–3341, ext. 494. Fax (601) 688–3017. Conducts missions to support the development of the Space Shuttle main engines; conducts research and development in remote sensing and other space applications.

NASA Missions

The following chronological list reflects the long line of projects managed or coordinated by various NASA offices that dealt primarily with astronomical endeavors.

★ **Explorer 1**—The first successful United States Earth satellite was launched January 31, 1958.

★ **Pioneer 3**—Launched Dec. 6, 1958, reached an altitude of 63,580 miles. This mission proved the existence of a second Van Allen radiation belt.

★ **Pioneer 4**—Launched March 3, 1959, was the United States's first successful Moon probe. Measured particles and fields in a flyby; entered heliocentric orbit.

★ **Ranger 3**—Launched in 1962 toward the Moon. No television pictures received of the lunar surface, but good data received on levels of gamma radiation.

★ **Ranger 4**—Launched April 23, 1962. It impacted on the Moon after the failure of a timer resulted in a loss of control of the spacecraft.

★ **Ranger 5**—Launched October 18, 1962, but also failed.

★ **Mariner 2**—Launched August 27, 1962, this interplanetary spacecraft passed Venus at a distance of 21,685 miles, on December 14. Sent back information about the atmosphere of the planet.

★ **Ranger 6**—Launched January 1964, was the first of a series of four spacecraft designed to obtain high-resolution television pictures of the lunar surface. Impacted on the Moon February 2, 1964, but the camera system failed to operate.

★ **Ranger 7**—Launched July 28, 1964, the craft radioed to Earth 4,316 pictures of the Moon's surface, some of which proved to have 2,000 times the resolution of the pictures produced by the best Earth-based telescopes. Photographed area of the Mare Cognitum.

★ **Mariner 3**—Launched November 5, 1964, toward Mars. Signal lost nine hours after launch and 76,000 miles from Earth when battery power depleted. Mariner 3 is in orbit around the Sun.

★ **Mariner 4**—Launched November 28, 1964 on a 228–day mission to Mars.

★ **Ranger 8**—Launched February 17, 1965. It landed on the Moon February 8 after transmitting 7,137 pictures of the Sea of Tranquility and highlands bordering its southwestern shore.

★ **Ranger 9**—Launched March 21, 1965, this was the final mission in the lunar photo-reconnaissance series. Ranger 9 came within 2.76 miles of its aiming point on the floor of the crater Alphonsus. It sent back 5,814 high-resolution pictures of the Moon.

★ **Surveyor 1**—Launched May 30, 1966, this was the first Surveyor spacecraft successfully launched and soft landed on the Moon June 1, 1966. It returned 11,150 pictures of the landing site in the Ocean of Storms near the crater Flamsteed.

★ **Surveyor 2**—Launched September 20, 1966, the craft began tumbling and crash landed in the crater Copernicus September 22, 1966.

★ **Surveyor 3**—Launched April 16, 1967, it landed on the Moon April 19, 1967 in the Ocean of Storms. It returned 6,315 pictures, including a solar eclipse as seen from the Moon.

★ **Mariner 5**—Launched June 12, 1967 to Venus on a flyby mission.

★ **Surveyor 4**—Launched July 14, 1967 to the lunar sea Sinus Medii. The spacecraft failed during the terminal descent to the surface.

★ **Surveyor 5**—Launched September 8, 1967, it returned data on the lunar soil, and indicated it was basaltic, found magnetic materials in the soil, and returned 19,006 pictures.

★ **Surveyor 6**—Launched November 6, 1967, and landed in Sinus Medii November 9. This mission carried a camera with polarizing filters for a study of the polarizing of light from the lunar surface. More than 30,000 pictures were transmitted during its two weeks of operation. Surveyor 6 was the first spacecraft to be launched from an extraterrestrial body. On November 17, 1967, it was commanded to fire its three vernier engines and the craft moved eight feet.

★ **Mariner 5**—On October 19, 1967, it encountered Venus at a distance of 45 million miles from Earth. The craft had traveled more than 200 million miles and passed the planet at a closest approach of about 2,500 miles.

★ **Surveyor 7**—Launched January 6, 1968, toward a January 9 landing on the Moon north of the crater Tycho. This was the first Surveyor targeted for the lunar highlands and the first used for purely scientific objectives. Earlier Surveyors had fulfilled Apollo objectives for exploration of Apollo landing sites. The spacecraft returned 21,038 television pictures of the surface, as well as data on soil composition from magnet assemblies.

★ **Mariner 6 & 7**—Mariner 6 launched to Mars February 23, 1969—followed by Mariner 7 on March 27. The 850–pound spacecraft were launched by Atlas-Centaur boosters on flyby trajectories. Mariner 6 encountered Mars on July 31, 1969 at a closest approach of 2,134 miles, transmitting 50 far-encounter TV pictures and 24–near encounter images. Mariner 7 encountered Mars on August 4, at a closest approach of approximately 2,200 miles.

★ **Mariner 8 & 9**—Mariner 8, launched May 1971 toward Mars orbit, was lost, but Mariner 9 successfully went into Mars orbit on November 13, 1971. Through May of 1972, Mariner 9 returned almost 7,000 pictures and thousands of spectral measurements. The photographs yielded a map covering 100 percent of the planet.

★ **Mariner 10**—Launched November 3, 1973, to Venus and Mercury. This was the first Mercury mission to use the gravity-assist technique (Venus to Mercury). Mariner 10 photographed Venus with ultraviolet filters, revealing atmospheric circulation patterns not visible from Earth. At Mercury, photographs revealed a lunar-like surface; a thin atmosphere of helium; and a magnetic field.

★ **Pioneer 10**—In 1972, this mission captured the first close-up pictures of Jupiter's Great Red Spot and planetary atmosphere; it carries a plaque with intergalactic greetings from Earth.

★ **Pioneer 11**—This spacecraft passed by Jupiter in 1973 at a distance of 26,725 miles above cloud tops; used Jupiter's gravity to swing it back across the Solar System to Saturn; took pictures of Saturn from within 13,300 miles of cloud tops.

★ **Helios 2**—Launched January 15, 1976, and flew in an elliptical orbit to within 41 million km of the Sun, measuring solar wind, corona, electrons, and cosmic rays.

★ **Pioneer Venus 1**—In 1978 studied cloud cover and planetary topography.

★ **Pioneer Venus 2**—In 1978 measured atmosphere of Venus top to bottom.

★ **Viking**—On August 20, 1975 and June 19, 1976, two Viking orbiter-lander spacecraft were launched toward Mars. Viking 1 began orbiting Mars June 19, 1976 and its lander reached the surface in the Chryse Planitia region July 20. Viking 2 reached Mars orbit August 7, and landed in the Utopia Planitia on September 3. During the primary mission, which lasted until mid-November, the Vikings took more than 10,000 pictures from orbit and the surface. Viking missions searched for microbial life; performed organic and mineralogical studies of the Martian soil; studied physical and magnetic properties of the soil; made daily weather reports and listened for seismic activity. No conclusive evidence of life found.

★ **Voyager**—During the summer of 1977, two Voyager spacecraft were launched toward Jupiter, Saturn, and beyond. The primary mission was to fly by the planets Jupiter and Saturn, capturing photographs and conducting other science experiments. The two craft later flew by Uranus and Neptune. Some spectacular photos were returned to Earth by the craft. They also discovered new moons around each of the planets they visited.

★ **Solar Maximum Mission**—Launched in 1980, the spacecraft contributed valuable data on solar cycles. SMM also provided the first measurements of sunspots in three dimensions, as well as detection of emissions from Supernova 1987a.

★ **The Infrared Astronomical Satellite**—Launched January 25, 1983. The joint mission with the Netherlands, the United Kingdom, and the U.S. carried a 22.5–inch refrigerated telescope to measure the infrared energy, or heat emissions, from dust, gas, stars, galaxies, and other objects that are difficult or impossible to detect with conventional optical telescopes.

★ **Project Magellan**—Launched May 4, 1989, toward Venus, with the goal of completing mapping the planet's surface landforms. This was the first planetary mission launched by the space shuttle.

Magellan arrived at Venus on August 10, 1990.

★ **Galileo**—Launched October 18, 1989, the Galileo spacecraft was the second planetary mission to be launched by the space shuttle. It is expected to arrive at Jupiter in December 1995. It will be the first to make direct measurements from an instrumented probe within Jupiter's atmosphere, and the first craft to conduct long-term observations of the planet.

★ **Cosmic Background Explorer, (COBE)**—Launched on November 18, 1989, to study the origin and dynamics of the Universe and seek evidence supporting the theory that the Universe began with a "Big Bang."

★ **ROSAT**—The Roentgen satellite was launched June 1, 1990, and is a joint project of Germany, the United Kingdom, and the United States. The goal is to map the entire sky in X-rays and then use a High-Resolution Imager built at the Smithsonian Astrophysical Observatory to make detailed studies of selected subjects.

★ **Ulysses**—Launched October 6, 1990, this is a cooperative international mission developed by NASA and the European Space Agency. The mission will explore the Sun and the heliosphere at previously unexplored high solar latitudes. It will make detailed measurements of the Sun's corona, the origin and acceleration of the solar wind into space, and the composition and acceleration of energetic atoms

from the Sun. It first will go toward Jupiter, where it will be projected out of the ecliptic plane toward the Sun's southern pole. It is scheduled to reach the Sun's south pole in May 1994 and to conclude its investigation in September 1995 at the Sun's north pole.

★ **Hubble Space Telescope**—Authorized in 1977 and launched in 1990, the space telescope is named for American astronomer Edwin P. Hubble. Hubble's observations from Mount Wilson Observatory in the 1920s established the reality of galaxies besides our own and led him to conclude that the Universe is expanding. Among the telescope's five science instruments are:

- The Wide Field/Planetary Camera, the space telescope's general-purpose camera;

- The Faint Object Camera, designed to study extremely distant stars and galaxies;

- The Faint Object Spectrograph, which will examine the chemistry of extremely faint objects;

- The High-Resolution Spectrograph, designed to study faint objects in the ultraviolet portion of the light spectrum;

- The High-Speed Photometer, which will measure the brightness of space objects and changes in brightness over time.

Planned Missions

★ **Extreme Ultraviolet Explorer**—Scheduled for launch in 1991, the instrument will conduct a two-year all-sky survey in the band between the ultraviolet and X-ray ranges.

★ **Mars Observer**—The Mars Observer mission will expand the discoveries of Mariner 9 and Viking by making a two-year global scientific survey of Mars. The mission is planned for a launch in 1992, and is scheduled to arrive at Mars in 1993. The scientific objectives are to: determine the global elemental and mineralogical characters of the surface material; define the global topography and gravitational field; establish the nature of the magnetic field; determine the time and space distribution, abundance, source, and sinks of volatile material and dust over a seasonal cycle; explore the atmosphere.

★ **Cassini Mission**—Tentatively scheduled for launch in 1996, it will fly past the asteroid Maja in 1997, and execute a gravity-assist flyby past Jupiter in 2000 for a four-year study of the Saturnian system. After entering orbit around Saturn, Cassini will send a probe to pass through the atmosphere of Titan, Saturn's largest moon. Additional plans call for up to 40 targeted flybys of Saturn's moons, including 36 close encounters of Titan, two of Iapetus, and one each of Enceladus and Dione.

★ **CRAF, Comet Rendezvous Asteroid Flyby**—To be launched in 1995 to fly by the asteroid Hamburga in 1998, and then to rendezvous with comet Kopff in the year 2000 for a three-year period of intensive study. CRAF will implant a penetrator in the comet's nucleus to analyze for the first time the solid material of which a comet is made.

★ **Gamma-Ray Observatory**—The second of four planned "Great Observatories" in space, this mission is designed to investigate gamma radiation, the most energetic of all forms of radiation, and its violent sources—pulsars, quasars, and black holes. It will be managed by Goddard. It is a joint development of the U.S., Germany, the Netherlands, the United Kingdom, and the European Space Agency.

★ **Advanced X-ray Astrophysics Facility**—The third of the Great Observatories is scheduled for launch in 1997. It is designed to obtain high resolution imagery from celestial X-ray sources and to study black holes, the contribution of hot gas to the mass of the Universe, clusters and superclusters of galaxies, and the existence of "dark matter" in the Universe. It is managed by Marshall Space Flight Center.

★ **Space Infrared Telescope Facility**—The fourth in the planned series of Great Observatories. The launch date is tentatively set for near the end of the century. The observatory will study areas of prime interest that have been identified by earlier infrared observatories, such as infrared sources at the edge of the Universe, cosmic births of stars and galaxies, and the "missing mass"—that 90 percent of matter in the Universe that cannot be seen.

9

THE HISTORY OF ASTRONOMY

WHO'S WHO OF ASTRONOMY

Throughout the long centuries of humanity's study of the heavens, individual astronomers have played key roles, sometimes revolutionary roles, not only in science, but in society. Some contributors initiated leaps forward in the technology of observing the skies, while others painstakingly catalogued and classified data that enabled us to know more about the Universe around us. In many instances, especially before the twentieth century, the astronomers were in essence "amateurs" who taught themselves astronomy, and in turn taught the rest of us. Of course, not all discoveries resulted in giant leaps forward, as did the work of Nicolaus Copernicus that moved the Earth from the center of the Universe to a less glorious position. Many times, simple improvements in instruments enabled others to make the leap. Galileo, for example, did not invent the telescope, but he certainly understood its significance and turned it to ground-breaking astronomical research.

The following who's who of astronomers and other scientists shows how the science of astronomy advanced, slowly at times, over the centuries.

★ **John Couch Adams** (1819–1892). An Englishman who analyzed the ir-

regularities in the motion of Uranus and uncovered evidence that a planet, now called Neptune, existed beyond the orbit of Uranus. At the same time, LeVerrier, a French mathematician, independently came to the same conclusion. This discovery confirmed the gravitational theory and ranks as one of the great scientific achievements.

★ **Aristotle** (lived in Greece about 350 B.C.). A philosopher and scientist who used the astronomical knowledge of his time to formulate a theory that dominated astronomy for nearly 1800 years. Aristotle believed the Earth was at the center of the Universe, and that the Sun, the planets, and the stars revolved around it.

★ **Halton "Chip" Arp** (1924–). A controversial astronomer currently on the staff at the Max Planck Institute for Physics and Astrophysics, Germany, who has questioned the fundamental premise of extragalactic astronomy: he has raised doubts that the redshifts of galaxies beyond the Local Group arise from the Doppler effect.

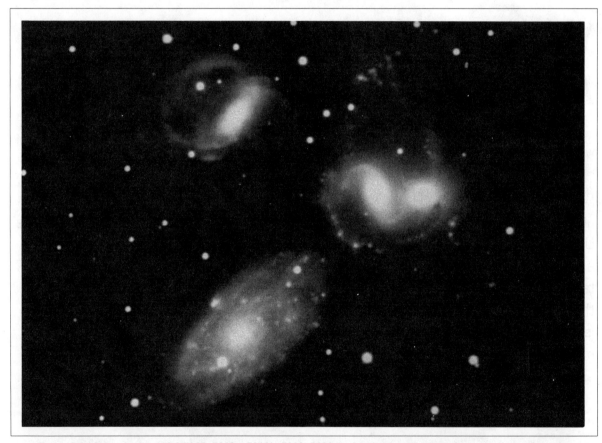

Four of the five galaxies (NGC 7317, 7318a, 7318b, 7319, 7320) in Stephan's quintet, in the constellation Pegasus. This system has been used to tout the theory that the redshift is not truly a distance indicator, because NGC 7320, the galaxy toward the bottom of the photo, shows a much smaller redshift than the other four, although it appears to be a member of the group. (National Optical Astronomy Observatories/W. Schoening/N. Sharp)

★ **Walter Baade** (1893–1960). Made contributions to stellar astronomy. His correction to the Cepheid scale led to a doubling of the estimated size of the Universe.

★ **Harold Delos Babcock** (1882–1968). An American astronomer who made major contributions in spectroscopy and studies of the Sun, especially solar magnetism.

★ **Edward Emerson Barnard** (1857–1923). A professional photographer initially, Barnard became one of the world's premier observers, and independently discovered at least fourteen comets. He worked at the Lick and Yerkes observatories.

★ **Johann Bayer** (1572–1625). Published a star atlas in 1603 that assigned Greek letters in alphabetical order to the stars in each constellation, usually in order of brightness. Those designations are used today.

★ **Friedrich Wilhelm Bessel** (1784–1846). Bessel was working at the Konigsberg Observatory in Germany in 1838 when he announced the stellar parallax of 61 Cygni. This was the first star whose distance was measured directly, using trigonometric parallax. Bessel obtained 61 Cygni's parallax with a telescope called a heliometer. In a sense this was the start of stellar astronomy and astrophysics.

★ **Hans Bethe** (1906–). Developed theories in the 1930s about the nuclear reactions inside stars—specifically, the fusion of hydrogen atoms into a helium atom.

★ **Tycho Brahe** (1546–1601). A Danish astronomer who perfected observations before the age of the telescope. His observations were accurate to the limit of naked-eye measurements. Some have called him the greatest astronomical observer before the advent of the telescope. Brahe worked diligently to measure angles, and constantly tested his observations of star and planet positions with the tables of other astronomers.

★ **Sherburne Wesley Burnham** (1838–1921). An American astronomer who worked at Lick and Yerkes Observatories. He discovered more than 1,300 double stars and produced a catalogue of double stars. He was one of the original astronomers when the Lick Observatory opened.

★ **W.W. Campbell** (1862–1938). An American astronomer and director of the Lick Observatory who pioneered the study of the radial velocities of stars and made major contributions to planetary science.

★ **Annie Jump Cannon** (1863–1941). An American astronomer who worked at the Harvard College Observatory. Her major emphasis was on stellar spectra, and she was the major contributor to the **Draper Catalogue**, published in 1924.

★ **Gian Domenico Cassini** (1625–1712). The first of four generations of Italian astronomers. He discovered a narrow, dark band on the surface of the rings around Saturn, which bears his name. Most of his later work was done in Paris. He also discovered several moons around Saturn, and added greatly to measurements of the distance of Mars from Earth.

★ **Nicolaus Copernicus** (1473–1543). A Polish-born scientist who proposed a then-heretical view among Europeans that the Sun, and not the Earth, was the center of the Solar System. In the year of his death, he published **De Revolutionibus** which set forth his assumptions.

★ **H.D. Curtis** (1872–1942). An American astronomer who worked at the Lick Observatory, and in 1920 correctly supported the "island-universe" theory of the galaxies in debates with Harlow Shapley.

★ **J.L.E. Dreyer** (1852–1926). Developed the **New General Catalogue of Nebulae and Clusters of Stars (NGC)** in 1888, and in 1895, the **Index Catalogue of Nebulae.** Dreyer also was a historian who wrote extensively about the lives of astronomers, especially Tycho Brahe.

★ **Arthur Stanley Eddington** (1882–1944). An English astronomer who concentrated on cosmology and the evolution of stars.

★ **Albert Einstein** (1879–1955). The most famous of the scientists who developed theories about the Universe. Einstein is known for his theory of relativity, the special theory of relativity, the equivalence of mass and energy, and cosmological considerations. He revolutionized the way we think about the Universe and time.

★ **Johann Franz Encke** (1791–1865). Used mathematics to "discover" the comet that bears his name. Actually Jean Louis Pons, of the Marseilles Observatory, spotted the comet on more than one pass by the Earth, but it took Encke's calculations to determine that the comets Pons had discovered actually were a single comet which orbited the Sun in a period of 3.5 years. Encke reportedly never viewed the comet through a telescope.

★ **Eratosthenes** (born in Egypt about 273 B.C.). Measured the size of the Earth through mathematical formulas. His measurements, based on the distance between two cities on the same line of longitude and the shadows cast by a stick at each city at the same time of day, essentially match those obtained by more exact methods today.

★ **Camille Flammarion** (1842–1925). A French astronomer who wrote numerous popular books and articles. He also was known for his study of Mars.

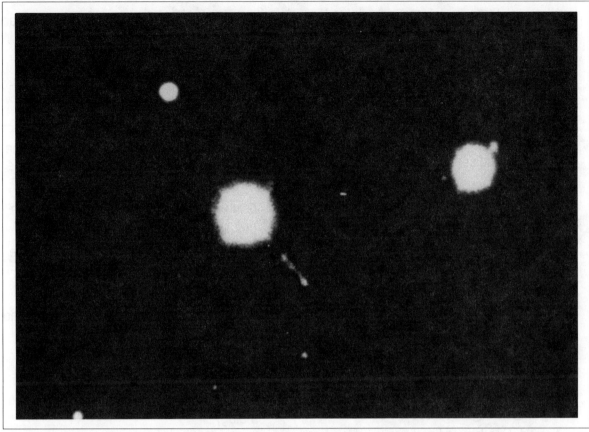

The visible part of 3C 273, a quasar in the constellation Virgo. (National Optical Astronomy Observatories)

★ **John Flamsteed** (1646–1719). The first Astronomer Royal of the Greenwich Observatory. He excelled in producing stellar catalogs and lunar tables based on his observations.

★ **Jean Bernard Leon Foucault** (1819–1868). A French physicist who created a giant pendulum to demonstrate the Earth's rotation. In addition, he laid the foundation for modern telescope making. He devised tests, including the Foucault knife-edge test, to analyze the curvature of a mirror.

★ **Galileo Galilei** (1564–1642). A contemporary of Kepler who was the first to use a telescope for astronomical observations. He also was among the first scientists of his time to use experimental investigations rather than interpreting old texts. He accepted the Copernican theory, which eventually landed him in trouble with Church officials of his era. Galileo found that, contrary to theories current at the time, the heavens did indeed change. He discovered sunspots and the moons around Jupiter, and noticed the odd shape of Saturn even though his meager telescope could not distinguish the rings. His findings set in motion a flood of astronomical study that revolutionized the way we view our Universe.

★ **George Gamow** (1904–1968). A Russian astrophysicist who studied stellar evolution and made several contributions to the field.

★ **John Goodricke** (1764–1786). An Englishman who was the first to record observations on the variations in light from the star Algol. Goodricke accounted for the variations in light by theorizing that either a large body was revolving around the star, or that the star had dark spots that were periodically turned toward Earth. His conjecture of an eclipsing body revolving around Algol eventually was confirmed. Goodricke also discovered two other naked-eye variables: Beta Lyrae and Delta Cephei.

★ **Jesse Greenstein** (1909–). An expert on the spectra of stars and quasars; the first (along with partner Maarten Schmidt) to discover quasars.

★ **Leonid Grishchuk** (1941–). A Soviet expert on gravity waves.

★ **George E. Hale** (1868–1938). Hale was known for his solar work, and also is mainly responsible for the building of the Hale Telescope, a 200–inch reflector at Palomar.

★ **Asaph Hall** (1829–1907). An observer at the U.S. Naval Observatory who discovered the moons of Mars, in part, he once said, because he was tired of reading that "Mars has no moons." Hall also observed the other planets and double and variable stars during his years at the Observatory.

★ **Edmund Halley** (1656–1742). Known for the comet that bears his name, Comet Halley, Halley predicted the return of the comet based on mathematics, but never saw its return. He was instrumental in getting Isaac Newton's theories published.

★ **Stephen Hawking** (1942–). An English mathematician and astronomer who has made fundamental contributions to cosmology.

★ **Caroline Herschel** (1750–1848). Discovered eight comets and numerous star clusters and nebulae as she worked with her brother, William Herschel. She also revised John Flamsteed's star catalogue.

★ **John Frederick William Herschel** (1792–1871). The son of William Herschel, he contributed to double star astronomy from his observatories in England and South Africa. He also discovered hundreds of deep-sky objects in both hemispheres and developed techniques for visual photometry.

★ **William Herschel** (1738–1822). An Englishman who discovered Uranus and hundreds of double stars, and also catalogued thousands of nebulae. Herschel's observations led him to believe that the Sun, like other stars, moved through space. He also gained fame in the astronomy community via his catalogues of nebulae and star clusters.

★ **Ejnar Hertzsprung** (1973–1967). A Danish astrophysicist who discovered the giant and dwarf divisions of stars. He and H.N. Russell are responsible for the Hertzsprung-Russell Diagram, in which stars are plotted by their spectral type and their absolute magnitudes.

★ **Johannes Hevelius** (1611–1687). Made accurate studies of the Moon's surface and also drew a star catalogue.

★ **Jeremiah Horrocks** (1619–1641). Born in a village near Liverpool, England, Horrocks was the first to predict and observe a transit of Venus across the disk of the Sun.

★ **Fred Hoyle** (1915–). A British astronomer who has made major contributions to astrophysics and cosmology. He supports the steady-state theory of the Universe.

★ **Edwin P. Hubble** (1889–1953). First measured the distance to the Andromeda Galaxy by using Cepheids. He classified galaxies, grouping them by sizes and shapes, and established that many nebulae actually are galaxies. He measured space out to 500 million light years—farther than any previous survey had. Hubble's study of the galaxies led him to conclude they are moving away from Earth, which supported the concept that the Universe originated in a cosmic explosion. Those observations led to Hubble's law: the more distant the galaxy from Earth, the faster it moves away.

★ **Lady Maragret Huggins** (1848–1915). An early pioneer for women in astronomy. She and her husband, William, were pioneers in the use of the spectroscope and published numerous articles on their work on stellar spectrum.

★ **Christian Huygens** (1629–1695). Devised new methods of forming accurate tools and grinding and polishing lenses. With his improved instruments, he discovered Titan, a moon of Saturn. Although an accomplished astronomer, Huygens eventually concentrated his attention on optics.

★ **Karl G. Jansky** (1905–1949). An American engineer who detected radio emissions from the Milky Way in 1931. This was the start of radio astronomy.

★ **Pierre Jules Cesar Janssen** (1824–1907). A French astronomer who survived several adventures, including revolutions, escape from a besieged city by hot air balloon, and expeditions to far countries, in his quest to explore one star, the Sun. Janssen turned a spectroscope on the Sun and advanced our knowledge of the elements it contains.

The M42 nebula, the middle "star" in the sword of Orion, was one of the objects that looked suspiciously like a comet to Charles Messier. (Courtesy of Vista)

★ **James Keeler** (1857–1900). An early director of the Lick Observatory.

★ **Johannes Kepler** (1571–1630). Born in Weilder-Stadt, Wurttemberg, in Germany, Kepler was a mathematician by training who became an early convert to the principles of the Copernican system. He served as an assistant to Tycho Brahe and after Brahe's death, obtained possession of most of Tycho's records. Kepler developed mathematical formulas that allowed him to predict the motions of the planets.

- **Kepler's First Law:** Each planet moves about the Sun in an orbit that is an ellipse, with the Sun at one focus of the ellipse.

- **Kepler's Second Law** (The Law of Areas): The straight line joining a planet and the Sun sweeps out equal areas in space in equal intervals of time.

- **Kepler's Third Law:** The squares of the sidereal periods of the planets are in direct proportion to the cubes of the semi-major axes of their orbits.

★ **Gerard P. Kuiper** (1905–1973). Director of the Jet Propulsion Laboratory from 1960 until 1973 and founder of the Lunar and Planetary Laboratory at Tucson, Arizona. He studied lunar and planetary subjects, especially in connection with spacecraft.

★ **Henrietta Leavitt** (1867–1921). Observed Cepheids in the Lesser Magellanic Cloud, and discovered she could draw a smooth curve or period-luminosity curve, which other astronomers used to calculate distances to other galaxies.

★ **Jean Joseph LeVerrier** (1811–1877). A French astronomer whose work led to the discovery of Neptune in 1846. He used mathematics to calculate the orbit, and the planet was found easily by observers using his predictions.

★ **Percival Lowell** (1855–1916). A U.S. astronomer who developed controversial theories about life on Mars. He also studied other planets, and established an observatory in Flagstaff, Arizona. He predicted the existence of a ninth planet, but Pluto was not discovered until fourteen years after his death. Lowell, technically an amateur, did much to promote astronomy in the United States.

★ **Donald H. Menzel** (1901–1976). An American astronomer who concentrated on solar research and published several popular books on astronomy.

★ **Charles Messier** (1730–1817). A French astronomer who prepared one of the earliest catalogues of nebulous objects in the sky. A comet hunter, Messier developed the catalogue as an aid to detecting objects that might be mistaken for comets. Astronomers still use his 103 designations of objects such as M81 in Ursa Major to identify them.

★ **Rudolf Minkowski** (1895–1976). Concentrated his research upon supernovas and studies of stellar evolution. He also was a pioneer in radio astronomy.

★ **Isaac Newton** (1643–1727). An Englishman who formulated the basic laws of modern mechanics and applied them to the Universe. He was one of the most celebrated of the early scientists, even in his own time, and contributed much to the scientific way of thinking. His "laws" of gravity and motion opened the way for advancements in nearly every technological field, and especially in the science of astronomy. Newton's Laws of Motion:

- The First Law (Inertia): in the absence of any outside influence, an object at rest tends to remain at rest, and an objection in motion tends to remain in motion, in a straight line, and at a constant speed.

- The Second Law: The strength of a force is equal to the amount of mass involved times the acceleration it undergoes: F = ma.

- The Third Law: For every action there is an equal and opposite reaction.

★ **Seth Barnes Nicholson** (1891–1963). American astronomer who did extensive studies of the moons of Jupiter and discovered several asteroids.

★ **Jan H. Oort** (1900–1989). A Dutch astronomer who advanced the theory that trillions of comets surround the Solar System in a sphere about 50,000 A.U. in radius, far outside Pluto's orbit.

★ **Theodor von Oppolzer** (1841–1886). Compiled a "Canon" that contains detailed information on all 8,000 solar eclipses and 5,200 lunar eclipses between 1208 B.C. and A.D. 2161.

★ **E.C. Pickering** (1846–1919). An American astronomer who was a pioneer in stellar spectroscopy. His contributions include the detection of the first spectroscopic binary (Mizar A).

★ **W.H. Pickering** (1858–1938). The brother of E.C. Pickering. Worked mainly with the Solar System. He was the first to find a satellite by photographic methods (Phoebe, a moon of Saturn), and produced a photographic atlas of the Moon, showing each section of the lunar surface.

★ **John S. Plaskett** (1865–1941). A Canadian astronomer who researched the nature of hot, early-type stars.

★ **Jean Louis Pons** (1761–1831). A French astronomer who specialized in comet-hunting. He was not formally trained as an astronomer, but eventually recorded thirty-six comet discoveries.

★ **Claudius Ptolemy**. A Greek astronomer who developed a detailed theory of the Universe around A.D. 140. Like Aristotle's, his theory placed the Earth at the center of the Universe, but attempted to explain retrograde motion of the planets. His theory included epicycles and deferents, which meant the planets circled about a line that also circled the Earth.

★ **Grote Reber** (1912–). An American engineer who built his own radio telescope at age twenty-five and pioneered research in the field.

★ **Ole Roemer** (1644–1710). Obtained a first value of the velocity of light, and also was the first to invent a transit instrument, which increased the accuracy in the determination of time and right ascensions.

★ **Henry Norris Russell** (1877–1957). An American astronomer mainly remembered for his work on stellar evolution, and as a co-designer of the Hertzsprung-Russell Diagram.

★ **Martin Ryle** (1918–1984). A British radio astronomer whose observations disproved the steady-state theory of the Universe. He also improved the design of radio telescopes.

★ **Allan Sandage** (1926–). An American astronomer known for his theories and studies of the Universe, its structure and size. He followed in Hubble's footsteps in trying to determine the extent and make-up of the Universe.

★ **Giovanni Schiaparelli** (1935–1910). An Italian astronomer best remembered for his planetary work, especially his 1877

reports in which he described "canals" on Mars.

★ **Bernhard Schmidt** (1879–1935). Inventor of the Schmidt telescope.

★ **Maarten Schmidt** (1930–). Along with Greenstein, discovered quasars.

★ **Heinrich Samuel Schwabe** (1794–1875). German-born astronomer who began a series of observations in 1825 which led to the discovery that sunspots followed a periodic schedule of about ten years. His careful, exact records actually began as an attempt to find a planet inside the orbit of Mercury. Initially, his findings were not noticed by the astronomical community.

★ **Karl Schwarzschild** (1873–1916). A German astronomer who studied stellar evolution and distribution, and developed the Schwarzschild radius, which, in part, offers an explanation of why "Black Holes" might exist.

★ **Harlow Shapley** (1885–1972). An American astronomer who was the first to give an accurate estimate of the size and shape of the Galaxy. He also incorrectly argued that galaxies were not separate "island universes," but a part of the Milky Way galaxy.

★ **Friedrich Wilhelm Struve** (1793–1864). A German astronomer who worked in Russia. He was a pioneer in double star astronomy. His son, Otto W. Struve

(1818–1905), also was known as a double star observer.

★ **Kip Thorne** (1940–). An American who has concentrated much of his efforts on theoretical analysis of gravity waves.

★ **Clyde W. Tombaugh** (1907–). In 1930, discovered the planet Pluto while working at the Lowell Observatory.

★ **Fred L. Whipple** (1906–). Developed the most widely accepted theory on the composition of comets. Whipple originated the idea that the nucleus of a comet is like a "dirty snowball" and is a few kilometers across.

★ **Yakov Borisovich Zel'dovich** (1913–1987). A Soviet astrophysicist who ranked among the top physicists of this century. He helped formulate a theory explaining the nuclear chain reactions in the atomic bomb. Later he concentrated on exploring the time just after the Big Bang.

★ **Fritz Zwicky** (1898–1974). A Swiss astronomer who emigrated to America. He specialized in studies of external galaxies, and was a vocal opponent of current theories of cosmology that place quasars far outside our galaxy.

ASTRONOMY TIMELINE

Nobody knows just when early humans began recording their observations of the heavens. The names of the constellations, for example, can be traced back to several civilizations that undoubtedly borrowed the designations from earlier cultures. Archaeological evidence, however, establishes that as early as 2000 B.C., Sumerians were recording constellations. The Egyptians, Babylonians, early Greeks, early Chinese, and peoples of the Euphrates Valley also kept records of the comings and goings of the constellations of the night sky.

In many cultures, constellations were given mystical powers; astrologers used their knowledge of the planets and the stars to foretell the future. Although these developments marked the early beginnings of astronomy, the "science" as we know it today did not develop for many centuries after humans began recording data.

The following timeline gives a brief history of the development of astronomy, from the days of the astrologers to today's astrophysicists and cosmologists.

★ **2000 B.C.:** Sumerians made records of the constellations. These most likely were based on early observations by other civilizations. Priests dominated the early astronomy observations, and the practice of astrology grew.

★ **1000 B.C.:** The Egyptians developed calendars based on Sirius, the brightest star in the sky.

★ **600 B.C. to 350 B.C.:** The Greeks attempted to explain the motion of the planets by making theoretical models of the Solar System. They also furthered the use of astrology as a predictor of events on Earth. The long-range impact of Greek thought, however, centered around the philosophy of Aristotle, who summarized knowledge of his day, including astronomy, into a philosophy that held sway for the next 1800 years. Aristotle believed that the Earth was at the center of the Universe, and that the planets and Sun circled about it. He developed a theory that the Universe was made of fifty-five celestial spheres that fit around each other.

★ **273 B.C.:** Eratosthenes developed a means to measure the Earth's circumference. His measurements were near the ones obtained by today's scientists. This was a demonstration that humans could hope to actually measure the size of the Earth.

★ **A.D. 140:** Claudius Ptolemy, a Greek astronomer living in Alexandria, Egypt, presented a detailed theory of the Universe that explained the retrograde motion of the planets, with the Earth at the center of the Universe. Versions of Ptolemy's ideas and his tables of planetary motions were accepted for nearly 1500 years.

★ **Middle Ages:** During this time, roughly from 476 until the 1500s, there were no major astronomical findings. Educated people relied on copies of older works, and there was little direct observation or research. The Arabs kept detailed records of the heavens, and their names for many of the stars are used today. In the Far East, the Chinese developed early catalogues, but retreated from the "scientific method" later adopted by Western Europe.

★ **1543:** In 1543 Nicolaus Copernicus published **De Revolutionibus (Concerning Revolutions),** which set forth the idea of a heliocentric system in which the Earth and the planets circled about the Sun. This was the first major advance in the science of astronomy in hundreds of years. Prior to this, the theories of Aristotle and Ptolemy had dominated astronomy. During the Middle Ages, only the Arabs had systematically studied the heavens, and they relied heavily on the seriously flawed work of Ptolemy.

★ **Late 1500s:** Tycho Brahe used giant sextants, steel quadrants, and armillary spheres to make astronomical observations. His data and recordings, of an accuracy unknown until that time, were made without benefit of the telescope. Tycho Brahe's observations led him to detect a new star, and to discover that the heavens were not always unchanging. His data eventually was given to his assistant, Johannes Kepler, who further advanced the science of astronomy.

★ **1608:** Dutch spectacle-maker Hans Lippershey invented the first telescope.

★ **1609:** Johannes Kepler published his book, **Astronomia Nova (The New Astronomy),** in which he outlined the first two of his three laws based on his observations. (See **Who's Who of Astronomy** above for a summary of his laws.) The work by Kepler, and later by Galileo, essentially changed the way educated people viewed their world.

★ **1609–1610:** In late 1609 and early 1610, Galileo Galilei turned a new instrument at the skies, and the rush of ideas that began with the Renaissance took another leap forward. Galileo pointed a telescope at the Moon, Jupiter, Saturn, and the stars. His observations, printed in **Sidereus Nuncius (The Starry Messenger)** detected flaws in the basic Ptolemaic theory and led him to support the theory that the Sun, and not the Earth, was the center of the Universe. Galileo's findings eventually created a controversy with the Roman Catholic Church, which objected to his models of the Universe as representing physical truths. He later was forced to recant his views, but other scientists already were using the data and coming to the same conclusions.

★ **1687:** This year saw the publication of **The Principia,** in which Isaac Newton described how the motions of the planets and comets could be explained by the same law of gravitation that governed objects on Earth. His three laws of motion had a tremendous impact on science. (See **Who's Who of Astronomy** above.)

★ **Late 1700s:** This period saw a resurgence of astronomy, as scientists like Sir William Herschel began exploring the heavens with ever more powerful telescopes. In 1781 Herschel discovered Uranus. He also launched ambitious plans to explore the Universe beyond the Solar System via large telescopes.

During this time, telescopes and observatories grew in size and capability.

★ **1846:** Neptune discovered after astronomers noticed a discrepancy in the orbit of Uranus.

★ **Mid–1800s:** During this time several astronomers worldwide began serious study of astrophysics, or the study of the physical characteristics of celestial bodies. Astronomers in Europe and the United States began using spectroscopy to study the stars and the Sun.

★ **1917:** Albert Einstein published his theories of general relativity. His findings led astronomers to expand their theories of the universe.

★ **1920–1930:** Several astronomers began studying galaxies and determined that they were, in fact, outside the Milky Way Galaxy. This pushed back the Universe to nearly unfathomable limits.

★ **1920s:** Astronomers developed the "Big Bang" theories after a series of investigations showed galaxies moving away from the Earth at great speeds. The work of Edwin Hubble greatly enhanced the theory of the "Big Bang."

★ **1930:** Clyde Tombaugh discovered the planet Pluto.

★ **1931:** K.G. Jansky, of the Bell Telephone Laboratories, discovered radio radiation coming from the stars.

★ **1936:** Grote Reber built the first antenna designed to receive cosmic radio waves.

★ **Late 1940s:** The giant Hale Telescope at the Palomar Observatory in California saw first light, and astronomers once again pushed back the edge of the Universe. Also during this period, the first large-scale investigations using radio telescopes began.

★ **1957:** The Soviet Union launched the Sputnik spacecraft, often referred to as the beginning of the Space Age.

★ **1960:** Radio sources were connected with what appeared to be stars. It wasn't until 1963 that the radio sources were identified as quasi-stellar-radio sources, or quasars.

★ **1967:** Pulsars discovered in the constellation Vulpecula.

★ **1969:** Humans first set foot on the Moon. The decade of the 1960s was the first in which a number of space probes were launched to the planets. See Chapter 8, U.S. Space-based Astronomy Projects.

★ **1970s:** Missions landed on Mars, Venus, and the Moon, and flew by several planets.

★ **1976:** Viking 1 and Viking 2 landed on the surface of Mars, sent back stunning photos, and tested for evidence of life. Initial results indicated a chemical reaction that resembled some form of life, but further studies seemed to indicate that life does not exist on the surface of Mars.

★ **1979:** Pioneer 11 flew by Saturn.

★ **1980:** Voyager 1 flew by Saturn and sent back photos that revealed hundreds of rings around the planet.

★ **1981:** Voyager 2 followed Voyager 1, and added even more data to the growing bank of information on Saturn.

★ **1982:** Soviet spacecraft Veneras 13 and 14 landed on Venus and sent back photos of the surface of the planet.

★ **1986:** Voyager 2 passed by Uranus, confirming the existence of partial rings and discovering additional moons not seen from Earth-based telescopes.

★ **1989:** Voyager 2 reached Neptune, recorded data about the planet, its moons, and magnetic field, and, on its way out of the Solar System, sent back a photo of all the planets except Pluto.

★ **1990:** The Hubble Telescope was placed in orbit around the Earth.

★ **1991:** Project Galileo took the first close-up photo of an asteroid.

10 ASTRONOMY EDUCATION

WHAT'S REQUIRED FOR AN ASTRONOMY DEGREE

What type of courses might you take in an astronomy program? At the Ohio State University, once you're beyond the introductory offerings, the following classes are available: Basic Astrophysics and Planetary Astronomy; Stellar, Galactic, and Extragalactic Astronomy and Astrophysics; Methods of Astronomical Observation; Introduction to Celestial Mechanics; Stellar Astronomy; Introduction to Astrophysics; Extragalactic Astronomy; Solar System; Astronomical Uses of Applied Mathematics; Properties of Stars and Galactic Structure; Single Stars; Observed Properties of Stars; Binary Stars; Advanced Topics in Astrophysics; Astronomical Instrumentation and Data Analysis; Stellar Systems and Interstellar Matter. Additionally, there are honors courses and seminars that focus on research, research problems, and topics of current interest. The program at OSU is fairly typical of what you would find at universities across the United States and Canada.

Astronomy as a career is not particularly wide open. There are approximately 3,500 professional astronomers at work in the United States; of that number, 60 percent teach at colleges, 30 percent work for the government, and the remainder hold various jobs in industry. Astronomers often spend a few intense days a year collecting information at observing sites, and spend much of the rest of the year analyzing the data. Observing time is at a premium, since the number of astronomers far outnumbers available observing time at most sites. It's worth remembering, though, that the training you receive with a degree in astronomy includes extensive education in math, physics, computers, and other sciences, and qualifies you for jobs such as science teacher, science writer, computer programmer, or researcher.

DEGREE PROGRAMS IN ASTRONOMY

The following universities and colleges offer majors in astronomy as a separate discipline. Many institutions not listed, however, offer opportunities to study astronomy as a separate academic subject within the physics department. In fact, astronomy is often considered a sub-field of physics.

For more information about universities or colleges with astronomy programs, write to their Admissions Office or Astronomy Department.

★ **Agnes Scott College,** East College Ave., Decatur, GA 30030. Tel. (404) 371–6430. A non-profit college for women, with an undergraduate enrollment of approximately 500. Semester calendar.

★ **Amherst College,** Amherst, MA 01002. Tel. (413) 542–2000. Undergraduate enrollment approximately 1,500. Semester calendar.

★ **Ball State University,** Muncie, IN 47306. Tel. (317) 289–1241. Undergraduate enrollment approximately 15,000. Quarter calendar.

★ **Bates College,** Lewiston, ME 04240. Tel. (207) 786–6255. Undergraduate enroll-

ment approximately 1,500. Semester calendar.

★ **Beloit College,** Beloit, WI 53511. Tel. (608) 365–3391. Undergraduate enrollment approximately 1,000. Semester calendar.

★ **Benedictine College,** 2nd and Division, Atchison, KS 66002. Tel. (913) 367–5340. Undergraduate enrollment approximately 900. Semester calendar.

★ **Boston University,** 121 Bay State Rd., Boston, MA 02215. Tel. (617) 353–2000. Undergraduate enrollment approximately 27,000.

Stellar Astronomy Programs

For students planning to major in astronomy, a good college with a good reputation can boost chances of finding jobs in the field or being accepted into graduate school upon graduation. Dr. Jack Gourman has rated undergraduate programs in several majors, including astronomy, in the seventh edition of his book, **The Gourman Report,** published by National Education Standards in 1989.

His rankings of the top astronomy programs, based on student-to-professor ratios and quality of teaching, include:

1. California Institute of Technology
2. University of California, Berkeley
3. Harvard and Radcliffe
4. Cornell
5. University of Wisconsin
6. MIT
7. University of Arizona
8. University of Maryland
9. University of Michigan
10. University of California at Los Angeles
11. Yale
12. Case Western University
13. University of Illinois
14. University of Texas
15. University of Virginia
16. University of Washington
17. University of Kansas
18. Indiana University
19. Northwestern University
20. University of Pennsylvania
21. Ohio State University
22. Pennsylvania State University
23. University of Minnesota
24. University of Oklahoma
25. University of Southern California

In Astrophysics, Gourman rates the schools as follows:

1. MIT
2. Cal Tech
3. Princeton
4. Indiana University
5. University of Minnesota
6. Harvard & Radcliffe
7. Purdue University
8. University of Pennsylvania
9. University of Virginia
10. University of Oklahoma

★ **Brigham Young University,** Provo, UT 84602. Tel. (801) 378–4511. Undergraduate enrollment approximately 28,000. Semester calendar.

★ **Brooklyn College of City University of New York,** Bedford Avenue and Avenue H, Brooklyn, New York 11210. Tel. (718) 780–5485. Undergraduate enrollment approximately 14,000. Semester calendar.

★ **Bryn Mawr College,** Bryn Mawr, PA 19010. Tel. (215) 645–5000. A private school. Semester calendar.

★ **California Institute of Technology**, 1201 East California Blvd., Pasadena, CA 91125. Tel. (818) 356–6811. Undergraduate enrollment approximately 1,800. Quarter calendar.

★ **Case Western Reserve University,** 2040 Adelbert Rd., Cleveland, OH 44106. Tel. (216) 368–2000. Undergraduate enrollment approximately 8,000. Semester calendar.

★ **Colgate University,** Hamilton, NY 13346. Tel. (315) 824–1000. Undergraduate enrollment approximately 2,700. Semester calendar.

★ **Cornell University,** Ithaca, NY 14853. Tel. (607) 255–1000. Undergraduate enrollment approximately 18,000. Semester calendar.

★ **Denison University,** Granville, OH 43023. Tel. (614) 587–0810. Undergraduate enrollment approximately 2,000. Semester calendar.

★ **Drake University,** Twenty-Fifth & University Avenue, Des Moines, IA 50311. Tel. (515) 271–2011. Undergraduate enrollment approximately 5,500. Semester calendar.

★ **Earlham College,** 701 National Road West, Richmond, IN 47374. Tel. (317)

983–1200. Undergraduate enrollment approximately 1,100. Three sessions per year, no summer classes.

★ **Georgia State University,** Atlanta, GA 30303. Tel. (404) 658–2000. Undergraduate enrollment approximately 22,000. Quarter calendar.

★ **Hampshire College,** West Street, Amherst, MA 01002. Tel. (413) 549–4600. Undergraduate enrollment approximately 1,000. Semester calendar.

★ **Harvard University,** Cambridge, MA 02138. Tel. (617) 495–1000. Undergraduate enrollment approximately 18,000. Semester calendar.

★ **Haverford College,** Haverford, PA 19041. Tel. (215) 896–1350. Undergraduate enrollment approximately 1,100. Semester calendar.

★ **Howard University,** 2400 Sixth St., NW, Washington DC 20059. Tel. (202) 636–6100. Undergraduate enrollment approximately 11,000. Semester calendar.

★ **Indiana University,** Bryan Hall 100, Bloomington, IN 47405. Tel. (812) 332–0211. Undergraduate enrollment more than 30,000. Semester calendar.

★ **Johns Hopkins University,** Charles and 34th Streets, Baltimore, MD 21218. Tel. (301) 338–8000. Undergraduate enrollment approximately 11,000. Semester calendar.

★ **Lehman College of City of New York,** Bedford Park Boulevard West, Bronx, NY 10468. Tel. (212) 960–8881. Undergraduate enrollment approximately 11,000. Semester calendar.

★ **Louisiana State University and A&M College,** Baton Rouge, LA 70803. Tel. (504) 388–3202. Undergraduate enrollment approximately 29,000. Semester calendar.

★ **Mankato State University,** Mankato, MN 56001. Tel. (507) 389–6767. Undergraduate enrollment approximately 13,000. Quarter calendar.

★ **Massachusetts Institute of Technology (MIT),** 77 Massachusetts Ave., Cambridge, MA 02139. Tel. (617) 253–1000. Undergraduate enrollment approximately 10,000. Semester calendar.

★ **Michigan State University,** East Lansing, MI 48824. Tel. (517) 355–8332. Undergraduate enrollment approximately 31,000. Quarter calendar.

★ **Mount Holyoke College,** South Hadley, MA 01075. Tel. (413) 538–2000. Undergraduate enrollment approximately 2,000. Semester calendar.

★ **Mount Union College,** 1972 Clark Ave., Alliance, OH 44601. Tel. (216) 821–5320. Undergraduate enrollment approximately 1,000. Semester calendar.

★ **Northern Arizona University,** NAU Box 4084, Flagstaff, AZ 86011. Tel. (602) 523–9011. Undergraduate enrollment approximately 13,000. Semester calendar.

★ **Northwestern University,** Department of Physics and Astronomy, 2145 Sheridan Rd., Evanston, IL 60208–3112. Tel. (312) 491–3741. Undergraduate enrollment approximately 16,000. Quarter calendar.

★ **Ohio State University,** Department of Astronomy, 174 West 18th Ave., Columbus, OH 43210–1106. Tel. (614) 292–6446. Undergraduate enrollment approximately 40,000. Quarter calendar.

★ **Ohio Wesleyan University,** Delaware, OH 43015. Tel. (614) 369– 4431. Undergraduate enrollment approximately 1,000. Semester calendar.

★ **Pennsylvania State University,** University Park, PA 16802. Tel. (814) 865–4700. Undergraduate enrollment approximately 35,000. Semester calendar.

★ **Pomona College,** 333 North College Way, Claremont, CA 91711. Tel. (714) 621–8000. Undergraduate enrollment approximately 1,300. Semester calendar.

★ **Saint Mary's University,** Robie St., Halifax, Nova Scotia, Canada B3H 3C3.

★ **San Diego State University,** San Diego, CA 92182. Tel. (619) 265–5200. Undergraduate enrollment approximately 35,000. Semester calendar.

★ **San Francisco State University,** 1600 Holloway Ave., San Francisco, CA 94132. Tel. (415) 338–1111. Undergraduate enrollment approximately 26,000. Semester calendar.

★ **Smith College,** Northampton, MA 01063. Tel. (413) 584–2700. Undergraduate enrollment approximately 3,000. Semester calendar.

★ **Sonoma State University,** 1801 East Cotali Ave., Rohnert Park, CA 94928. Tel. (707) 664–2880. Undergraduate enrollment approximately 5,000. Semester calendar.

★ **State University of New York at Stony Brook,** Stony Brook, NY 11794. Tel. (516) 632–6868. Undergraduate enrollment approximately 1,000. Semester calendar.

★ **Swarthmore College,** Swarthmore, PA 19081. Tel. (215) 328–8300. Undergraduate enrollment approximately 1,200. Semester calendar.

★ **Texas Christian University,** Fort Worth, TX 76129. Tel. (817) 921–7490. Undergraduate enrollment approximately 5,000. Semester calendar.

★ **Tufts University,** Medford, MA 02155. Tel. (617) 381–3170. Undergraduate enrollment approximately 5,000. Semester calendar.

★ **University of Arizona,** 1111 North Cherry, Tucson, AZ 85721. Tel. (602) 621–6524. Undergraduate enrollment approximately 23,000. Semester calendar.

★ **University of British Columbia,** Vancouver, British Columbia, Canada, V6T 1Z2. Tel. (604) 228–3014. Undergraduate enrollment approximately 15,000.

★ **University of California/Berkeley,** Berkeley, CA 94720. Tel. (415) 642–0200. Undergraduate enrollment approximately 22,000. Semester calendar.

★ **University of California at Los Angeles,** Los Angeles, CA 90024. Tel. (213) 825–3101. Undergraduate enrollment approximately 24,000. Quarter calendar.

★ **University of Chicago,** Chicago, IL 60037. Tel. (312) 702–8650. Undergraduate enrollment approximately 3,000. Quarter calendar.

★ **University of Florida,** Gainesville, FL 32611. Tel. (904) 392–1365. Undergraduate enrollment approximately 23,000. Semester calendar.

★ **University of Georgia,** Athens, GA 30602. Tel. (404) 542–2112. Undergraduate enrollment approximately 19,000. Quarter calendar.

★ **University of Illinois,** Urbana, IL 61801. Tel. (217) 333–6548. Undergraduate enrollment approximately 25,000. Semester calendar.

★ **University of Iowa,** Iowa City, IA 52242. Tel. (319) 335–1548. Undergraduate enrollment approximately 17,000. Semester calendar.

★ **University of Kansas,** Lawrence, KS 66045. Tel. (913) 864–3911. Undergraduate enrollment approximately 17,000. Semester calendar.

★ **University of Manitoba,** Winnipeg, Manitoba, Canada R3T 2N2. Tel. (204) 474–8810. Undergraduate enrollment approximately 20,000.

★ **University of Maryland,** College Park, MD 20742. Tel. (301) 454–5550. Undergraduate enrollment approximately 22,000. Semester calendar.

★ **University of Massachusetts** at Amherst, Amherst, MA 01003. Tel. (413) 545–0222. Undergraduate enrollment approximately 17,000. Semester calendar.

★ **University of Michigan,** Ann Arbor, MI 48109. Tel. (313) 764–7433. Undergraduate enrollment approximately 22,000. Trimester calendar.

★ **University of Minnesota/Twin Cities Campus,** Minneapolis, MN 55455. Tel. (612) 624–5555; 1–800–826–0750 (out-of-state). Undergraduate enrollment approximately 16,000. Quarter calendar.

★ **University of Nebraska,** Lincoln, NE 68588. Tel. (402) 472–2023. Under-

graduate enrollment approximately 16,000. Semester calendar.

★ **University of New Mexico,** Albuquerque, NM 87131. Tel. (505) 277–2446. Undergraduate enrollment approximately 13,000. Semester calendar.

★ **University of North Carolina,** Chapel Hill, NC 27599. Tel. (919) 966–3621. Undergraduate enrollment approximately 14,000. Semester calendar.

★ **University of Oklahoma,** Norman, OK 73072. Tel. (405) 325–2251. Undergraduate enrollment approximately 12,000. Semester calendar.

★ **University of Pennsylvania,** Philadelphia, PA 19104. Tel. (215) 898–7507. Undergraduate enrollment approximately 9,000. Semester calendar.

★ **University of Pittsburgh,** Pittsburgh, PA 15260. Tel. (412) 624–7488. Undergraduate enrollment approximately 13,000. Terms.

★ **University of Rochester,** Rochester, NY 14627. Tel. (716) 275–3221. Undergraduate enrollment approximately 5,000. Semester calendar.

★ **University of Southern California,** Los Angeles, CA 90089. Tel. (213) 743–2311. Undergraduate enrollment approximately 14,000. Semester calendar.

★ **University of Tennessee,** Knoxville, TN 37996. Tel. (615) 974–2184. Undergraduate enrollment approximately 15,000. Semester calendar.

★ **University of Texas,** Austin, TX 78712. Tel. (512) 471–7601. Undergraduate enrollment approximately 38,000. Semester calendar.

★ **University of Toronto,** Toronto, Ontario, Canada M5S 1A3. Tel. (416) 978–2190. Undergraduate enrollment approximately 32,000. Terms.

★ **University of Victoria,** Box 1700, Victoria, British Columbia, Canada V8W 2Y2.

★ **University of Virginia,** Department of Astronomy, P.O. Box 3818, Charlottesville, VA 22903–0818. Tel. (804) 924–7751. Undergraduate enrollment approximately 11,000. Semester calendar.

★ **University of Washington,** Seattle, WA 98195. Tel. (206) 543–9686. Undergraduate enrollment approximately 22,000. Quarter calendar.

★ **University of Western Ontario,** London, Ontario, Canada N6A 3K7. Tel. (519) 661–2150. Undergraduate enrollment approximately 20,000. Semester calendar.

★ **University of Wisconsin,** 50 Lincoln Dr., Madison, WI 53706. Tel. (608) 262–1234. Undergraduate enrollment approximately 44,000. Semester calendar.

★ **University of Wyoming,** University Station, WY 82071. Tel. (307) 766–1121. Undergraduate enrollment approximately 10,000. Semester calendar.

★ **Valdosta State College,** North Patterson, GA 31698. Tel. (912) 247–3335. Undergraduate enrollment approximately 6,000. Quarter calendar.

★ **Vanderbilt University,** Nashville, TN 37212. Tel. (615) 322–2561. Undergraduate enrollment approximately 5,000. Semester calendar.

★ **Vassar College,** Poughkeepsie, NY 12601. Tel. (914) 437–7300. Undergraduate enrollment approximately 2,300. Semester calendar.

★ **Villanova University,** Villanova, PA 19085. Tel. (215) 645–4500. Undergraduate enrollment approximately 12,000. Semester calendar.

★ **Wellesley College,** Wellesley, MA 02181. Tel. (617) 235–0320. Undergraduate enrollment approximately 2,000. Semester calendar.

★ **Wesleyan University,** Middleton, CT 06457. Tel. (203) 347–9411. Undergraduate enrollment approximately 3,000. Semester calendar.

★ **West Chester University of Pennsylvania,** University Avenue and High Street, West Chester, PA 19383. Tel. (215) 436–1000. Undergraduate enrollment approximately 10,000. Semester calendar.

★ **Western Connecticut State University,** 181 White St., Danbury CT 06810. Tel. (203) 797–4297. Undergraduate enrollment approximately 6,000. Semester calendar.

★ **Western Washington University,** 516 Hight St., Bellingham, WA 98225. Tel. (206) 676–3000. Undergraduate enrollment approximately 8,500. Quarter calendar.

★ **Whitman College,** 345 Boyer Ave., Walla Walla, WA 99362. Tel. (509) 527–5111. Undergraduate enrollment approximately 1,200. Semester calendar.

★ **Williams College,** Main Street, Williamstown, MA 01267. Tel. (413) 597–3131. Undergraduate enrollment approximately 2,000.

★ **Yale University,** New Haven, CT 06810. Tel. (203) 436–0300. Undergraduate enrollment approximately 11,000. Semester calendar.

Astrophysics Programs

★ **Boston University.** See above listing.

★ **California Institute of Technology.** See above listing.

★ **Colgate University.** See above listing.

★ **Columbia College,** 116th Street and Broadway, New York, NY 10027. Tel. (212) 280–1754. Undergraduate enrollment approximately 18,000. Semester calendar.

★ **Harvard University.** See above listing.

★ **Howard University.** See above listing.

★ **Indiana University.** See above listing.

★ **Johns Hopkins University.** See above listing.

★ **Lehman College of City of New York.** See above listing.

★ **Marlboro College.** See above listing.

★ **Massachusetts Institute of Technology (MIT).** See above listing.

★ **New Mexico Institute of Mining and Technology,** Campus Station, Socorro, NM 87801. Tel. (505) 835–5011. Undergraduate enrollment approximately 1,100. Semester calendar.

★ **Pacific Union College,** Angwin, CA 94508. Tel. (707) 965–6311. Undergraduate enrollment approximately 1,400. Quarter calendar.

★ **Princeton University,** Princeton, NJ 08544. Tel. (609) 452–3000. Undergraduate enrollment approximately 6,000. Semester calendar.

★ **Purdue University,** West Lafayette, IN 47907. Tel. (317) 494–2145. Undergraduate enrollment approximately 33,000. Semester calendar.

★ **San Francisco State University.** See above listing.

★ **University of Akron,** 302 East Buchtel Ave., Akron, Ohio 44325. Tel. (216) 375–7111. Undergraduate enrollment approximately 25,000. Semester calendar.

★ **University of Minnesota**. See above listing.

★ **University of New Mexico.** See above listing.

★ **University of Oklahoma.** See above listing.

★ **University of Pennsylvania.** See above listing.

★ **University of Virginia.** See above listing.

★ **University of Wyoming.** See above listing.

★ **Wesleyan University.** See above listing.

★ **Williams College.** See above listing.

SCHOLARSHIPS, GRANTS, AND INTERNSHIPS

★ **American Astronomical Society**, 2000 Florida Ave., NW, Suite 300, Washington, DC 20009. Tel. (202) 328–2010. The Society is the major organization of professional astronomers in the United States, Canada, and Mexico. See the **National and Special Interest Groups** section in Chapter 2 for a description of its activities.

The AAS operates three grant programs: the Small Research Grant Program, which helps unsupported astronomers cover some costs of research; the International Travel Grant Program, which helps American astronomers with travel expenses; and the Chretien Awards, which promote observational astronomy on an international basis.

★ **American Museum of Natural History,** office of Grants & Fellowships, Central Park West at 79th, New York, NY 10024. Scholarships in the sciences. Deadline of Jan. 15, each year. Write for more information.

★ **Annie J. Cannon Award in Astronomy,** sponsored by the American Association of University Women Education Foundation, 2401 Virginia Ave. NW, Washington, D.C. 20037. Tel. (202) 785–7736. A $1,000 award for women under 35.

★ **Carnegie Institution of Washington,** 1530 P St. NW, Washington, D.C. 20005. Tel. (202) 387–6400. A postdoctoral fellowship for $1,500 annually.

★ **Challenger Seven Fellowship Program,** 1101 King St., Suite 190, Alexandria, VA 22314. Tel. (703) 683–9740. The Fellowship awards $5,000 to professional educators or those on temporary leave from professional education. Awarded for innovative projects that are technology-driven and space-related.

★ **Dudley Observatory,** 69 Union Ave., Schenectady, NY, 12308. Tel. (518) 382–7583. Ralph A. Alpher, administrator. The Observatory no longer is involved in active research, but gives annual awards. These include the Ernest F. Fullman Award, which is an annual competition for funds in support of an innovative research project in astronomy or astrophysics; and the Herbert C. Pollock Award, an annual competition for support of a project in the history of astronomy or astrophysics. Each award currently is funded at $10,000 annually. The Observatory also sponsors the Dudley Award, which is an on-going program of career development to provide start-up research

funds in amounts up to $8,000 to new, untenured faculty members at colleges and universities in New York state.

★ **Lunar & Planetary Institute,** 3303 NASA Road 1, Houston, TX, 77058. Internships. Write for more information.

★ **Maria Mitchell Observatory,** 3 Vestal St., Nantucket, MA 02554. Tel. (617) 228–9273. Internships.

★ **National Radio Astronomy Observatory,** Edgemont Rd., Charlottesville, VA 22901. Tel. (804) 296–0223. Summer student programs.

★ **National Science Foundation,** Fellowship Office, National Research Council, 2101 Constitution Ave., N.W., Washington, D.C. 20418. Provides fellowships for students majoring in science or engineering. Must complete a special NSF application and take the Graduate Record Examination. Write for more information.

★ **The Planetary Society,** 65 N. Catalina Ave., Pasadena, CA 91106. Tel. (818) 793–5100. The Society gives five $1,000 awards to college students majoring in engineering or science and planning a career in planetary-related science. Scholarships are based on merit, and requirements include a written essay on a relevant topic. The competition is open to Planetary Society members or individuals nominated by members. The Society also sponsors the following awards/scholarships:

■ **New Millennium Committee High School Scholarships.** Up to $5,000 in scholarships available each year to high school students planning careers in planetary and space sciences. The amount of each award depends on the qualifications of the applicants. To be eligible, a student must be a member of The Planetary Society or the nominee of a member and be in the final year of secondary school. Awards are made on the basis of SAT or ACT scores, scholastic achievement, letters of recommendation, accomplishments showing leadership and creativity, and a written essay.

■ **Mars Institute Student Contest.** The contest is open to all high school and college students. The $1,000 prize is awarded for the best essay on a topic selected by Dr. Chris McKay, the Society's Mars Institute Coordinator. The essays should be in the form of a detailed proposal, which is judged by a panel of distinguished scientists and engineers.

■ **National Merit Scholarship.** The Society sponsors a four-year college scholarship given to an outstanding high school student through the National Merit Scholarship program. The scholarship goes to a student planning to major in one of the disciplines that make up the planetary sciences. The National Merit Scholarship Corporation administers the scholarship.

★ **Tombaugh Scholars Program,** NMSU Foundation, Inc., Box 3590, Las Cruces, NM 88003. Sponsored by New Mexico State University, the scholarship is open to young astronomers. The program is designed to aid two to three postdoctoral students a year, with recipients having the opportunity to use the 3.5–meter telescope at Apache Point, New Mexico.

SUMMER CAMPS AND SCHOOLS

★ **Astronomy Camps,** sponsored by the University of Arizona Alumni Association, 1111 N. Cherry Ave., Tucson, AZ 85721. Tel. (602) 621–5233 or 1–800– BEAT–ASU outside of Arizona. These camps are designed for students and adults. Offers a beginning astronomy camp, advanced camp, and adult camp.

The camps typically include tours of Kitt Peak National Observatory and the University of Arizona Mirror Laboratory, plus daily lectures, demonstrations, and recreational activities. Tuition for the young adult camp is $485, and includes lodging, meals, transportation in Tucson, and all materials. The adult camp tuition is $275 or $350.

★ **The Colorado Springs School,** 21 Broadmoor Ave., Colorado Springs, CO 80906. Tel. (719) 475–9747. Opportunity for students in grades K–12 to work with astronomers at Kitt Peak.

★ **Consortium for Undergraduate Research and Education in Astronomy,** Department of Physics, Wright Laboratory, Oberlin College, Oberlin, OH 44074–1088. Contact Professor Joseph L. Snider, CUREA Director. Tel. (216) 775–8335. Open to undergraduate physics or astronomy majors, with junior or senior standing, who are considering a career in science or science teaching. Offers a summer program at Mount Wilson observatory. The $750 cost covers room, board, and tuition. Students receive a hands-on course in solar, planetary, and stellar astronomy and astrophysics.

★ **International Space University,** 636 Beacon St., Boston, MA 02215. An association founded in 1987, the ISU is designed to expose students from many countries to the aerospace program. The coursework is grouped into eight dis-ciplines: architecture, business and management, engineering, life sciences, physical sciences, policy and law, resources and manufacturing, and satellite applications. It operates as a summer program; classes are held at various universities and research centers around the world.

★ **Mississippi Student Space Station,** sponsored by the Russell C. Davis Planetarium, P.O. Box 22826, Jackson, MS 39225–2826. Tel. (601) 960–1550. Offers two or three camps each summer, open to a "select group" of seventh- and eighth-grade students from across the state and nation who want to study space sciences. Students chosen by application. Application deadline is mid-May each year. Total cost for the 14–day program is $1,200. Tuition assistance is available.

★ **Space Center,** P.O. Box 533, Alamogordo, NM 88311–0533. Tel. (505) 437–2840. Sponsors a summer space science camp for grades three through nine.

★ **United States Space Camp,** One Tranquility Base, Huntsville, AL 35807–7015. This NASA-sponsored camp is designed to teach aspiring astronauts or astronomers about the U.S. space program and space shuttle operations. The Space Camp and Space Academy are open to students at different levels, starting with elementary-school students through high school students. Adult programs also are available.

The programs are offered in Alabama and Florida; costs start at $450. Scholarships and other financial aid sometimes are available. For brochure, write to the Space Camp. Call 1–800–63–SPACE for reservations.

TEACHING RESOURCES

With the added emphasis on science in the classroom, more and more educators will be seeking creative ways to teach astronomy. Fortunately, a variety of kits, laboratory experiments, posters, and so forth have been designed to ease curious youngsters into the beauties of the Universe. Astronomy educators can obtain many of these materials for their classes at little or no cost. The organizations and companies below are excellent sources of teaching materials.

★ **The Association of Astronomy Educators,** Physics Department, University of Wisconsin, LaCrosse, WI 54601. Contact Robert Allen. The AAE encourages improvements in the curriculum of astronomy courses, publishes a newsletter with teaching tips and resources, and has an "Astronomy Education Material Resource Guide," which lists curricula and resources available for cost.

★ **Kalmbach Publishing Co.,** 21027 Crossroads Circle, P.O. Box 1612, Waukesha, WI 53187. Tel (414) 796–8776. The publishers of **Astronomy** magazine also offer for sale posters, videos, books, and other items related to the space program and astronomy. NASA mission patches and educational materials also available.

★ **MMI Corporation,** 2950 Wyman Parkway, P.O. Box 19907, Baltimore, MD 21211. Tel. (301) 366–1222. Fax (301) 366–6311. Slides, videos, and teaching manuals available. Has a wide range of educational materials designed for high school or college level instructors. Videos of all types, including some for telescope users, and instructional material for clubs or schools. Free catalog for educators; $2 for others.

★ **NASA.** See below.

★ **Sky Publishing Corporation,** 49 Bay State Rd., Cambridge, MA 02138. Tel. (617) 864–7360. The publishers of **Sky & Telescope** offer a series of educational lessons on astronomy, designed for use in the classroom at various levels.

★ **The Universe in the Classroom,** a newsletter for teaching astronomy. The project is co-sponsored by the Astronomical Society of the Pacific, the American Astronomical Society, the Canadian Astronomical Society, and the International Planetarium Society. Each issue includes non-technical articles on new developments in the exploration of the Universe, practical classroom activities, and suggested visual aids. To be included on the mailing list, write to: Astronomical Society of the Pacific, Teachers' Newsletter, Dept. N, 390 Ashton Ave., San Francisco, CA 94112.

NASA

The National Aeronautics and Space Administration has volumes of materials, slides, booklets, videos, and other teaching aids available for educators. Most are available via mail-order. Additionally, there are a number of offices throughout the country where educators can review materials for their classes in the sciences, especially aviation, astronomy, and rocketry.

For more information, write to, or visit, one of the following offices.

★ **NASA CORE (Central Operation of Resources for Education),** 15181 Route 58 S., Oberlin, OH 44074. Tel. (216) 774–1051, ext. 293. Serves as the national distribution center for NASA-produced educational materials. Provides videos, audio/visuals, transparencies, NASA memorabilia, etc., to teachers and groups sponsoring educational programs. CORE is designed to help teachers unable to visit one of the many teacher resource centers around the country. Filmstrips, videos, and slides cover topics such as the history of space travel, careers in space, Comet Halley, views of the sky, novas and supernovas, etc. The center also distributes information on various education conferences dealing with space and astronomy.

NASA Teacher Resource Centers

NASA Teacher Resource Centers are selected sites where educators can preview the materials available from NASA. These sites include NASA centers, universities, and museums. For the address of the NASA center nearest you, consult the list below.

If you live in **Alaska, Arizona, California, Hawaii, Idaho, Montana, Nevada, Oregon, Utah, Washington,** or **Wyoming,** contact:

NASA Ames Research
Mail Stop T025
Moffett Field, CA 94035
(415) 604–3574
or
NASA Jet Propulsion Laboratory
Mail Code CS–530
4800 Oak Grove Drive
Pasadena, CA 91103
(818) 354–6916

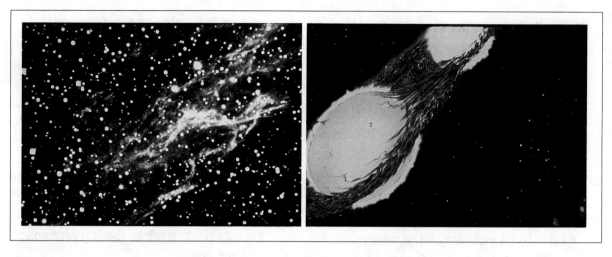

Examples of images available through NASA Teacher Resource Centers: left, the Veil Nebula (NGC 6992) in Cygnus; right, binary star showing exchange of matter between components. (Courtesy of National Aeronautics and Space Administration)

If you live in **Florida, Georgia, Puerto Rico,** or the **Virgin Islands,** contact:

NASA Kennedy Space Center
Education Resource Library
Mail Code ERL
JFK Space Center, FL 32899
(407) 867–4090 or (407) 867–9383

If you live in **Illinois, Indiana, Michigan, Minnesota, Ohio,** or **Wisconsin,** contact:

NASA Lewis Research Center
Mail Stop 8–1
21000 Brookpark Road
Cleveland, OH 44135
(216) 433–2017

If you live in **Connecticut, Washington, D.C., Delaware, Massachusetts,**

Maryland, Maine, New Hampshire, New Jersey, New York, Pennsylvania, Rhode Island, or **Vermont,** contact:

NASA Goddard Space Flight Center
Mail Code 130.3
Greenbelt, MD 20771
(301) 286–8570
or
NASA Wallops Flight Facility
P.O. Box 98/Building J–17
Wallops Island, VA 23337
(804) 824–2298

If you live in **Colorado, Kansas, North Dakota, Nebraska, New Mexico, Oklahoma, South Dakota,** or **Texas,** contact:

NASA Johnson Space Center
Mail Code AP–42

Houston, TX 77058
(713) 483–8696

If you live in **Kentucky, North Carolina, South Carolina, Virginia,** or **West Virginia,** contact:

NASA Langley Research Center
Mail Stop 146
Hampton, VA 23665–5225
(804) 864–3293

If you live in **Alabama, Arkansas, Iowa, Louisiana, Missouri,** or **Tennessee,** contact:

Alabama Space & Rocket Center
ATTN: NASA Teacher Resource Center
Tranquility Base
Huntsville, AL 35807
(205) 544–5812

In **Mississippi,** contact:

NASA Stennis Space Center
Building 1200
Stennis Space Center, MS 39529–6000
(601) 688–3338

NASA Regional Teacher Resource Centers

The following Resource Centers are independent sites designated by NASA to receive NASA materials and to serve as Teacher Resource Centers.

Museum of Science & Industry
57th St. and Lakeshore Dr.
Chicago, IL 60637
(312) 684–1414, ext. 429/449

Parks College of St. Louis University
400 Falling Springs Rd.
Cahokia, IL 62206
(618) 337–7500

University of the District of Columbia
Science and Engineering Center
Mail Stop 4201
4200 Connecticut Ave., NW
Washington, D.C. 20008
(202) 282–3677

National Air & Space Museum
Smithsonian Institution
Education Resource Center, P–700
Washington, D.C. 20560
(202) 786–2109

Mankato State University
P.O. Box 52
Mankato, MN 56001
(507) 389–1516

University of Evansville
School of Education
1800 Lincoln Ave.
Evansville, IN 47714
(812) 479–2393

Oklahoma State University
300 North Cordell
Stillwater, OK 74078–0422
(405) 744–7015

Central Michigan University
Ronan Hall
Mount Pleasant, MI 48859
(517) 774–4387

Northern Michigan University
Olson Library Media Center
Marquette, MI 49855
(906) 227–2117

The City College
NAC 5/224
Convent Ave. at 138th St.
New York, NY 10031
(212) 690–6993

University of Pittsburgh
823 William Pitt Union
Pittsburgh, PA 15260
(412) 648–7010

Bossier Parish Community College
2719 Airline Drive
Bossier City, LA 71111
(318) 746–7754

Kansas Cosmosphere and Space Center
1100 N. Plum
Hutchinson, KS 67501
(316) 662–2305

Waterfield Library
Murray State University
Murray, KY 42071
(502) 762–4420

Vermont College of Norwich University
Schulmaier Hall
Montpelier, VT 05602
(802) 828–8765

Wheeling Jesuit College
316 Washington Avenue
Wheeling, WV 26003
(304) 243–2455

Southern University-Shreveport
610 Texas St., Suite 307
Shreveport, LA 71101
(318) 674–3444

University of Wisconsin at LaCrosse
Morris Hall, Room 200
LaCrosse, WI 54601
(608) 785–8650

Mississippi Delta Community College
P.O. Box 177, Highway #3
Moorhead, MS 38761
(601) 246–5631, ext. 126

Luna & Planetary Laboratory
Space Science Building
University of Arizona
Tucson, AZ 85721
(602) 621–2234

U.S. Space Foundation
1525 Vapor Trail
Colorado Springs, CO 80916
(719) 550–1000

University of North Carolina
J. Murrey Atkins Library
Charlotte, NC 28223
(704) 547–2559

St. Cloud University
Center for Information Media
720 Fourth Ave., S.
St. Cloud, MN 56301–4498
(612) 255–2062

Delaware Teacher Center
Brandywine School District
Administrative Office

1000 Pennsylvania Avenue
Claymont, DE 19703
(302) 792-3858

Oakland University
NASA Teacher Resource Center
216 O'Dowd Hall
Rochester, MI 48309-4401
(313) 370-4165

Appendixes

The Twenty Brightest Stars

Star	Constellation	Spectral Type	Apparent Magnitude
Sirius	Canis Major	A1 V	-1.46
Canopus	Carina	F0 Ia	-0.72
Arcturus	Bootes	K2 IIIp	-0.2
Rigil Kentaurus	Centaurus	G2 V	0.00
Vega	Lyra	A0 V0	.03
Capella	Auriga	G8 III	0.08
Rigel	Orion	B8 Ia	0.12
Procyon	Canis Minor	F5 IV	0.38
Betelgeuse	Orion	M2 Iab	0.50
Achernar	Eridanus	B5 IV	0.46
Beta Centauri	Hadar	B1 II	0.61
Altair	Aquila	A7 IV-V	0.77
Aldebaran	Taurus	K5 III	0.85
Spica	Virgo	B1 V	0.98
Anatares	Scorpius	M1 1b	0.96
Fomalhaut	Piscis Austrinus	A3 V	1.16

Pollux	Gemini	K0 III	1.14
Deneb	Cygnus	A2 Ia	1.25
Beta Crucis	Crux	B0 III	1.25

Spectral Sequence

Spectral Class	Color	Approximate Temperature (K)
O	Blue	>30,000–60,000
B	Blue	10,000–30,000
A	Blue	7,500–10,000
F	Blue to White	6,000–7,500
G	White to Yellow	5,000–6,000
K	Orange to Red	3,500–5,000
M	Red	<3,500

Astronomical Constants

Light-year: 5,880,000,000,000 miles

Parsec: approximately 3.26 light-years or 19.2 trillion miles

Velocity of light: 186,281 miles per second

Astronomical unit (mean distance from sun to earth): 92,900,000 miles

Mean distance from Earth to Moon: 238,854 miles

Equatorial radius of the Earth: 3,963.34 statute miles

Polar radius of the Earth: 3,949.99 statue miles

Earth's mean radius: 3,958.89 statue miles

Equatorial circumference of Earth: 24,902 miles

Sun's diameter: 864,000 miles

Tropical year (time elapsing between two passages in succession of the Sun through the same equinox): 265.2422 days

Sidereal year (year measured with units that depend upon the apparent diurnal movement of the stars): 365.2564 days

Sidereal month (month measured with units that depend upon the apparent diurnal movement of the stars): 27.3217 days

Synodic month (time elapsing between two successive passages of the Moon between the Earth and the Sun): 29.5306 days

Sidereal day (day measured with units that depend upon the apparent diurnal movments of the stars): 23 hours 56 minutes 4.091 seconds of mean solar time

Mean solar day: 24 hours 3 minutes 56.555 seconds of sidereal time.

Units of Angular Measure

The most common units of angular measure used in astronomy are:

ARC MEASURE:

One circle contains 360 degrees = $360°$;

$1°$ contains 60 minutes of arc = $60'$;
$1'$ contains 60 seconds of arc = $60''$.

TIME MEASURE:

one circle contains 24 hours = 24^h;
1^h contains 60 minutes of time = 60^m;
1^m contains 60 seconds of time = 60^s.

RADIAN MEASURE:

one circle contains 2(pi) radians.

A radian is the angle at the center of a circle subtended by a length along the circumference of the circle equal to its radius. Since the circumference of a circle is 2(pi) times its radius, there are 2(pi) radians in a circle.

Temperature Scales

Fahrenheit (F): water freezes at 32° and boils at 212°F.

Centigrade (C): water freezes at 0° and boils at 100°C.

Kelvin or absolute (K): water freezes at 273° and boils at 373°K.

The Kelvin scale is most often used in astronomy. Kelvin degrees have the same value as Centigrade degrees, since the defference between the freezing and boiling points of water is 100 degrees in each.

On the Fahrenheit scale, water boils at 212 degrees and freezes at 32 degrees; the difference is 180 degrees.

To convert Kelvin degrees to Fahrenheit, first subtract 273 from the Kelvin scale, which gives you the Centigrade temperature. Then multiply the result by $\frac{9}{5}$ and add 32. For example, if you want to find the Fahrenheit temperature of a star with a Kelvin temperature of 5,000, follow these steps:

> Subtract 273 from 5000 (5000 − 273 = 4727 C)
> Multiply by 9 (4727 x 9 = 42543)
> Divide by 5 (42543 ÷ 5 = 8508.6)
> Add 32 (8508.6 + 32 = 8540.6 F)

To convert Fahrenheit degrees to Centrigrade and then to Kelvin, use this formula: (Fahrenheit − 32) x $\frac{5}{9}$ = Centigrade. Add the Centigrade temperature to 273 to get the Kelvin temperature.

Metric Conversion Chart

INTO METRIC		
If you know	Multiply **length** by	To get
inches	2.54	Centimeters
feet	30	Centimeters
yards	0.91	Meters
miles	1.6097	Kilometers

If you know	Multiply **length** by	To get
Millimeters	0.04	Inches
Centimeters	0.4	Inches
Meters	3.3	Feet
Kilometers	0.62	Miles

The Greek Alphabet

α	Alpha	Al-fuh
β	Beta	Bey-tuh
γ	Gamma	Gam-uh
δ	Delta	Dell-tuh
ε	Epsilon	Epp-sih-lon
ζ	Zeta	Zay-tuh
η	Eta	Ay-tuh
θ	Theta	Thay-tuh
ι	Iota	I-oh-tuh
κ	Kappa	Cap-uh
λ	Lambda	Lam-duh
μ	Mu	Mew or Moo
ν	Nu	New or Noo
ξ	Xi	Zi
ο	Omicron	Ohm-ih-krawn
π	Pi	Pie
ρ	Rho	Row
σ	Sigma	Sig-muh
τ	Tau	Taw

υ	Upsilon	Up-sih-lon
φ	Phi	Fie
χ	Chi	Kie
ψ	Psi	Sie
ω	Omega	Oh-me-guh

The Constellations

Latin Name	Genitive*	English Meaning	Abbreviation	Approximate Position
Andromeda	Andromedae	Princess of Ethiopia	And	1 +40
Antila	Antliae	Pump	Ant	10 –35
Apus	Apodis	Bird of Paradise	Aps	16 –75
Aquarius	Aquarii	Water Bearer	Aqr	23 –15
Aquila	Aquilae	Eagle	Aq	20 +5
Ara	Arae	Altar	Ara	17 –55
Aries	Arietis	Ram	Ari	3 +20
Auriga	Aurigae	Charioteer	Aur	6 +40
Bootes	Bootis	Herdsman	Boo	15 +30
Caelum	Caeli	Graving Tool	Cae	5 –40
Camelopardus	Camelopardis	Giraffe	Cam	6 –40
Cancer	Cancri	Crab	Cnc	9 +20
Canes Venatici	Canum Venaticorum	Hunting Dogs	CVn	13 +40
Canis Major	Canis Majoris	Big Dog	CMA	7 –20

* The genitive for of a constellation's name is used after the Greek letter used to designate a star's relative brightness within the constellation. For example, Deneb, the brightest star in Cygnus, is alpha Cygni.

Canis Minor	Canis Minoris	Little Dog	CMi	8	+5
Capricornus	Capricorni	Goat	Cap	21	−20
Carina	Carinae	Keel	Car	9	−60
Cassiopea	Casiopeiae	Queen of Ethiopia	Cas	1	+60
Centaurus	Centauri	Centaur	Cen	13	−50
Cepheus	Cephei	King of Ethiopia	Cep	22	+70
Cetus	Ceti	Sea Monster (Whale)	Cet	2	−10
Chamaeleon	Chamaeleontis	Chameleon	Cha	11	−80
Circinus	Circini	Compasses	Cir	15	−60
Columba	Columbae	Dove	Col	6	−60
Coma Berenices	Comae Berenices	Berenice's Hair	Com	13	+20
Corona Australis	Coronae Australis	Southern Crown	CrA	19	−40
Corona Borealis	Coronae Borealis	Northern Crown	CrB	16	+30
Corvus	Corvi	Crow	Crv	12	−20
Crater	Crateris	Cup	Crt	11	−15
Crux	Crucis	Southern Cross	Cru	12	−60
Cygnus	Cygnis	Swan	Cyg	21	+40
Delphinus	Delphini	Dolphin	Del	21	+10
Dorado	Doradus	Swordfish	Dor	5	−65
Draco	Draconis	Dragon	Dra	17	+65
Equuleus	Equulei	Little Horse	Equ	21	+10
Eridanus	Eridani	River Eridanus	Eri	3	−20
Fornax	Fornacis	Furnace	For	3	−30
Gemini	Geminorum	Twins	Gem	7	+20
Grus	Gruis	Crane	Gru	22	−45
Hercules	Herculis	Hercules, Son of Sezus	Her	17	+30
Horologium	Horologii	Clock	Hor	3	−60

Hydra	Hydrae	Sea Serpent	Hya	10	−20
Hydrus	Hydri	Water Snake	Hyi	2	−75
Indus	Indi	Indian	Ind	21	−55
Lacerta	Lacertae	Lizard	Lac	22	+45
Leo	Leonis	Lion	Leo	11	+15
Leo Minor	Leonis Minoris	Little Lion	LMi	10	+35
Lepus	Leporis	Hare	Lep	6	−20
Libra	Librae	Scales	Lib	15	−15
Lupus	Lupi	Wolf	Lup	15	−45
Lynx	Lyncis	Lynx	Lyn	8	+45
Lyra	Lyrae	Lyre or Harp	Lyr	19	+40
Mensa	Mensae	Table	Men	5	−80
Microscopium	Microscopii	Microscope	Mic	21	−35
Monoceros	Monocerotis	Unicorn	Mon	7	−5
Musca	Muscae	Fly	Mus	12	−70
Norma	Normae	Level	Nor	16	−50
Octans	Octantis	Octant	Oct	22	−85
Ophiuchus	Ophiuchi	Holder of Serpent	Oph	17	0
Orion	Orionis	Orion, the Hunter	Ori	5	+5
Pavo	Pavonis	Peacock	Pav	20	−65
Pegasus	Pegasi	Pegasus, Winged Horse	Peg	22	+22
Perseus	Persei	Perseus, the Hero Who Saved Andromeda	Per	3	+45
Phoenix	Phoenicis	Phoenix	Phe	1	−50
Pictor	Pictoris	Pasel	Pic	6	−55
Pisces	Piscium	Fish	Psc	1	+15
Piscis Austrinus	Piscis Austrinus	Southern Fish	PsA	22	−30
Puppis	Puppis	Ship's Stern	Pup	8	−40

Pyxis	Pyxidis	Ship's Compass	Pyx	9	−30
Reticulum	Reticuli	Net	Ret	4	−60
Sagitta	Sagittae	Arrow	Sge	20	+10
Sagittarius	Sagittarii	Archer	Sgr	19	−25
Scorpiu	Scorpii	Scorpion	Sco	17	−40
Sculptor	Sculptoris	Sculptor	Scl	0	−30
Scutum	Scuti	Shield	Sct	19	−10
Serpens	Serpentis	Serpent	Ser	17	0
Sextans	Sextantis	Sextant	Sex	10	0
Taurus	Tauri	Bull	Tau	4	+15
Telescopium	Telescopii	Telescope	Tel	19	−50
Triangulum	Trianguli	Triangle	Tri	2	+30
Triangulum Australe	Trianguli Australis	Southern Triangle	TrA	16	−65
Tucana	Tucanae	Toucan	Tuc	0	−65
Ursa Major	Ursae Majoris	Big Bear	UMA	11	+50
Ursa Minor	Ursae Minoris	Little Bear	UMi	15	+70
Vela	Velorum	Ship's Sail	Vel	9	−50
Virgo	Virginis	Virgin	Vir	13	0
Volans	Volantis	Flying Fish	Vol	8	−70
Vulpecula	Vulpeculae	Fox	Vul	20	+25

Note: The four constellations Carina, Puppis, Pyxis, and Vela originally formed the single constellation, Argo Navis, named after the Argonauts' ship.

Messier Objects

The findings by the French comet hunter Charles Messier showcase galaxies, clusters, and nebulae. Messier began the list in the 1770s as an attempt to separate the objects from the comets he sought. Today, many of the objects remain the subject of intense study by professionals. The Messier objects are a favorite of amateur astronomers, and include some of the most interesting views in the sky, even for smaller telescopes. Many clubs hold Messier Marathons in the spring as amateurs attempt to spot as many of the objects as possible in a single "marathon" viewing session.

M1—bright nebula in Taurus (Crab Nebula, NGC 1952)

M2—globular cluster in Aquarius (NGC 7089)

M3—globular cluster in Canes Venatici (NGC 5272)

M4—globular cluster in Scorpius (NGC 6121)

M5—globular cluster in Serpens (NGC 5904)

M6—open cluster in Scorpius (Butterfly Cluster, NGC 6405)

M7—open cluster in Scorpius (NGC 6475)

M8—bright nebula in Sagittarius (Lagoon Nebula, NGC 6523)

M9—globular cluster in Ophiuchus (NGC 6333)

M10—globular cluster in Ophiuchus (NGC 6254)

M11—open cluster in Scutum (Wild Duck Cluster, NGC 6705)

M12—globular cluster in Ophiuchus (NGC 6218)

M13—globular cluster in Hercules (Great Cluster in Hercules, Hercules Cluster, NGC 6205)

M14—globular cluster in Ophiuchus (NGC 6402)

M15—globular cluster in Pegasus (NGC 7078)

M16—bright nebula in Serpens (Eagle Nebula, NGC 6611)

M17—bright nebula in Sagittarius (Checkmark Nebula, Horseshoe Nebula, Omega Nebula, Swan Nebula NGC 6618)

M18—open cluster in Sagittarius (NGC 6613)

M19—globular cluster in Ophiuchus (NGC 6273)

M20—bright nebula in Sagittarius (Trifid Nebula, NGC 6514)

M21—open cluster in Sagittarius (NGC 6531)

M22—globular cluster in Sagittarius (NGC 6656)

M23—open cluster in Sagittarius (NGC 6494)

M24—starcloud in Sagittarius (Delle Caustiche, Small Sagittarius Cloud)

M25—open cluster in Sagittarius (IC 4725)

M26—open cluster in Scutum (NGC 6694)

M27—planetary nebula in Vulpecula (Dumbbell Nebula, NGC 6853)

M28—globular cluster in Sagittarius (NGC 6626)

M29—open cluster in Cygnus (NGC 6913)

M30—globular cluster in Capricornus (NGC 7099)

M31—galaxy in Andromeda (Andromeda Galaxy, NGC 224)

M32—galaxy in Andromeda (NGC 221)

M33—galaxy in Triangulum (Pinwheel Galaxy, NGC 598)

M34—open cluster in Perseus (NGC 1039)

M35—open cluster in Gemini (NGC 2168)

M36—open cluster in Auriga (NGC 1960)

M37—open cluster in Auriga (NGC 2099)

M38—open cluster in Auriga (NGC 1912)

M39—open cluster in Cygnus (NGC 7092)

M40—double star in Ursa Major

M41—open cluster in Canis Major (NGC 2287)

M42—bright nebula in Orion (Great Nebula in Orion, NGC 1976)

M43—detached portion of M42 (NGC 1982)

M44—open cluster in Cancer (Beehive Cluster, Manger, Praesepe Cluster, NGC 2632)

M45—open cluster in Taurus (Pleiades, Seven Sisters)

M46—open cluster in Puppis (NGC 2437)

M47—open cluster in Puppis (NGC 2422)

M48—open cluster in Hydra (NGC 2548)

M49—galaxy in Virgo (NGC 4472)

M50—open cluster in Monoceros (NGC 2323)

M51—galaxy in Canes Venatici (Whirlpool Galaxy, Lord Rosse's Nebula, NGC 5194 and 5195)

M52—open cluster in Cassiopeia (NGC 7654)

M53—globular cluster in Coma Berenices (NGC 5024)

M54—globular cluster in Sagittarius (NGC 6715)

M55—globular cluster in Sagittarius (NGC 6809)

M56—globular cluster in Lyra (NGC 6779)

M57—planetary nebula in Lyra (Ring Nebula, NGC 6720)

M58—galaxy in Virgo, (NGC 4579)

M59—galaxy in Virgo (NGC 4621)

M60—galaxy in Virgo (NGC 4649)

M61—galaxy in Virgo (NGC 4303)

M62—globular cluster in Ophiuchus and Scorpius (NGC 6266)

M63—galaxy in Canes Venatici (Sunflower Galaxy, NGC 5055)

M64—galaxy in Coma Berenices (Blackeye Galaxy, NGC 4826)

M65—galaxy in Leo (NGC 3623, pair with M66)

M66—galaxy in Leo (NGC 3627, pair with M65)

M67—open cluster in Cancer (NGC 2682)

M68—globular cluster in Hydra (NGC 4590)

M69—globular cluster in Sagittarius (NGC 6637)

M70—globular cluster in Sagittarius (NGC 6681)

M71—globular cluster in Sagitta (NGC 6838)

M72—globular cluster in Aquarius (NGC 6981)

M73—open cluster in Aquarius (NGC 6994)

M74—galaxy in Pisces (NGC 628)

M75—globular cluster in Sagittarius (NGC 6864)

M76—planetary nebula in Perseus (Butterfly Nebula, Cork Nebula, Little Dumbbell Nebula, NGC 650 and 651)

M77—galaxy in Cetus (NGC 1068)

M78—bright nebula in Orion (NGC 2068)

M79—globular cluster in Lepus (NGC 1904)

M80—globular cluster in Scorpius (NGC 6093)

M81—Dwarf B Galaxy in Ursa Major

M81—galaxy in Ursa Major (Bode's Nebulae with NGC 3034, NGC 3031)

M81—group cluster of galaxies in Ursa Major

M82—galaxy in Ursa Major (with NGC 3031, NGC 3034 member of M81 group)

M83—galaxy in Hyrda (NGC 5236)

M84—galaxy in Virgo (NGC 4374)

M85—galaxy in Coma Berenices (NGC 4382)

M86—galaxy in Virgo (NGC 4406)

M87—galaxy in Virgo (NGC 4486, Virgo A Galaxy)

M88—galaxy in Coma Berenices (NGC 4501)

M89—galaxy in Virgo (NGC 4552)

M90—galaxy in Virgo (NGC 4569)

M91—error in Messier Catalogue or possibly galaxy in Coma Berenices (NGC 4548)

M92—globular cluster in Hercules (NGC 6341)

M93—open cluster in Puppis (NGC 2447)

M94—galaxy in Canes Venatici (NGC 4736)

M95—galaxy in Leo (NGC 3351, pair with M96)

M96—galaxy in Leo (NGC 3368, pair with M95)

M97—planetary nebula in Ursa Major (Owl Nebula, NGC 3587)

M98—galaxy in Coma Berenices (NGC 4192)

M99—galaxy in Coma Berenices (NGC 4254)

M100—galaxy in Coma Berenices (NGC 4321)

M101—galaxy in Ursa Major (Pinwheel Galaxy, NGC 5457)

M101—group cluster of galaxies in Ursa Major

M102—accidental re-observation of M101?

M103—open cluster in Cassiopeia (NGC 581)

M104—galaxy in Virgo (Sombrero Galaxy, NGC 4594)

M105—galaxy in Leo (NGC 3379)

M106—galaxy in Canes Venatici (NGC 4258)

M107—globular cluster in Ophiuchus (NGC 6171)

M108—galaxy in Ursa Major (NGC 3556)

M109—galaxy in Ursa Major (NGC 3992)

M110—galaxy in Andromeda (NGC 205)

Planetary Data

Name	Equatorial Radius (km)	Mean Density (g/cm^3)	Surface Gravity (Earth = 1)	Sidereal Period (Days)	Inclination of Equator to Orbit (degrees)	Known Moons
Mercury	2,439	5.43	0.378	87.96	0.0	0
Venus	6,052	5.24	0.894	224.68	177.3	0
Earth	6,378.14	5.515	1	365.25	23.45	1
Mars	3,393.4	3.94	0.379	686.95	25.19	2
Jupiter	71,398	1.33	2.54	4,337	3.12	16
Saturn	60,000	0.70	1.07	10,760	26.73	17
Uranus	26,071	1.30	0.8	30,700	97.86	15
Neptune	24,764	1.64	1.2	60,200	29.56	8
Pluto	1,150	2.03	0.01	90,780	120	1

Meteor Showers

On almost any clear night you can spot several sporadic meteors each hour. During a shower, however, several meteors may be visible each minute. Most showers occur at the same time each year; the result of the Earth passing through the orbits of comets, such as Comet Halley. The duration depends on how spread out the meteoroids are in the comet's orbit. The rate at which meteors are visible increases after midnight on the night of a shower, in part because that side of the Earth then is turned to it and plows through the debris. A full moon, or even bright city lights, can dramatically reduce the number of meteors visible. Meteor watching organizations (see the **National and Special Interest Groups** section in Chapter 2) ask their members to count the number of meteors visible during showers. The best showers of the year are the Perseids, in August, with up to 68 meteors visible per hour; the Leonids, in November, with up to 100 per hour visible; and the Geminids, in December, with up to 58 visible per hour. This is one area in which amateurs can contribute data to professionals, especially by working with one of the many groups that monitor meteor showers.

Name	Date of Maximum	Duration	Approximate Limits	Number per Hour at Maximum	Source	Constellation
Quadrantids	Jan. 4	1 day	Jan. 1-6	110	------	Bootes
Zeta Bootids	Mar. 9	3 days	Mar. 9-12	10		Bootes
Lyrids	April 22	2 days	April 19-24	12	Comet 1861 I	Hercules
Eta Aquarids	May 5	3 days	May 1-8	20	Comet Halley	Aquarius
June Lyrids	June 15	11 days	June 10-21	12	------	Lyra
Ophiuchids	June 20	9 days	June 17-26	15	------	Ophiuchus
Capricornids	July 26	37 days	July 26-Aug. 15	6	------	Capricornus
Delta Aquarids	July 27-28	7 days	July 15-Aug. 15	35	------	Aquarius
Alpha Capricornids	Aug. 2	40 days	July 15-Aug. 25	8	------	Capricornus
Iota Aquarids	Aug. 6	40 days	July 15-Aug. 25	6	-------	Aquarius
Perseids	Aug. 12	5 days	July 25-Aug. 18	68	Comet 1862 III	Cassiopeia

Kappa Cygnids	Aug. 20	3 days	Aug. 19-22	4	------	Cygnus
Beta Cassiopeids	Sept. 11	8 days	Sept. 7-15	10	------	Cassiopeia
Draconids	Oct. 10	1 day	Oct. 10	variable	------	Draco
Orionids	Oct. 2	12 days	Oct. 16-26	30	Comet Halley	Orion
Taurids	Nov. 8	Spread out	Oct. 20-Nov. 30	12	Comet Encke	Taurus
Cepheids	Nov. 9	4 days	Nov. 7-11	8	------	Cassiopeia
Leonids	Nov. 17	Spread out	Nov. 15-19	10	Comet 1866 I	Leo
Andromedids	Nov. 20	21 days	Nov. 15-Dec. 6	variable	------	Cassiopeia
Geminids	Dec. 14	3 days	Dec. 7-15	58	3200 Phaethon	Gemini
Ursids	Dec. 22	7 days	Dec. 17-24	6	------	Ursa Minor

Solar Eclipses

DATE	TYPE	DURATION (minutes)	LOCATION
January 4, 1992	annular	11:42	Over Pacific Ocean
June 30, 1992	total	5:20	Atlantic Ocean
May 10, 1994	annular	6:14	Eastern Pacific Ocean, North America, Atlantic Ocean, NW Africa
November 3, 1994	total	4:24	South America, southern Atlantic Ocean
April 29, 1995	annular	6:38	Pacific Ocean, S. America
October 24, 1995	total	2:10	Asia, Borneo, Pacific Ocean

The Elements

Atomic Number	Symbol	Element	Weight
1	H	Hydrogen	1.01
2	He	Helium	4.00
3	Li	Lithium	6.94
4	Be	Beryllium	9.01
5	B	Boron	10.81
6	C	Carbon	12.01
7	N	Nitrogen	14.01
8	O	Oxygen	16.00
9	F	Fluorine	19.00
10	Ne	Neon	20.18
11	Na	Sodium	22.99
12	Mg	Magnesium	24.31
13	Al	Aluminum	26.98
14	Si	Silicon	28.09
15	P	Phosphorus	30.97
16	S	Sulfur	32.07
17	Cl	Chlorine	35.45
18	Ar	Argon	39.94
19	K	Potassium	39.10
20	Ca	Calcium	40.08
21	Sc	Scandium	44.96
22	Ti	Titanium	47.88
23	V	Vanadium	50.94
24	Cr	Chromium	52.00
25	Mn	Manganese	54.94
26	Fe	Iron	55.85
27	Co	Cobalt	58.93
28	Ni	Nickel	58.69
29	Cu	Copper	63.55
30	Zn	Zinc	65.39
31	Ga	Gallium	69.72
32	Ge	Germanium	72.61
33	As	Arsenic	74.92
34	Se	Selenium	78.96
35	Br	Bromine	79.90
36	Kr	Krypton	83.80

37	Rb	Rubidium	85.47
38	Sr	Strontium	87.62
39	Y	Yttrium	88.91
40	Zr	Zirconium	91.22
41	Nb	Niobium	92.91
42	Mo	Molybdenum	95.94
43	Tc	Technetium	(98)*
44	Ru	Ruthenium	101.07
45	Rh	Rhodium	102.91
46	Pd	Palladium	106.42
47	Ag	Silver	107.87
48	Cd	Cadmium	112.41
49	In	Indium	114.82
50	Sn	Tin	118.71
51	Sb	Antimony	121.75
52	Te	Tellurium	127.60
53	I	Iodine	126.90
54	Xe	Xenon	131.29
55	Ss	Cesium	132.91
56	Ba	Barium	137.33
57	La	Lanthanum	138.91
58	Ce	Cerium	140.12
59	Pr	Praseodymium	140.91
60	Nd	Neodymium	144.24
61	Pm	Promethium	(145)
62	Sm	Samarium	150.36
63	Eu	Europium	151.97
64	Gd	Gadolinium	157.25
65	Tb	Terbium	158.93
66	Dy	Dysprosium	162.50
67	Ho	Holmium	164.93
68	Er	Erbium	167.26
69	Tm	Thulium	168.93
70	Yb	Ytterbium	173.04
71	Lu	Lutetium	174.97
72	Hf	Hafnium	178.49

* Values in parentheses are the most stable of the important isotopes.

73	Ta	Tantalum	180.95
74	W	Tungsten	183.85
75	Re	Rhenium	186.21
76	Os	Osmium	190.2
77	Ir	Iridium	192.22
78	Pt	Platinum	195.08
79	Au	Gold	196.97
80	Hg	Mercury	200.59
81	Ti	Thallium	204.38
82	Pb	Lead	207.2
83	Bi	Bismuth	208.98
84	Po	Polonium	(209)
85	At	Astatine	(210)
86	Rn	Radon	(222)
87	Fr	Francium	(223)
88	Ra	Radium	(226)
89	Ac	Actinium	(227)
90	Th	Thorium	232.04
91	Pa	Protactinium	231.04
92	U	Uranium	238.03
93	Np	Neptunium	(237)
94	Pu	Plutonium	(244)
95	Am	Americium	(243)
96	Cm	Curium	(247)
97	Bk	Berkelium	(247)
98	Cf	Califorinium	(251)
99	Es	Einsteinium	(252)
100	Fm	Fermium	(257)
101	Md	Mendelevium	(258)
102	No	Nobelium	(259)
103	Lr	Lawrencium	(260)
104	Unk	Unnilquadium	(261)
105	Unp	Unnilpentium	(252)
106	Unh	Unnilhexium	(263)
107	Uns	Unnilseptium	(262)
108	Uno	Unniloctium	(265)
109	Une	Unnilennium	(266)

GLOSSARY

Aberration of starlight: The tiny apparent displacement of stars resulting from the motion of the Earth through space.

Absolute magnitude (M): The magnitude a celestial object would appear to have if it were at a distance of 10 parsecs.

Absolute visual magnitude (Mv): The absolute magnitude of an object measured through a special yellowish filter that approximates the visual range of the human eye.

Absolute zero: −273 degrees C or zero degrees Kelvin, the temperature at which all molecular motion stops.

Absorption nebula: A nebula seen in silhouette as it absorbs light from behind; also called a dark nebula.

Altitude: Angular distance (usually measured in degrees) above the horizon.

Analemma: The figure eight representing the equation of time and the variation of the Sun's altitude in the sky during the course of a year.

Angstrom: A unit of wavelength or distance, equivalent to 1/10,000 micrometer or 1/10,000,000,000 meter.

Annular eclipse: A solar eclipse in which a ring—an annulus—of solar photosphere remains visible.

Aphelion: The farthest point from the Sun in an object's orbit around it.

Apparent magnitude (m): Magnitude as seen by an observer.

Apparent solar time: Time determined by the actual position of the Sun in the sky; corresponds to time on most sundials.

Asterism: A noticeable pattern of stars that makes up part of one or more constellations; not a constellation itself.

Asteroid: A minor planet, smaller than any major planet in our Solar System; not one of the satellites (moons) of a major planet such as the Earth or Jupiter.

Astronomical unit (A.U.): The average distance from the Earth to the Sun, which equals 149,598,770 kilometers, or about 93 million miles.

Autumnal equinox: The intersection of the ecliptic and the celestial equator that the Sun passes each year on its way to southern (negative) declinations.

Baily's beads: A chain of several bright "beads" of white light, visible just before or after totality at a solar eclipse. The effect occurs when bits of photosphere shine through valleys at the Moon's edge. See also **Diamond-ring effect.**

Bayer designations: The Greek letters assigned to the stars in a constellation, usually in order of brightness, by Johann Bayer in his sky atlas (1603).

Belts: Dark bands in the clouds on giant planets such as Jupiter; compare with zones.

Binary star: A double star; a system containing two or more stars. In an eclipsing binary, one star goes behind the other periodically, changing the total amount of light we see.

Black hole: A region of space in which mass is packed so densely that (according to Einstein's general theory of relativity) nothing, not even light, can escape.

Blueshifts: When a body emitting light approaches you, the wavelengths of light shift slightly in the direction of the blue on the spectral line (and appear shorter). Objects with a blueshift are moving toward the Earth.

Cassini's division: The major division in Saturn's rings, which separates the A-ring from the B-ring.

Celestial equator: The imaginary great circle that lies above the Earth's equator on the celestial sphere.

Celestial longitude: Longitude measure (in degrees) along the ecliptic to the east from the vernal equinox.

Celestial poles: The points in the sky where the Earth's axis, extended into space, intersects with the celestial sphere.

Celestial sphere: The imaginary sphere surrounding the Earth, with the stars and other astronomical objects attached to it.

Cepheid variable: A star that varies in the manner of delta Cephei. The absolute magnitudes of these variable stars can be calculated from their periods of variation; by comparing the absolute and apparent magnitudes, the distances to these stars and the galaxies they are in can be determined.

Chromosphere: A layer in the Sun and many other stars just above the photosphere. During eclipses, the solar chromosphere glows reddish from hydrogen emission.

Circumpolar: Refers to a star, asterism, or constellation that is close enough to the celestial pole that, from the latitude at which you are observing it, never appears to set.

Collimation: The alignment of telescope optics.

Comet: A body—probably resembling a "dirty snowball" between 0.1 km and 100 km across—that travels through the Solar System in an elliptical orbit of random inclination to the ecliptic. A comet grows a tail if it comes close enough to the Sun.

Conjunction: The alignment of two celestial bodies that occurs when they reach the same celestial longitude. The bodies then appear approximately closest to each other in the sky. See also **Inferior conjunction, Superior conjunction.**

Constellation: One of the 88 parts into which the sky is divided; also refers to the historical, mythological, or other figures that represented earlier divisions of the sky.

Contact(s): The stage(s) of an eclipse, occultation, or transit when the edges of the apparent disks of astronomical bodies seem to touch. At a solar eclipse, first contact is when the advancing edge of the Sun first touches the Moon; second contact is when the advancing edges of the

Sun touches the other side of the Moon, beginning totality; third contact is when the trailing edge of the Sun touches the trailing edge of the Moon, ending totality; and fourth contact marks the end of the eclipse.

Corona: The outermost layer of the Sun and many other stars; a faint halo of extremely hot (million-degree) gas.

Cosmic String: A new theory in astrophysics that holds that the phase change undergone by the Universe was not perfect in the initital stages. There is a possibility of a defect in space-time, which may mean the old type of space-time exists. According to the theory, the strings would be left over from the Big Bang; early studies, however, have ruled out at least the simplest forms of cosmic strings.

Crepe ring: Saturn's inner ring, also know as the C-ring, which extends inward to the planet from the brightest ring (B-ring).

Crescent: One of the phases of the Moon or the inner planets (Venus and Mercury) as seen from the Earth, caused by the relative angles of sunlight and the observer's viewpoint. From spacecraft, crescent phases of the Earth, Mars, Jupiter, and Saturn also have been seen.

Declination: The celestial coordinate analogous to latitude, usually measured in degrees, minutes, and seconds of arc north (+) or south (-) of the celestial equator.

Diamond-ring effect: An effect created as the total phase of a solar eclipse is about to begin, when the last Baily's bead—a remaining bit of photosphere—glows so intensely by contrast with the Sun's faint corona that it looks like the jewel on a ring. Also refers to the equivalent phase at the end of totality.

Doppler Effect: A change in wavelength that occurs when the source of waves and the receiver are moving relative to each other. Scientists use the Doppler Effect to determine the radial velocity of an object, or its speed toward or away from us, and how fast it is moving toward or away from us.

Double star: A system containing two or more stars. In a true double, the stars are physically close to each other, in an optical double, they lie in approximately the same direction from the Earth and thus appear close to each other, but are actually far apart. See also **Binary star.**

Earthshine: Sunlight reflected off the Earth, which lights the side of the Moon that does not receive direct sunlight.

Eclipse, lunar: The passage of the Moon into the Earth's shadow.

Eclipse, solar: The passage of the Moon's shadow across the Earth. See also **Annular eclipse, Contact(s), Penumbra, Umbra.**

Ecliptic: The apparent path the Sun follows across the sky during the year; the same path is also followed approximately by the Moon and planets.

Ejecta blanket: Chunks of rock, usually extending from one side of a crater, that were ejected during the crater's formation.

Elongation: Angular distance in celestial longitude from the Sun in the sky.

Emission lines: Extra radiation at certain specific wavelengths in a spectrum, compared with neighboring wavelengths (colors).

Emission nebula: A gas cloud that receives energy from a hot star, allowing it to give off radiation in emission lines such as those of hydrogen. The characteristic reddish radiation of many emission nebulae is mostly from the hydrogen-alpha line.

Encke's division: A thin division in the A-ring of Saturn.

Ephemeris Time: The official system of mean solar time, used to calculate data for tables of changing astronomical phenomena (ephemerides). Ephemeris Time differs only slightly from Universal time.

Equation of time: The variation of local apparent solar time minus local mean solar time over the year.

Equinox: One of the two intersections of the ecliptic and the celestial equator. See **Autumnal equinox, Vernal equinox.**

Filament: A dark region snaking across the Sun; a prominence seen in projection against the solar disk.

Fireball: An extremely bright meteor, usually with an apparent magnitude brighter than –5; some fireballs are as bright as magnitude –20.

Flamsteed number: The number assigned to a star in a given constellation, in order of right ascension, in the 1725 catalogue of John Flamsteed.

Galactic: Pertaining to our galaxy, the Milky Way Galaxy.

Galactic cluster: An irregular grouping of stars of a common and possibly recent origin. Also called an open cluster.

Galactic equator, galactic poles: The equator and poles in a coordinate system in which the equator is placed along the plane of our galaxy, the Milky Way Galaxy.

Galaxy: A giant collection of stars, gas, and dust. Our galaxy, the Milky Way Galaxy, contains 1 trillion times the mass of our Sun.

Giant: A star brighter and larger than most stars of its color and temperature. Stars become giants (normally red giants) when they use up all the hydrogen in their cores and leave the "main sequence" part of their life cycle. See also **Supergiant.**

Gibbous: A phase of a moon or planet in which more than half the side we see is illuminated.

Globular cluster: A spherical grouping of stars of a common origin; globular clusters and the stars in them are very old.

Graben: On the surface of the Earth, the Moon, or other planets or moons, a long and narrow region between two faults that has subsided.

Half moon: The first-quarter or third-quarter phase, when half the visible side of a moon is illuminated.

Hour angle: The sidereal time elapsed since an object was on the meridian, or, if the hour angle is negative, before the object reaches the meridian. (The hour angle equals the difference between the right ascension of an object and of your meridian.)

Hour circle: A line along which right ascension is constant, lying on a great circle that passes through the celestial poles and the object.

Hubble's Law: The relationship between the velocity and distance of galaxies and other distant objects; it shows that the Universe is expanding.

Hydrogen-alpha line: The strongest spectral line of hydrogen in the visible part of the spectrum. It falls in the red, so that an emission hydrogen-alpha line is red; an absorption hydrogen-alpha line is the absence of that wavelength of red.

Inferior conjunction: The conjunction in which a planet whose orbit is inside that of the Earth passes between the Earth and the Sun.

Intrinsic brightness: The amount of energy (usually light) an object gives off; its true brightness, independent of the effects of distance or dimming by intervening material.

Ionized hydrogen: Hydrogen that has lost its electron; ionized hydrogen gas, commonly found in stars and nebulae, has free protons and free electrons.

Julian day: The number of days since noon on 1 January 4713 B.C. Variable-star observers and other astronomers commonly calculate the interval between dates of events by subtracting Julian days, eliminating the necessity to keep track of leap years and other calendar details.

Libration: The turning of the visible face of the Moon, which allows us to see different amounts of the lunar surface around the limb or edge.

Light-year: The distance that light travels in a year, which equals 9,460,000,000,000 km or 63,240 A.U. (astronomical units).

Limb: The edge of the apparent disk of an astronomical body, such as the Sun, Moon, or a planet.

Magnitude: A logarithmic scale of brightness, in which each change of five magnitudes is equivalent to a change by a factor of 100. Adding one magnitude corresponds to a decrease in brightness by a factor of 2.512. See also **Absolute magnitude** and **Apparent magnitude.**

Main-sequence star: A star in the prime of its life, when hydrogen inside it is undergoing nuclear fusion; such stars form a band—the main sequence—across a graph of stellar temperatures vs. stellar brightness.

Maxima: The times when a variable star reaches its maximum brightness.

Mean solar time: Time as kept by a fictitious "mean" sun that travels at a steady rate across the sky throughout the year.

Meridian: The great circle passing through the celestial poles and your zenith.

Messier Catalogue: The list of 103 nonstellar, deep-sky objects compiled by Charles Messier in the 1770s, and subsequently expanded to 109 or 110 objects.

Meteor: A meteoroid streaking across the sky; a shooting star.

Meteorite: The part of a meteoroid that survives its passage through the Earth's atmosphere.

Meteoroid: A small chunk of rock or metal in the Solar System, often spread throughout a comet's orbit; sometimes a chip of an asteroid.

Meteor shower: The appearance of many meteors during a short period of time, as the Earth passes through a comet's orbit.

Minima: The times of a variable star's minimum brightness.

Mira variable: A long-period variable star like the star omicron Ceti (Mira).

Nebula: A region of gas or dust in a galaxy that can be observed optically. See also **Emission nebula, Absorption nebula,** and **Reflection nebula.**

Neutron star: A small (20–km diameter), dense star (up to a billion tons per cubic cm) resulting from the collapse of a dying star to the point where only the fact that its neutrons resist being pushed still closer together prevents further collapse.

NGC: The prefix used before numbers assigned to nonstellar objects in the New General Catalogue, published by J.L.E. Dreyer in 1888.

Nova: A newly visible star, or one that suddenly increases drastically in brightness.

Nutation: A small, nodding motion of the Earth's axis of rotation with a period of 19 years; this motion is superimposed on precession.

Oblate: A nonspherical shape formed by rotating an ellipse around its narrower axis; the equatorial diameter of an oblate body (such as Jupiter) is greater than its polar diameter.

Occultation: The hiding of one celestial body by another.

Open cluster: An irregular grouping of stars of a common and possibly recent origin. Also called a galactic cluster.

Opposition: The point in a planet's orbit at which its celestial longitude is 180 degrees from that of the Sun. A planet at opposition is visible all night long.

Parsec: The distance from which 1 A.U. appears to subtend or cover 1 second of arc; 1 parsec equals 3.261633 light-years.

Penumbra: At an eclipse, the part of the Earth or Moon's shadow from which part of the solar disk is visible. Also refers to the outer, less dark portion of a sunspot.

Perihelion: The farthest point from the Sun in an object's orbit around it.

Photosphere: The visible surface of the Sun or of another star.

Planetary nebula: A shell of gas ejected by a dying star that contains about as much mass as the Sun.

Polar tufts: Small spikes visible in the solar corona near the Sun's poles, formed by gas following the Sun's magnetic field.

Position angle: The angle, centered at the brighter component of a double star, that an observer follows counterclockwise from north around to the fainter component.

Precession: The slow drifting of the orientation of the Earth's axis over a period of 26,000 years. Also refers to its effect on the location of the equinoxes, and thus on the coordinate system of right ascension and declination used to plot positions of stars and other objects.

Prominence: Gas suspended above the solar photosphere by the Sun's magnetic field; ordinarily visible at the solar limb. A prominence glows reddish during eclipses because of its characteristic hydrogen-alpha radiation.

Proper motion: Apparent angular motion across the sky, shown as a change in an object's position with respect to the background stars.

Pulsar: A rotating neutron star that gives off sharp pulses of radio waves with a period ranging from about 0.001 to 4 seconds.

Quasar: A "quasi-stellar object" with an extremely large redshift; presumably a powerful event going on in the central region of a galaxy. According to Hubble's Law, quasars must be among the most distant objects in the Universe.

Radiant: The location on the celestial sphere from which meteors in a given shower appear to radiate, because of perspective.

Red-giant: A swollen star; a stage occurring at the end of a star's main-sequence period of life. See also **Giant.**

Redshifts: When an object emitting light is moving away from a source, the visible light appears shifted to the red on the spectral line. Objects receding from the Earth have a redshift.

Reflecting telescope: A telescope that uses a mirror in the principal stage of forming an image.

Reflection nebula: A dust cloud that reflects a star's light to us.

Refracting telescope: A telescope that uses a lens in the principal stage of forming an image.

Retrograde motion: The apparent backward (westward) loop in a planet's motion across the sky over a lengthy period of time. Copernicus explained it as a projection effect caused when the Earth overtakes another planet as they both orbit the Sun.

Revolution: The orbiting of a planet or other object around the Sun or another central body.

Right ascension: The angle of an object around the celestial equator, measured in hours, minutes, and seconds eastward from the vernal equinox.

Rotation: The spinning of a planet or other object on its axis.

Separation: The annular distance (measured in degrees, minutes and seconds of arc) between components of a double star.

Shadow bands: Light and dark bands that appear to sweep across the ground in the minutes before and after totality at a solar eclipse; caused by irregularities in the Earth's upper atmosphere.

Sidereal time: Time by the stars; technically, the hour angle of the vernal equinox, which is equal to the right ascension of objections on your meridian.

Solar flare: An explosive eruption on the Sun reaching temperatures of millions of degrees. Note: a flare is not a prominence.

Solstices: The positions of the Sun when it reaches its northern-most declination (in northern-hemisphere summer) or southern-most declination (in northern-hemisphere winter).

Spectral line: A wavelength of the spectrum at which the intensity is greater than (an emission line) or less than (an absorption line) neighboring values.

Spectral type: One of several temperature classes—OBAFGKM, in decreasing order of temperature—into which stars are placed, based on analyses of their spectra.

Spectrum: The radiation from an object spread out into its component colors, wavelengths, or frequencies.

Star cloud: One of several regions of the Milky Way where great numbers of stars appear.

Streamers: Large-scale structures in the Sun's corona, usually near the solar equator, shaped by the Sun's magnetic fields.

Supergiant: A star brighter and larger than even giants of the same color and temperature. Only the most massive stars become supergiants, after passing through the giant stage.

Superior conjunction: The conjunction in which a planet whose orbit is inside that of the Earth passes on the far side of the Sun with respect to the Earth.

Supernova: The explosion and devastation of a very massive star.

Supernova remnant: Gas left over from a supernova that can be seen in the sky or detected from it by radio or X-ray emission. (The Crab Nebula, for example, can be detected all three ways.)

Surface brightness: The brightness of a unit area of an object's surface. For spread-out objects such as nebulae, the surface brightness determines the amount of contrast the object has against the background sky, and whether the object's surface is bright enough to make an image on your retina. Even though the object's total brightness may be high, it still may be hard to see if it is spread out enough so that its surface brightness is low.

Synodic: Related to the alignment of three bodies, often the Earth, the Sun, and a third body, such as the Moon or a planet.

Terminator: The edge of the lighted region of a moon or planet; the line between day and night.

Train: A path left in the sky by a meteor.

Transient Lunar Phenomena (TLP's): Changes, such as emissions of gas, observed on the Moon.

Transit: The passage of an inner planet (Mercury or Venus) across the Sun's disk as seen from Earth, or of a moon (such as one of Jupiter's Galilean satellites) across its planet's disk. Also, the passage of an object across an observer's meridian.

Umbra: At an eclipse, the part of the Moon or Earth's shadow from which the solar disk is entirely hidden. Also refers to the inner, darker portion of a sunspot. See also **Penumbra.**

Universal Time (U.T.): Solar time at the meridian of Greenwich, England.

Variable star: A star whose apparent brightness changes over time.

Vernal equinox: The intersection of the ecliptic and the celestial equator that the Sun passes on its way to northern declinations. Spring.

Zenith: The point directly overhead (wherever an observer is), 90 degrees above the horizon.

Zodiac: Traditionally, a set of 12 constellations through which the Sun, Moon, and planets pass in the course of a year. Actually, that band of the sky contains many more parts of constellations, and because of precession, the Sun is no longer in the constellations associated with its "traditional" dates at those times.

Zones: Bright bands in the cloud layers of the giant planets Jupiter, Saturn, Uranus, and Neptune.

Corporate Index

PUBLICATIONS INDEX

SUBJECT INDEX

Q

Quasars, 217, 218, 223, 224, 227

R

Radio astronomy, 219, 221, 223, 227
Rainwater Observatory & Planetarium, 158
Ranger missions, 205, 206
Reber, Grote, 223, 227
Redshifts, of galaxies, 214
Reflectors. **See** Newtonians
Refractors, pros and cons of, 87–88
Relativity, theory of, 165, 216
Resolution, of telescopes, 91
Resolving power, 91
N.A. Richardson Astronomical Observatory, 148
River Ridge Observatory, 145
Roberts Observatory, 155
Roemer, Ole, 223
ROSAT, 209
Royal Astronomical Society of Canada, 44
Warren Rupp Observatory, 162
Russell, Henry Norris, 223
Ryle, Martin, 223

S

San Fernando Observatory, 148
San Francisco State University Observatory, 148–49
Sandage, Allan, 223
Satellites and probes, NASA, 205–9
Saturn
   moons of, 210, 216, 219, 222

NASA probes to, 208, 210
   rings of, 216, 217, 227
   white spot on, 84
Schiaparelli, Giovanni, 223
Schmidt, Bernhard, 223
Schmidt, Maarten, 223
Schmidt-Cassegrain telescope, 89
Scholarships, for astronomy students, 238–40
Schwabe, Heinrich, 223
Schwarzschild, Karl, 223
Schwarzschild radius, 223
Science North Solar Observatory, 168
Search for Extraterrestrial Intelligence. **See** SETI
Seares, Frederick H., 159
SETI
   books about, 11–12
   telescopes used for, 162
Shapley, Harlow, 148, 159, 216, 223
Shattuck Observatory, 159
Sidereus Nuncius, 226
Sirius, 225
Slides, of astronomical objects, 28–31
Smithsonian Astrophysical Observatory, 27, 44, 83
Society of Meteoritophiles, 44
Society for Scientific Exploration, 80
Software, astronomy, 19–22
Solar magnetism, 215
Solar Maximum, 208
Solar observations, 82
Solar probes, 208, 209
Solar System, books about, 9–10
Sommers-Bausch Observatory, 150
Sonoma State University Observatory, 149

ABOUT THE AUTHOR

Bob D. Gibson is an award-winning journalist whose work has appeared in such leading astronomy magazines as **Astronomy, Final Frontier,** and the National Space Society's **AD ASTRA.** An avid amateur astronomer, Gibson lives and star-gazes in Prospect, Ohio.